**Pentecostal Manifestos**

James K. A. Smith and Amos Yong, *Editors*

PENTECOSTAL MANIFESTOS will provide a forum for exhibiting the next generation of Pentecostal scholarship. Having exploded across the globe in the twentieth century, Pentecostalism now enters its second century. For the past fifty years, Pentecostal and charismatic theologians (and scholars in other disciplines) have been working "internally," as it were, to articulate a distinctly Pentecostal theology and vision. The next generation of Pentecostal scholarship is poised to move beyond a merely internal conversation to an outward-looking agenda, in a twofold sense: first, Pentecostal scholars are increasingly gaining the attention of those outside Pentecostal/charismatic circles *as* Pentecostal voices in mainstream discussions; second, Pentecostal scholars are moving beyond simply reflecting on their own tradition and instead are engaging in theological and cultural analysis of a variety of issues from a Pentecostal perspective. In short, Pentecostal scholars are poised with a new boldness:

- Whereas the first generation of Pentecostal scholars was careful to learn the methods of the academy and then "apply" those to the Pentecostal tradition, the next generation is beginning to interrogate the reigning methodologies and paradigms of inquiry from the perspective of a unique Pentecostal worldview.
- Whereas the first generation of Pentecostal scholars was faithful in applying the tools of their respective trades to the work of illuminating the phenomena of modern Pentecostalism, the charismatic movements, and (now) the global renewal movements, the second generation is expanding its focus to bring a Pentecostal perspective to bear on important questions and issues that are concerns not only for Pentecostals and charismatics but also for the whole church.
- Whereas the first generation of Pentecostal/charismatic scholars was engaged in transforming the anti-intellectualism of the tradition, the second generation is engaged in contributing to and even impacting the conversations of the wider theological academy.

PENTECOSTAL MANIFESTOS will bring together both high-profile scholars and newly emerging scholars to address issues at the intersection of Pentecostalism, the global church, the theological academy, and even broader cultural concerns. Authors in PENTECOSTAL MANIFESTOS will be writing to and addressing not only their own movements but also those outside of Pentecostal/charismatic circles, offering a manifesto for a uniquely Pentecostal perspective on various themes. These will be "manifestos" in the sense that they will be bold statements of a distinctly Pentecostal interjection into contemporary discussions and debates, undergirded by rigorous scholarship.

Under this general rubric of bold, programmatic "manifestos," the series will include both shorter, crisply argued volumes that articulate a bold vision within a field as well as longer scholarly monographs, more fully developed and meticulously documented, with the same goal of engaging wider conversations. Such PENTECOSTAL MANIFESTOS are offered as intrepid contributions with the hope of serving the global church and advancing wider conversations.

**PUBLISHED**

James K. A. Smith, *Thinking in Tongues: Pentecostal Contributions to Christian Philosophy* (2010)

Frank D. Macchia, *Justified in the Spirit: Creation, Redemption, and the Triune God* (2010)

Wolfgang Vondey, *Beyond Pentecostalism: The Crisis of Global Christianity and the Renewal of the Theological Agenda* (2010)

Amos Yong, *The Spirit of Creation: Modern Science and Divine Action in the Pentecostal-Charismatic Imagination* (2011)

Nimi Wariboko, *The Pentecostal Principle: Ethical Methodology in New Spirit* (2011)

Steven M. Studebaker, *From Pentecost to the Trinitarian God: A Pentecostal Theology of the Trinity* (2012)

Mark J. Cartledge, *The Mediation of the Spirit: Interventions in Practical Theology* (2015)

# The Mediation of the Spirit

*Interventions in Practical Theology*

Mark J. Cartledge

WILLIAM B. EERDMANS PUBLISHING COMPANY
GRAND RAPIDS, MICHIGAN / CAMBRIDGE, U.K.

Published 2015 by

Wm. B. Eerdmans Publishing Co.

2140 Oak Industrial Drive N.E., Grand Rapids, Michigan 49505 /

P.O. Box 163, Cambridge CB3 9PU U.K.

Printed in the United States of America

21  20  19  18  17  16  15       7  6  5  4  3  2  1

**Library of Congress Cataloging-in-Publication Data**

Cartledge, Mark J., 1962-
     The mediation of the spirit: interventions in practical theology / Mark J. Cartledge.
          pages       cm       — (Pentecostal manifestos)
     Includes bibliographical references and index.
     ISBN 978-0-8028-6955-5 (pbk.: alk. paper)
     1. Pentecostal churches — Doctrines.   2. Theology, Practical.
     3. Theology, Doctrinal.   4. Pentecostalism.   I. Title.

     BX8762.Z5C37   2015
     230'.994 — dc23

                                                                2015002952

www.eerdmans.com

# Contents

# Acknowledgments

I am very grateful to the editors of the Pentecostal Manifestos series for the invitation to write a book addressing the academic constituency of practical theology from a Pentecostal and charismatic perspective. It has been a natural and important development for me, and I have appreciated the opportunity. A number of people read chapters and draft versions of this book, and I am in their debt. I am grateful to Allan Anderson, Zoë Bennett, Bonnie Miller-McLemore, Stephen Pattison, and Amos Yong for reading the manuscript and raising important and critical issues. I have tried to address most of them as best as I am able. Of course, it goes without saying that any outstanding weaknesses in the text remain entirely my own responsibility. Rick Osmer kindly offered to endorse this book, and I am extremely grateful for his endorsement.

I have presented papers from this research to both Pentecostal and charismatic studies conferences and practical theology conferences. I am most grateful to colleagues in these largely separate academic communities for their comments and suggestions made both in formal discussion and informally. Thank you.

In the Centre for Pentecostal and Charismatic Studies at the University of Birmingham, there is a thriving community of young (and not so young) scholars, and its seminars have been a highlight of my academic work. In addition to standard seminars, extra seminars (for those interested in "constructive theology") have been convened by some students, usually over a cup of coffee or tea. On at least two occasions, my work has been the subject of rigorous discussion there, and I have appreciated the dialogue immensely.

It is always a humbling experience to have your work deconstructed by your own students, but they have always been gracious, which increases my respect for them even more. I am especially grateful to Dik Allan, Elmer Chen, Matt Churchouse, Simo Frestadius, Rony Kristanto, Dieter Quick, Debbie Newson, Denise Ross, and Selena Su, who provided comment and feedback during one memorable seminar. I am also grateful to students in the Doctor of Practical Theology seminar at Birmingham for discussing my practical theology manifesto in detail, and to Stephen Pattison for inviting me to share my research.

This book was completed during what turned out to be a transitional phase of my life. During the very final stages of writing, I accepted the post of Professor of Practical Theology at Regent University School of Divinity, Virginia Beach, USA. Thankfully, I managed to carve out time to complete the book, and I am grateful for the opportunity to visit the historic Launde Abbey retreat house, where I was able to appreciate the rhythm of Anglican daily prayer, as well as the peace and tranquillity of such a beautiful environment. It was a necessary and timely "writing retreat."

I don't seem to be able to exist without the love of my life, Joan. Once again I am in her debt after yet another writing project has made it to completion. She is my greatest supporter and fan, even though she knows me like no other person in the world. My daughter, Becky, is studying theology, much to my surprise, and it is a joy to discuss theology with her and to appreciate how it has the capacity not just to expand the intellect but to ignite the spirit as well. Trying to explain the thesis of this book to an undergraduate was an important step in clarification, at least for me. I am grateful for her love and hope that she finds some usefulness for this book in her life, even beyond studies for her degree. In my experience, theology can become a lifelong preoccupation even after one's (first) degree has been completed!

*       *       *

I am grateful to the following publishers for allowing me permission to republish previously published material. Permission has been gratefully received for the following pieces.

Although I have rewritten most of it for this book, some of chapter 1 was published previously as Mark J. Cartledge, "Practical Theology," in *Studying Global Pentecostalism: Theories and Methods,* edited by A. Anderson, M. Bergunder, A. Droogers, and C. Van der Laan, pp. 268-85, © 2010 by the Regents of the University of California. Published by the University of California Press. http://www.ucpress.edu/book.php?isbn=9780520266629.

Part of chapter 2 was published as Mark J. Cartledge, "The Use of Scripture in Practical Theology: A Study of Academic Practice," *Practical Theology* 6, no. 3, pp. 271-83, © 2013 Maney Publishing. http://www.maneyonline.com/pra and http://www.metapress.com/content/122841.

# Introduction

This book has been a number of years in the pipeline. It took some time before I actually cleared my desk of the demands of other writing projects to create some space and attend to it. It began, as projects often do, with a conversation, in this case with Amos Yong, one of the series editors who was visiting the UK. I became convinced of its feasibility while eating a meal with him and my wife in a Moroccan restaurant in Birmingham. How often it is that theology and food live in close harmony and lead to writing decisions!

The Pentecostal Manifestos series seeks to identify a theological domain outside of Pentecostal and charismatic scholarship and address particular issues in that domain with a view to engaging in a broader theological conversation. I regard my field of study as located within Pentecostal and charismatic studies, and I approach this field from both empirical studies (including social scientific perspectives) and theology, so that I find myself located within the discipline of practical theology, and especially its empirical approach. Primarily, I move from the one to the other, although occasionally I have worked rather separately in both domains from either sociological or theological perspectives. This project gave me an opportunity to reverse my normal direction of study (from practical theology to Pentecostal and charismatic studies) and to ask how Pentecostal and charismatic theological perspectives might inform and contribute to the discourse of practical theology. In other words, how might insights and knowledge gained from research into theology from a Pentecostal and charismatic perspective interject into the discourse of practical theology? It builds on my earlier work and extends my thinking and contribution quite considerably (see chap. 1).

In this book I used scholars who have identified themselves as either Pentecostal or charismatic in some way.[1] In general, they have self-identified with the spirituality and worldview of the contemporary Pentecostal and charismatic movements. Put simply, this spirituality gives priority to an *encounter* with the person of the Holy Spirit in the scholar's theological narrative and the personal and corporate *transformation* that results from such an encounter. Expression is given to a worldview that includes the immanence of the Holy Spirit in the practice of worship, through extended periods of praise and prayer, the use of the charismata or gifts of the Spirit in congregational life, and witness to the presence of the kingdom of God through signs and wonders, including healings and miracles. A Pentecostal and charismatic perspective refers to positions arising from within this spirituality and worldview, even if there is considerable diversity among those who self-identify with this tradition. Generally, I have not attempted to differentiate between types of Pentecostals or charismatics, for example, classical, renewalist, and third wave, but use the designation "P/C" to refer to the group as a whole. It is not meant to homogenize the very real differences between traditions; it is simply a shorthand abbreviation for the sake of convenience.

Given the focus of the Pentecostal Manifestos series, my study seeks to make a distinctive contribution to the discipline of practical theology from a P/C perspective (and therefore the designation "Pentecostal" in this context implies "charismatic" as well). In particular, it aims to draw upon selected elements of P/C scholarship to appreciate how key texts drawn from the Acts of the Apostles, together with the concept of experience (and in particular "religious experience"), can be elucidated by means of pneumatology. It uses the notion of "mediation" as a way of giving an account of how pneumatology provides a connection between the two different kinds of theological discourse. From this discussion, the study seeks to make at least two clear "interventions" into the domain of practical theology (chaps. 5 and 6). That is, it seeks to interrupt the existing discourse and to challenge its account, but also to suggest different ways of theologizing leading to a modification of the practical-theological agenda.

To achieve this goal, the study first performs two context-defining ex-

---

1. See the descriptions in Mark J. Cartledge, "Charismatic Spirituality," in *The Bloomsbury Guide to Christian Spirituality*, ed. Richard Woods and Peter Tyler (London: Bloomsbury, 2012), pp. 214-25; see also Mark J. Cartledge, "Pentecostalism," in *The Wiley-Blackwell Companion to Practical Theology*, ed. Bonnie J. Miller-McLemore (Oxford: Wiley-Blackwell, 2012), pp. 587-95, esp. pp. 588-89.

ercises by describing the existing state of play in these two fields. It identifies strands of literature in the field of P/C studies as they address issues normally associated with practical theology (chap. 1). In this chapter, I seek to illustrate the contributions that have been made to practical-theological discourse in recent years by scholars working from a P/C perspective. This is followed in chapter 2 by a turn to the wider practical-theological scholarship in order to ascertain how Scripture is used, how the concept of "experience" is described, and how pneumatology is understood and informs practical theology. From this interaction with the existing literature, an assessment is offered, which identifies certain weaknesses. In particular, it asks what kinds of gaps in practical-theological discourse might be identified in order to advance the discussion. These gaps help define the "problem" or deficit to be addressed and the research opportunity to be explored.

In a "nutshell," often the problem is that P/C practical theologians are largely detached from the mainstream practical theology academy. They tend to be working out of an evangelical applied theological model, with the addition of liberationist and empirical strands. However, they have supplemented this model with an *experiential* dimension, and in particular, experience of the Holy Spirit, as an accompanying aspect to the approach. This is sometimes framed in terms of an ecclesial tradition, especially by classical Pentecostals. Positively put, this threefold approach of Scripture, experience, and pneumatology provides a set of lenses through which to view the broader practical-theological literature. When this is done, it is discovered that the mainstream literature has severe weaknesses in precisely these areas, which invite comment from a P/C perspective.

The following two chapters offer a constructive theological proposal that aims to address the deficits described in practical theology. Chapter 3 considers the nature of pneumatology using the concept of mediation. It draws on the most recent discussion of religious experience and mediation of the Holy Spirit among P/C theologians and situates this discussion within broader Protestant theology. Chapter 4 proposes an original analysis of key narratives in the Acts of the Apostles regarding Spirit reception and mediation. P/C Christians have used these narratives in constructing their theological identity, and so they are significant resources from within their tradition. Although the chapter draws upon the insights of biblical commentaries and other relevant literature, it fundamentally offers a *fresh reading* of the New Testament texts.

Having constructed a theological model of mediation that has relevance for ecclesial praxis, the book moves into a third phase by offering an intervention in the discourse of practical theology. This is achieved in two ways. First, chapter 5 provides a close reading of a single congregational study that has attempted to analyze the theology of an ecclesial community by paying attention to the espoused and operant theology embedded within the congregation. Perspectives from the Spirit-reception texts, and therefore of pneumatological mediation, are used to evaluate and contribute to a discussion of the significance of a particular study of a congregation. Finally, in chapter 6, we pick up one of the central theological loci identified at the end of chapter 4, namely, soteriology, and ask how this theme is presented in practical-theological discourse. From a critical analysis of the literature, this study seeks to make an original contribution to practical theology within the broader academy but one informed explicitly by the thesis of the study, namely, pneumatologically mediated soteriology. It argues that soteriology is central to practical theology, and in a P/C key it is best understood via the notion of mediation of the Holy Spirit in the church and the world.

This means that the study begins in a broad manner by looking at two fields before narrowing the focus to pneumatology and in particular the Acts of the Apostles. This narrow and in-depth analysis is then used to engage with a concrete study in order to reflect on its particularity before moving out more broadly again in terms of theological discourse within a discipline. Therefore, this movement from the broad to the narrow and back again should be considered a useful methodological process for allowing the breadth of the material to inform the depth of the focused analysis, and vice versa.

Some readers may wish to skip the literature surveys of chapters 1 and 2, especially if they are very familiar with both fields of study, and read their conclusions in order to understand the "problem" I am addressing. But I believe there is a need to illustrate the fields of study in order to elucidate the nature of the problem clearly. This is because the nature of this problem has not been defined previously in the field of practical theology. Therefore, I regard it as essential rather than peripheral reading, but I also understand that reading what amount to literature reviews can feel like a rather preliminary exercise.

Finally, there are many types of theology and there are many types of practical theology. This is a study first and foremost in practical *theology*, even if it is rather theoretical; it has a concern for ecclesial practice in society at its very heart. I do not present any empirical evidence in this study, and my engagement with a congregational study is by way of someone else's empirical research rather than my own. I also bring into the conversation literature from biblical studies, systematic theology, and practical theology. Again, this is deliberate in order to illustrate just how Scripture, tradition, and contemporary studies might be used creatively to inform constructive practical theology. For a change, I do not engage in a sustained conversation with the social sciences, even if I still regard this as an important aspect of practical theology. Of course, we all write from within specific traditions, be they academic traditions or belief systems of one kind or another (even nontheistic belief systems). It has been rather fashionable to denigrate the role of religious faith in the process of knowledge building, while at the same time allowing secular value judgments to predominate the assessment of what counts as "valuable academic knowledge." To comport with the nature of the Pentecostal Manifestos series, this book is written both as academic theology and as ecclesial theology in its engagement with society. Some might consider this controversial, especially those who think they are working within an intellectually superior, secular, autonomous, and critical academy. Increasingly, however, there is a view that knowledge, and what counts as "valuable knowledge," can be produced from many different sectors of society, and often through a process of collaboration and coproduction rather than independent and isolated enterprise. To facilitate the greater "coproduction" of knowledge between the academy and the church, in both its confessional and nonconfessional contexts, this study positions itself at the intersection of these two domains. Therefore, I invite my readers to appreciate this study as situated in both the academy and the church, but having implications for theological engagement with wider society as well.

# 1 Pentecostal and Charismatic Approaches to Practical Theology

## 1.1 Introduction

The discipline of practical theology has appeared to be in constant redefinition in recent times, although some consensus might at last be emerging. It was once regarded as the crown of theological study, which was placed toward the end of theological education for ordained ministry. At that point in the process all the necessary "hints and tips" were added under the rubric of *pastoralia*. In this context it was closely aligned to education for ministry, and by extension, church education in a broader sense. Thus would-be clergy learned how to preach, lead worship, conduct pastoral conversations with the insights of psychology, administer educational programs, and of course, integrate spirituality into ministerial practice. Fundamentally, with this model, the minister applies theological knowledge from elsewhere (the Bible, systematic theology, church history, and philosophy) to church leadership with the aid of *pastoralia*. This is often referred to as the formational or ministerial model. However, with the advent of *liberation theology*, there came a turn to contemporary praxis as the starting point, and in particular the use of Marxist social theory to diagnose the "problem" to be solved by liberating practices.[1] This meant that practical theology practitioners and academics used the hermeneutical tools of liberation theology to be suspicious about power relations and to emphasize the need for those on the margins

---

1. The most influential text is by Gustavo Gutiérrez, *A Theology of Liberation* (London: SCM, 1974).

to be heard and empowered. It has also been allied to mission theology, as liberation is conceived as part of the missionary imperative. This liberationist model of practical theology is now a very dominant one in the academy. The third model arises from the use of the social sciences by theologians in the twentieth century, in particular both qualitative and quantitative empirical research methods within the discourse of theology. This model was developed in Europe toward the end of the 1980s, although its roots in North America can be traced to the beginning of the twentieth century and the early work associated with the University of Chicago. European theologians started to consider the idea of theory development using the actual beliefs and practices of religious individuals and groups, rather than by simply reflecting on theological traditions historically. This model has been named *empirical theology*, but must not be confused with later versions of the Chicago School, which allied itself to process theology and philosophy. North American readers, in particular, must be aware of the very real differences here, even if there are common roots in both traditions.[2]

The International Academy of Practical Theology (IAPT) was founded in 1993 and now has around 135 members worldwide. It is probably best placed to comment on the nature of the discipline as it is practiced by academics globally.[3] This academy first acknowledged in 2005 the existence of these three strands of practical theology as represented by its members.[4]

---

2. Compare R. C. Miller, ed., *Empirical Theology: A Handbook* (Birmingham, Ala.: Religious Education Press, 1992), with Johannes A. van der Ven, *Practical Theology: An Empirical Approach* (Kampen: Kok Pharos, 1993).

3. Publications emerging from the academy include the following: Paul Ballard and Pamela Couture, eds., *Globalisation and Difference: Practical Theology in a World Context* (Cardiff: Cardiff Academic Press, 1999); Paul Ballard and Pamela Couture, eds., *Creativity, Imagination, and Criticism: The Expressive Dimension in Practical Theology* (Cardiff: Cardiff Academic Press, 2001); Pamela Couture and Bonnie Miller-McLemore, eds., *Poverty, Suffering, and HIV-AIDS: International Practical Theological Perspectives* (Cardiff: Cardiff Academic Press, 2003); Elaine Graham and Anna Rowlands, eds., *Pathways to the Public Square: Practical Theology in an Age of Pluralism* (Münster: LIT Verlag, 2005); Hans-Georg Ziebertz and Friedrich Schweitzer, eds., *Dreaming the Land: Theologies of Resistance and Hope* (Münster: LIT Verlag, 2007); Wilhelm Gräb and Lars Charbonnier, eds., *Secularization Theories, Religious Identity, and Practical Theology: Developing International Practical Theology for the 21st Century* (Münster: LIT Verlag, 2009); Edward Foley, ed., *Religion, Diversity, and Conflict* (Münster: LIT Verlag, 2011); Ruard R. Ganzevoort, Rein Brouwer, and Bonnie Miller-McLemore, eds., *City of Desires — a Place for God? Practical Theological Perspectives* (Münster: LIT Verlag, 2013).

4. Ruard Ganzevoort, the president of IAPT at the time, suggested this classification. I find it a useful way of classifying the material, even though individual authors can be found in more than one category.

They are not mutually exclusive categories, and scholars combine them according to their own commitments and interests. Nevertheless, there is an agreed common focus or direct object of inquiry, namely, contemporary religious praxis, that is, the value-laden practices of ecclesial and religious communities in global contexts. Of course, such a definition means that other areas or disciplines conceived in this manner can, in effect, become subdisciplines of practical theology, for example, mission, worship and liturgy, spirituality, and education. Therefore, overlap is inevitable, even if in all cases the horizon of interest is principally the contemporary one. For some, practical theology is more like a field of study than a narrower discipline. Personally, I tend to view practical theology more as a discipline, even if I acknowledge that others understand it as a broader field of study.

In what follows, I shall trace some representative contributions to practical theology from P/C perspectives in order to illustrate the kinds of approaches that are present. In this chapter, I do not intend to offer an exhaustive overview of the material. I have provided a more detailed survey of this material elsewhere.[5] I shall instead look at specific theologians to elucidate how they contribute to the landscape. I intend to provide a specific trail through the terrain that demonstrates three key characteristics in relation to practical theology. First, practical theologians in this tradition engage with Scripture in some significant way. They bring either biblical themes or specific texts into conversation with the contemporary situation. They sometimes do this in the context of a conscious "reading tradition" or a particular doctrinal commitment, for example, from Wesleyan Pentecostalism, while at other times they appear to be applicationist in a traditional evangelical sense of seeking to derive their theology from biblical texts without allowing other commitments to interfere (at least explicitly). Second, they relate the discussion in some way to their own experience, either "religious experience" in terms of spirituality or some kind of ecclesial, mission, or pastoral experience. Very often this experience is communal and shaped by worshiping practices. Third, they connect the use of Scripture and their experience by means of the person and work of the Holy Spirit. In other words, there is some coordination of these themes at work, yet the precise configuration of them depends on the topic of the discussion in question.

---

5. Mark J. Cartledge, "Practical Theology," in *Studying Global Pentecostalism: Theories and Methods,* ed. A. Anderson et al. (Berkeley and Los Angeles: University of California Press, 2010), pp. 268-85.

## 1.2 Formation, Worship, and Ministry

Practical theology has been understood historically as part of ministerial education for clergy and church leaders. In many respects this has not changed,
except that it is no longer conceived exclusively in these terms. In this model,
one first of all gets to grips with theology proper before applying such knowledge to pastoral problems or ministerial tasks. In many evangelical seminar-
ies this is the type of model that still predominates. It is fundamentally an
applied model, whereby Scripture is applied to ministerial tasks or pastoral
problems. At the heart of this model is the formation of the minister himself
or herself as a pastor being prepared to take charge of a congregation or a
church ministry of some kind. Many P/C practical theologians understand
themselves as providing training and resources for individuals and for communities that equip lay and ordained personnel for church-related ministry,
but this provision interfaces with spirituality, discipleship, and Christian
education. In this context, I focus on what has been termed "formation," but
also worship and specific ministerial practices, to demonstrate the kinds of
approaches that can be located in the sector.

On the subject of spiritual *formation* and leadership in the P/C tradition,
one of the most significant texts to emerge in the last twenty years is by Cheryl
Bridges Johns. In her book *Pentecostal Formation,* she adapts the educational
paradigm developed by the Brazilian Paulo Freire.[6] She critiques Freire in
the light of her theological commitments and then offers an approach to
catechesis for the Pentecostal tradition. Using the Hebrew notion of *'yada* as
personal knowledge of God, she critiques the concept of praxis on epistemo-
logical grounds.[7] Knowledge of God is accomplished more by the heart than
by the mind, and is active, intentional, and related to lived experience. This
kind of knowledge is primarily not about how much information a person
knows but is about the quality of life lived in response to God. This means that
knowledge grows and develops over time, because knowing God comes via a
loving relationship (1 John 4:7-8, 16, 20) and is displayed through obedience
to the will of God as it has been made known (1 John 2:3-5; 5:1-5).[8] For Johns

6. Cheryl Bridges Johns, *Pentecostal Formation: A Pedagogy among the Oppressed* (Sheffield: Sheffield Academic Press, 1993).

7. She argues that praxis is an insufficient basis upon which to know God and achieve hu-
man transformation because praxis may become distorted and self-serving. Johns, *Pentecostal
Formation,* pp. 37-38; cf. my discussion of her proposal in Mark J. Cartledge, *Practical Theology:
Charismatic and Empirical Perspectives* (Carlisle: Paternoster, 2003), pp. 45-47.

8. Johns, *Pentecostal Formation,* p. 36.

the context in which this knowledge is experienced is the community of the church, because it is the context of an encounter with the Holy Spirit in the experience of the people that results in transformation.

She offers an approach to discipleship and catechesis, which she defines as "the means whereby the Pentecostal community becomes aware of God's revelation and responds to this revelation in faithful obedience. The nature of this process should include the oral nature of a Pentecostal hermeneutic and the dynamics of Pentecostal liturgy. It includes a dynamic and active role of the Holy Spirit and emphasizes the full participation of all members of the community of faith."[9] The goal of this catechesis is to promote the Christian faith as it is lived out or actualized in both church and society. For Johns, Scripture is "the standard for the process and the outcome of the catechetical process."[10] However, this reception of the Bible is not simply in terms of information about God and the world; rather, it is placed within a dynamic relationship with the Holy Spirit, who speaks via the written word. The context of this interaction is the community of faith in its worshiping practices. Thus catechesis includes both human experience and the use of Scripture, existing in a dialectical relationship that nevertheless evaluates experience "by the norm of Scripture."[11]

To illustrate how this biblically informed epistemology and spirituality are expressed in relation to Scripture, she proposes a Pentecostal approach to Bible study. It includes a fourfold movement.[12] The Bible study begins with the sharing of personal testimony, through which issues in the lives of participants are discussed by the group. The presuppositions individuals bring to the text of Scripture are also shared. This is followed by a group exercise to search the Bible in a personal, humble manner, and which allows and expects the Holy Spirit to speak through the text. It is an inductive process that allows the literary genres of the different biblical books to be appreciated as revealing the thoughts and intentions of the author. The illumination of the Holy Spirit is regarded as essential if the members of the group are to experience a sense of being addressed directly by God. The third movement is to yield to the Holy Spirit as the will of God is known, and this means being obedient to join in with the mission of Christ to the world. The group asks:

9. Johns, *Pentecostal Formation*, p. 121.

10. Johns, *Pentecostal Formation*, p. 122.

11. Johns, *Pentecostal Formation*, p. 129.

12. Johns, *Pentecostal Formation*, pp. 130-40; also see Jackie D. Johns and Cheryl Bridges Johns, "Yielding to the Spirit: A Pentecostal Approach to Group Bible Study," *Journal of Pentecostal Theology* 1 (1992): 109-34.

What is the Spirit saying to the church? The fourth and final movement is the response to the call that emerges from the encounter. Transformation of individuals leads them to become people of conviction, which in turn leads to action. Opportunities are therefore provided that enable individuals and the group to respond in appropriate ways.

James P. Bowers advances an approach to Christian formation from an explicitly Wesleyan Pentecostal perspective.[13] This approach supplements Johns by adding a theological reading tradition to the use of Scripture, experience, and discipleship. Although he does not engage with biblical texts directly, his work provides a framework that resonates very strongly with the approach of Johns. He suggests that Pentecostals have suffered from an identity crisis that has, in effect, turned their approach to formation in a pragmatist and denominationally driven direction. His answer to this problem is to quarry the resources of the Wesleyan Pentecostal tradition; he suggests that the fivefold gospel (Jesus as savior, sanctifier, baptizer in the Holy Spirit, healer, and coming king) can offer formational experience of life in the Spirit to transform and energize individuals and communities. He sets up a discussion between Wesleyans and Wesleyan Pentecostals and reviews a number of topics, including "religious experience," which is pertinent to this study.

He discusses experience in terms of orientation, crisis, and process as well as the community and the individual. In terms of orientation, he affirms the Wesleyan tradition that understands soteriology as essentially transformational in the here and now, which naturally leads to an experiential form of Christianity. P/C Christians have been far more emotional in their experiences, and this has been challenged by Wesleyans, as has the appeal to other sources of theological knowledge such as reason and tradition. Experiences of grace have been understood in terms of both crisis and process. He notes the tension between both of these dimensions and argues that the moments of crisis should be placed within the broader process of spiritual and moral renewal. The relationship between the community and the individual is essential to authentic Christian experience. This is because redemption and holiness are shared communal experiences. He further suggests that the discipleship process can be translated into appropriate objectives and educational practices, for example, experiential knowledge, spiritual transformation, responsiveness and moral fullness, prophetic engagement,

---

13. James P. Bowers, "A Wesleyan-Pentecostal Approach to Christian Formation," *Journal of Pentecostal Theology* 6 (1995): 55-86.

covenant relationships, discernment of truth, vocational calls to mission, and ministry and kingdom-centered eschatological vision.[14] Having articulated these objectives, he then suggests that they can be applied to education programs, parenting initiatives, the church community, pastors and the eldership, small discipleship groups, church structures and decision-making processes, membership and church discipline, and the ministry of believers.[15]

The subject of formation is understood from a P/C perspective more deeply by considering the specific role that *worship* plays in shaping a communal worldview. Pentecostal traditions and spiritualities provide a set of lenses derived from the Bible through which to read the world and issues in society. R. Jerome Boone gives a helpful account of the main components of the P/C worshiping community as the key context for spiritual formation and thus links spirituality to church ministry.[16] For Boone the ethos of the community is rooted in the work of the Holy Spirit and cannot be understood apart from this presupposition. The ethos connects all the different kinds of experiences and practices, as well as expressions of affection and holiness. This ethos shapes the worshiping rituals. This means that the "role of the faith community as the mediator of reality necessitates a construct in which Christians — individually and corporately — are subjects of history."[17] They are shaped to become agents of change as they are themselves empowered by the person of the Holy Spirit experienced in this worshiping community. The congregational members achieve *communitas,* that is, egalitarian relationships, as they worship in the Spirit, which relativizes existing social status, as they move into a liminal (eschatological) reality. This egalitarianism is understood as being rooted in the gospel message itself (Gal. 3:28).

It is in this context that Boone says transformation is possible. He argues that the Pentecostal community offers a place of contradiction and confirmation.[18] The place of contradiction is brought about by the work of the Holy Spirit, who exposes prejudice and sin. Inner resistance to God is exposed by the Spirit as the difference between individual narratives and God's metanarrative is confronted. This tension is held and resolved in the church. The pain of conflict is carried by a community of hospitality, forgiveness, and acceptance. In this context of love, change is made possible through dialogue,

---

14. Bowers, "A Wesleyan-Pentecostal Approach," pp. 78-81.
15. Bowers, "A Wesleyan-Pentecostal Approach," pp. 81-85.
16. R. Jerome Boone, "Community and Worship: The Key Components of Pentecostal Christian Formation," *Journal of Pentecostal Theology* 8 (1996): 129-42.
17. Boone, "Community and Worship," p. 132.
18. Boone, "Community and Worship," p. 134.

which is both "factual and truthful."[19] In this dialogue shared values and goals can be discerned and covenant relationships established. "The reality revealed by the Word and Spirit and mediated through the faith community critiques both us and the world in which we live."[20] This means that the community is prophetic and provides an alternative society for its members, even as it is critiqued by the Spirit of God. It is a contrast society providing a countercultural critique, shining light into the darkness (Eph. 5:8).

These three P/C approaches to formation and discipleship have a number of strengths. They emphasize relational epistemology, which is important for Pentecostal spirituality, given its commitment to experiencing God through the person of the Holy Spirit. This feature is presuppositional and needs to be acknowledged as such. This knowledge is, of course, placed within a relational context of the ecclesial community, and its understanding of the Holy Spirit is expressed in ways that seem appropriate to the nature of Pentecostalism, with its focus on social and communal practices. These communal practices are critical in the socialization of individuals into Pentecostal identity and its negotiation with the outside world over time. This is linked to orality and the ways in which personal knowledge is communicated through oral modes of discourse, very often attributed to the person and work of the Holy Spirit directly, even though all experience of the Holy Spirit is in fact mediated in some sense (see chaps. 3 and 4). Despite this orality, there is a strong commitment to the use of the text of the Bible to understand and interpret experience, yet these P/C theologians are not naïve in their use of biblical texts, but rather acknowledge that reading traditions are in operation and provide a set of lenses through which to make sense of the various texts employed, but in a dialectical fashion whereby the text informs the experience and the experience reads the text. In this context it is good to see an appreciation of the relationship between crisis and process in religious experience, since both are very obviously signaled in the wider literature on the subject. Finally, conflict is not avoided but is considered inevitable, and through it a pneumatological critique within the community can lead to a self-critique that in turn leads to a greater prophetic witness in society.

In terms of weaknesses, this communal and relational epistemology could lead to a sociopragmatic hermeneutic that, in effect, does not allow critique from the outside of the community (except perhaps prophetically,

19. Boone, "Community and Worship," p. 135.
20. Boone, "Community and Worship," p. 135.

which may be mediated from within the community).[21] It has the capacity to domesticate voices that do not fit because of very strong socialization processes and ideological commitments. In addition, as I have noted elsewhere, pneumatology could be made subordinate to ecclesiology or to a dominant personality such that diversity of expression is minimized for the sake of conformity to a particular style or approach to church life. However, given the discussion of conflict and self-critical awareness noted above, we may be confident that scholars are at least giving some attention to this matter. The evangelical commitment to Scripture as the "norming norm" is evident in the discourse. Nevertheless, a trialectic tension is set up between Scripture, the Holy Spirit, and the community, which often appears to be resolved in terms of the community mediating the other two dimensions. This observation may suggest that the trialectic is ultimately unsustainable in Pentecostal hermeneutics, and this may result in authoritarianism or pragmatism or indeed both.

Given this *formational and ministry context,* and to illustrate the relationship of Scripture, experience, and the Holy Spirit in relation to ministry issues, I shall describe approaches to four areas: preaching, healing, deliverance, and social ministry. The following examples demonstrate how the relationship between these key components functions within the field of P/C theology.

John Gordy acknowledges that one of the weaknesses of P/C scholarship is that it has failed to reflect critically on the practice of *preaching.* He aims to address this weakness by exploring the nature of Pentecostal preaching, its internal dynamics and parameters, and by proposing a framework for understanding it.[22] Fundamentally, he regards preaching as prophetic in nature. "Truth put in the heart of the preacher by the Holy Spirit is proclaimed. He or she speaks the Word from God."[23] The expectation is that the effects of such preaching should mirror those found in the book of Acts: conviction of sin, increased faith, confrontation of the demonic, fear and reverence, spiritual gifts, and signs and wonders. The early Pentecostal preachers associated with the Azusa Street revival spoke out of their experience of being baptized in the Holy Spirit and having a deep communion with God. There are examples of clear preparation, as well as logical and clear communication, which go hand

21. See the discussion of sociopragmatic hermeneutics in Anthony C. Thiselton, *New Horizons in Hermeneutics* (London: HarperCollins, 1992), pp. 439-52.

22. John Gordy, "Toward a Theology of Pentecostal Preaching," *Journal of Pentecostal Theology* 10, no. 1 (2001): 81-97.

23. Gordy, "Toward a Theology," p. 88.

in hand with passion, conviction, and authority. However, the starting point for all Pentecostal preaching, according to Gordy, is the person of the Holy Spirit. "The Spirit is the One who illumines, indwells, intercedes, searches the heart, knows the mind of God, liberates, guides, bears witness to Christ, transforms, produces fruit in the life of the believer, bestows gifts, empowers, teaches, convicts of sin, reproves and regenerates."[24] Therefore, Gordy argues that the preacher must first wait for a message from the Holy Spirit for the people. The Spirit helps the preacher choose the biblical passage, focus on the important issues, and gain an understanding of the text. Thus all preparation and delivery are in the context of prayer and give the preacher not just the message but also a sense of authority. The prophetic dimension of the sermon is first experienced by the preacher before it is released to the congregation, with an expectation that signs and wonder will follow.

Another study, by Aldwin Ragoonath, suggests that by comparing Pentecostal preaching with Protestant and Roman Catholic preaching, it may be possible to define the contours of a distinctly Pentecostal approach. This is achieved by starting from an exegesis of Luke 4:16-20.[25] Instead of starting from experience of the Holy Spirit, this approach starts with the text of Scripture, from which an approach to ministry is derived. At first glance, it looks like a standard evangelical approach. However, when examined in more detail, it begins to look very different. The starting point for preaching is in fact the preachers' reexperiencing the text for themselves *before* they communicate the message to the congregation and assist the audience to reexperience the text.[26] This means that the preaching is relevant and alive; the text has been made real to the preachers first, and they then encourage a direct response from the congregation. This is at the heart of Pentecostal preaching for Ragoonath, but he places it within a number of other features. He argues that a distinctly Pentecostal preaching approach should contain eight features. Homiletics in this tradition (1) contains a commitment to the whole of the Scriptures; (2) operates from a Spirit worldview; (3) starts with the preacher reexperiencing the text and subsequently drawing out the symbolic meaning of it; (4) moves the congregation to experience the presence of God through the sermon; (5) seeks to preach to the needs of

24. Gordy, "Toward a Theology," p. 93.

25. Aldwin Ragoonath, "Pentecostal Preaching" (message at the 36th Annual Meeting of the Society for Pentecostal Studies, "The Role of Experience in Christian Life and Thought — Pentecostal Insights," Cleveland, Tenn., 2007), pp. 291-98.

26. Aldwin Ragoonath, *Preach the Word: A Pentecostal Approach* (Winnipeg: Agape Teaching Ministry of Canada, 2004), p. 103.

the congregation; (6) preaches in a variety of genres (topical, textual, need-centered, counseling, expository); (7) is not dependent on any particular mode of communication (monologues and dialogues); and (8) uses blocks of thought, especially when preaching from narratives. What is interesting about the use of biblical texts here is the relationship between the ministry of Jesus expressed in the Lukan mandate and the use of the Acts of the Apostles. This is a common feature of Pentecostal hermeneutics as applied to ministry practices.

Jacques P. J. Theron offers a practical-theological reflection on the subject of *healing* by considering Pentecostal theory in relation to the full gospel. He sees healing as "provided for all in the atonement," noting the biblical texts Isaiah 53:4-5, Matthew 8:17, and 1 Peter 2:24. He subsequently identifies practical-theological issues by studying the "faith communicative actions which relate to the healing ministry of Pentecostals."[27] He observes how the theory has been modified in the light of experience and raises issues for further consideration, made necessary because some people are not healed even though they exhibit faith in the power of the Holy Spirit to heal today. He explores the state of grassroots healing ministries and concludes that the process of prayer for healing is strongly determined by the nature of the illness. Where there is strong evidence that a medical procedure is the best course of action, prayer is often used alongside medical means, whereas in former generations medical support was ignored completely. He also considers the role of pastoral care among Pentecostals, whether manipulation is used and excessive claims are made in some cases, as well as the problem of how to respond to those who are not healed, prolonged illnesses, and the possibility of the demonic. He suggests that critical reflection is required that does not ignore some of these difficult issues. However, behind much of the discussion of healing today, Theron argues, is a bigger issue, namely, the influence of the Western worldview, which tends to deny supernatural causation: it is exclusively naturalistic. Therefore, healing practices in the Western world, or wherever the worldview predominates, can inhibit expectations. He also considers the Eucharist as a context for healing because of its link to the atonement. Anointing with oil has been important for Pentecostals, and this practice continues in many places. He wonders whether the congregational use of oil is a legitimate reading of James 5, upon which the practice is based but which assumes a domestic setting. Theron considers other pertinent

27. Jacques P. J. Theron, "Towards a Practical Theological Theory for the Healing Ministry in the Pentecostal Churches," *Journal of Pentecostal Theology* 14 (1999): 49-64 (esp. pp. 50, 52).

issues, namely, the relationship between the charismata, the gifts of healing, the ministry of healing, and the work of the Holy Spirit. He also discusses the use of healing teams, the terminology in use, the healing of societies, and the influence of non-Pentecostals on Pentecostals in the healing ministry. All these features suggest that the practice of prayer for healing in Pentecostal and charismatic Christianity is diverse, yet the practice itself remains central to Pentecostal identity and mission because of the biblical mandate to pray for the sick and the experiences of the work of the Holy Spirit.

My own reflection on the demonology of John Wimber in the context of a multidisciplinary discussion begins to open up the nature and problems associated with *deliverance* ministry.[28] It is worth considering his approach as a form of practical theology. Wimber placed his understanding of deliverance within the context of his healing theology. This theology is informed by four cosmological presuppositions, namely, that God does not directly will evil to exist; that he does directly remove evil; that sometimes he accomplishes his purposes through evil; and that in practice this means that the passive option is not always possible. In this context, he understands that healing is linked to repentance for sin as well as conflict with Satan. Healing should be regarded as holistic and encompassing all areas of life. The ministry of Jesus in the Gospels (especially Mark, although also parallel Synoptic accounts) is used as a model for Christian practice today, which is placed within an understanding of the in-breaking of the kingdom of God (Matt. 12:28); and this kingdom or reign is destroying the kingdom of Satan (1 John 3:8). He focuses on the idea of *demonization,* whereby Satan obtains some kind of grip on people's lives that results in sickness or affliction of some kind. The symptoms and effect of this kind of influence can vary from severe to mild. Spiritual battle through prayer allows Christians to release those who are influenced in this way. It is a model derived from Scripture, from which Wimber provides a set of guidelines to enable a deliverance ministry to be put into practice. These guidelines contain six foundational principles that provide the context for the ministry and include empowerment of the Holy Spirit. These principles are further defined in terms of values, for example, a healing environment where the Spirit is present and there is faith, as well as a step-by-step procedure through which a person can receive prayer for

---

28. Mark J. Cartledge, "Demonology and Deliverance: A Practical-Theological Case Study," in *Deliverance and Exorcism: Multidisciplinary Perspectives,* ed. William K. Kay and Robin Parry (Milton Keynes: Paternoster, 2011), pp. 243-63; John Wimber with Kevin Springer, *Power Healing* (London: Hodder and Stoughton, 1986).

healing. What is interesting about this analysis is the way Wimber begins from biblical texts and then advocates practical guidelines. His deliverance ministry has been shaped by both his reading of Scripture and his own experience of practice; the two mutually inform each other even if he starts chronologically with biblical texts. His approach reflects the dialectic noted above by Johns, even if the accent is on following a biblical model in a more standard evangelical manner.

Murray W. Dempster highlights the eschatological significance of Pentecostal *social ministries* in the context of mission; he asserts that they have proliferated in recent times (indeed, even more so since the publication of his article).[29] He argues that this development in practice has been motivated by a change in "social conscience," which is motivated by dire human need and terrible living conditions. In other words, the experience of human misery has informed and shaped a response. He suggests, however, that this emerging social commitment is still in tension with an eschatological expectation of the imminent return of Christ and the annihilation of the world. He seeks to address this tension by locating the problem within the context of the mission of the church. The day of Pentecost becomes the normative narrative for Pentecostals; the outpouring of the Holy Spirit as well as the hope of the return of Christ mark out the eschatological age. This relationship between mission, empowerment of the Holy Spirit, and eschatological hope provides a perspective from which to appreciate social concern. The Pentecost narrative demonstrates how the charismatic Spirit that anointed Jesus has been transferred to the church; with this transference come both power and ethical character. There is continuity between the ministry of Jesus and the church; a new redemptive society is born characterized by love, peace, justice, solidarity, sharing of resources, and respect. Dempster argues that social programs are essential to the ethical character of the kingdom of God, and this means that authentic gospel witness will contain their expression. The kingdom of God has been inaugurated in the ministry of Jesus, and its social dimension has been instantiated by the Lukan mandate (Luke 4:18-19) and the action of Jesus in the Gospel accounts. However, its full consummation remains outstanding until the parousia, which will signal not annihilation of creation (except for evil) but the transformation of the world. In this framework, social ministries are anticipations of God's ultimate transformation of creation within the kingdom of God. What is fascinating about

---

29. Murray W. Dempster, "Christian Social Concern in Pentecostal Perspective: Reformulating Pentecostal Eschatology," *Journal of Pentecostal Theology* 2 (1993): 51-64.

this description is that the ministry of the church in its social dimension is framed by eschatology but shaped by the day of Pentecost narrative. It is this biblical narrative that has a unique place in the Pentecostal imagination.

The strengths of these accounts lie in the view that ministry is embedded in and arises from spirituality, which permeates everything. The ministry is holistic and addresses every area of life. The spirituality, in turn, is based on a worldview that contains certain assumptions about reality, in particular spiritual reality and the person and work of the Holy Spirit. There is an engagement with Scripture via an experiential hermeneutic, which allows accessibility across congregational membership but can also filter the meaning of the text; therefore, it is both a strength and a weakness. As part of this hermeneutic, biblical models are indeed used, as in the Gospels of Luke and Mark, but there appears to be a limited wider discussion of biblical themes or intensive exegesis. There are some links to wider theological doctrinal content, for example, eschatology, which is both useful and necessary. However, in terms of weaknesses, a certain dualism seems to underlie the discussion in places, despite the holistic emphasis of ministry and the use of medicine, and this could be usefully complemented by a theology of creation and culture.

Drawing these different contributions together, I suggest that there is indeed a coordination of the use of Scripture, experience, and the work of the Holy Spirit from a Pentecostal and charismatic theological perspective. There is a supremacy given to the role of Scripture as well as a dialectic between experience and Scripture, as the Spirit is understood to be mediated by both sources. Also, wider concerns assist with the reading of Scripture and the performance of practices, and I noted the role of the Pentecostal reading traditions, doctrinal commitments, and, more fundamentally, a Pentecostal worldview. The ministry of Jesus is very much linked to the ministry of the church by means of the Holy Spirit, and for Pentecostals this transferring of anointing is signaled by the day of Pentecost narrative.

## 1.3 Liberation Theology

Liberation theology emerged in the twentieth century as a way of expressing theology as a form of action, as well as a way of giving a voice to the marginalized and oppressed. It is a theology offered from particular social contexts and pays attention to the needs of specific groups of people who have suffered injustice systematically in order to "liberate" them. Very often the theological reflection is based on social analysis of the contemporary situation, and the problem is remedied in terms of orthopraxis, or right action, informed by liberation motifs, such as the exodus. It has been expressed most obviously in non-Western contexts, in Latin America, Africa, and Asia. However, it has also been formulated and expressed in Western contexts, in black, feminist, and Hispanic theologies. In its Western expressions, especially among feminists, it has found a place within the discourse of practical theology. This is because theology as action leading to emancipation resonates very strongly with practical theology's commitment to doing theology holistically, not just thinking theologically. This liberationist strand is also present in P/C scholarship, but in a much more limited manner. I shall consider three examples of liberation theology, two from a Hispanic American perspective and one from a black British perspective.[30] I include them because they form a link between P/C perspectives and the academy of practical theology. Any serious attempt at literature mapping cannot ignore them, even if their influence is limited.

Eldin Villafañe, in his presidential address to the Society for Pentecostal Studies in 1996, challenged the society to consider liberation not in terms of liberal and Enlightenment ideals but in terms of the biblical promise that is linked to the gospel.[31] He argued that this liberation is part of the Spirit's work for personal and social transformation. This means that the Spirit has a political agenda for God's creation and works this out through the church in the world. The "politics of the Spirit" must, therefore, be understood as part of the reign of God in-breaking into history. Villafañe was critical of the "ecclesial theological politics" of postliberalism and argued that it fails to deliver in terms of social transformation, especially for those on the margins of society. Politics is about "community-creating life," and the role of the church is to participate in this kind of politics by means of the Holy Spirit. The church reads the signs of the times and provides the context out of which action takes place. Villafañe located the politics of the Spirit within the eschatological reign of God and saw the work of Jesus in the Gospel accounts as signaling this reign through a challenge to the powers (Matt. 12:28). This in-breaking reign is also linked to Pentecost and the church's experience of baptism in the Spirit as a continuation of the ministry of Jesus. It signals the reign of God, while not being identified with it. The institutions of the world

30. For an overview of liberation theology, see Christopher Rowland, ed., *The Cambridge Companion to Liberation Theology* (Cambridge: Cambridge University Press, 1999).

31. Eldin Villafañe, "The Politics of the Spirit: Reflections on a Theology of Social Transformation for the Twenty-first Century," *Pneuma: The Journal of the Society for Pentecostal Studies* 18, no. 2 (1996): 161-70.

and their associated politics are the arena of the Spirit in which there is a struggle for community. This means that Pentecostal action in the world is pneumatic, political discipleship guided by biblical teaching and paradigms of divine action demonstrating God's preferential option for the poor. All politics of the world are ultimately judged by the politics of the Spirit and holistic liberation.

This call addressed to the academic guild builds on his established proposal for a Hispanic American Pentecostal social ethic, which aims to participate in the reign of God, confront structural sin and evil, and fulfill a prophetic and vocational role for those baptized in the Spirit.[32] He believes his work *The Liberating Spirit* provides the first ever liberationist approach to social ethics, and it is worth considering in more detail. He uses the term "Hispanic" to designate a sociocultural group covering persons of Latin American origin, and the designation "Hispanic American" to refer to immigrants and their descendants now living in the USA. He understands the latter as an oppressed minority often living in the poorest neighborhoods of a city and being disadvantaged materially, educationally, and politically, if not spiritually. He argues that in the American context Hispanic Pentecostalism is the church of an oppressed minority that provides holistic support to this religious and cultural group. Hispanic Christianity can be characterized as a form of spirituality that emphasizes submission to the leading of the Holy Spirit, simplicity in worship, separation from the evils of the world, empowerment through Spirit baptism, and hope as anticipation of the fullness of the eschaton. It is associated with the marginalized and speaks prophetically on behalf of the poor. This embodied spirituality is informed and shaped by Scripture, as Villafañe says: "The Scriptures play an important role. . . . While indigenous Pentecostals have often been caricatured for their handling of Scripture — as fundamentalist, literalist or biblicist — with a certain amount of truth in it for sure, Scriptures, nevertheless, are read in an existential-spiritual manner."[33]

It is important to emphasize this hermeneutical point. Many Pentecostals read the text of Scripture in an experiential manner as inspired by the Holy Spirit in the context of the community of the church. Villafañe supports this hermeneutic by placing it within a set of theological parameters. These parameters are (1) contextual, as a response to the dominant "barrio culture";

32. Eldin Villafañe, *The Liberating Spirit: Towards a Hispanic American Social Ethic* (Grand Rapids: Eerdmans, 1993).

33. Villafañe, *The Liberating Spirit*, p. 130.

(2) spiritual, informed by Latin passion and symbolic mediation; (3) personalist and existentialist, expecting God to speak personally via Scripture and the Holy Spirit; (4) liberationist, providing solidarity with the poor and oppressed and freedom from bondage; (5) charismatic, where the experience of glossolalia colors all other spiritual experiences; and (6) egalitarian, where all are given the opportunity to prophesy. These factors become features of the Hispanic Pentecostal community of the church and its relationships internally and externally.

From the perspective of this sociocultural group, the church offers a critique of wider society. It declares that all is not well in the world. Indeed, the vision of the disinherited rejects totally those who reject them as insignificant and invisible. They feel alienated from wider society and its secular values and structures. Therefore, they offer a countercultural alternative as a form of protest. As a sociocultural entity, the church "posits its own counterpoint, whether by the authority of Scripture, community, charismatic person or the Spirit — thus providing an external and/or transcendent point of reference."[34] From this counterpoint of reference, it denounces what it sees as destructive factors in human society. The critique itself is informed, shaped, and resourced by a pneumatology whereby the Spirit is understood to be grieved by personal and social sin (Eph. 4:30) and convicts both Christian and non-Christian alike of their sinfulness (John 16:8-11). The presence of the Spirit is a sign of God's in-breaking reign as he brings order, restrains chaos, and offers support and help. In this way the church continues to participate in the anointing that Jesus experienced during his earthly ministry, which since Pentecost has been passed on to the ministry of the church. The church is not the same as the kingdom of God, but it is a visible expression of the kingdom and embodies and witnesses to it.[35]

For Villafañe this liberationist and pneumatological paradigm informs a distinctly Hispanic Pentecostal social ethic. This social ethic is constructed on two pillars: the role of Scripture and the role of love and justice. It emerges from an experience of the Spirit that produces love for the other who is oppressed and downtrodden (Rom. 5:5). Love is the source and motivation for life in the Spirit. The ethic itself is based on Galatians 5:25: "If we live in the Spirit, let us also walk in the Spirit" (NKJV). Living in the Spirit is understood to refer to all that the Spirit has done historically, in power encounters and in "charismatic" empowerment. Walking in the Spirit is understood as

---

34. Villafañe, *The Liberating Spirit*, p. 156.
35. Villafañe, *The Liberating Spirit*, p. 186.

participating in the reign of God, challenging structural sin and evil, and fulfilling the prophetic and vocational role of being Spirit-baptized believers.[36] The church is called to be a community of the Spirit in the world for the world, which means participating in political processes and seeking the peace of the city (Jer. 29:7). The role of the church, as empowered by the Holy Spirit, is to restrain evil, help establish conditions of justice, and work toward a peaceful moral order — in other words, to discern the presence and action of the Spirit and join in his existing witness to God's reign. This will include aspects of spiritual warfare against "principalities and powers" (Eph. 6:12) as they are manifest in social structures, since liberation is both personal and social. It is in this work of love and justice (Mic. 6:8) that the church fulfills its role as prophetic and its vocation as Spirit-baptized. This theological norm is based in Villafañe's reading, via Stronstad, of the Pentecostal narrative in Acts. Indeed, both the Holy Spirit and Scripture provide the ethical norms for this distinctly Hispanic American Pentecostal perspective, since revelation is regarded as dynamic and continuous, based on the *testimonium internum Spiritus sancti*. It is also based in the understanding that God is love (1 John 4:8, 16), and this is mediated by the Spirit's presence in the church for the sake of justice as "love rationally distributed."[37]

Samuel Solivan's work offers a complementary approach to Villafañe in the Hispanic Pentecostal liberationist tradition.[38] In particular, it seeks to address how Pentecostals respond on behalf of the socially and economically disadvantaged. The key concept Solivan uses to explore the liberation of American Hispanics is *orthopathos*, by which he means the "type of critical, theological and personal first-hand engagement with the biblical, theological and social reality of suffering and marginalized communities."[39] This concept attempts to bridge the gap between the related concepts of *orthodoxy* (right belief) and *orthopraxy* (right action). The focus on *pathos* places people's suffering and marginalization at the center rather than at the periphery. Historically, Pentecostalism has engaged much more extensively with the poor of Latin America, and their communities have provided empowerment and hope. With the migration of Hispanics to North America, Solivan seeks to articulate a liberation theology from a Pentecostal perspective that addresses this group that has been marginalized by society.

36. Villafañe, *The Liberating Spirit*, p. 195.

37. Villafañe, *The Liberating Spirit*, p. 214.

38. Samuel Solivan, *The Spirit, Pathos, and Liberation: Toward an Hispanic Pentecostal Theology* (Sheffield: Sheffield Academic Press, 1998).

39. Solivan, *Spirit, Pathos, and Liberation*, p. 11.

Solivan argues that this type of theology starts in two places: with the Scriptures and with the suffering of the people. They are "read" side by side. The Bible is read from the context of the poorest neighborhoods in the USA, and biblical models are used to resource identity, whether it be the exodus narrative and the compassion of God (Exod. 3:7-22), the Word becoming human (John 1:1-14), the power made perfect in human weakness (2 Cor. 12:9-13), or God's willingness to raise up those in despair (Jer. 29:4-14).[40] In these and other passages God is attentive to the needs of the poor and demonstrates a "kenotic empathy" toward the needs of humanity. Thus God identifies with the human condition in the incarnation, locates himself with the poor and the oppressed, and transforms the very condition of *pathos* in human experience, thus giving hope. For Solivan, it is the transforming power of the Scripture as mediated by the Holy Spirit in the lives of believers that gives it authority. It is the *testimonium internum Spiritus sancti* verified by experience. Only by the Holy Spirit can people and communities move from suffering to liberation and experience faith, hope, and love. Acts 2 affirms the diversity of both language and culture, of the existence of particularity as well as universality. It is the Holy Spirit that energizes respect for different languages and cultures as a means of God's desire for the liberation of all people. In many respects Solivan's work should be understood as a development of Villafañe's contribution, developing its ideas and giving it nuanced support.

I now turn to the UK and the work of Robert Beckford. He analyzed Pentecostalism within the context of the immigrant churches in order to propose a political theology for the black church.[41] By "black" he means immigrants in the UK from African Caribbean heritage; it is used as a term of resistance against white hegemony. In *Dread and Pentecostal* Beckford writes as a black British Pentecostal who sees baptism in the Spirit as a defining characteristic of this kind of Pentecostalism. He perceives the black church as a "shelter" or place of support and transformation that is characterized by the Spirit's presence among a family with close kinship ties. The black church must be driven by the Spirit, he affirms, since communion with the Spirit is essential to worshiping practices. This pneumatology is harnessed in favor of black Pentecostals. "Racialized subordination and White supremacist ideology are still prevalent. In opposition, pneumatology must be concerned

40. Solivan, *Spirit, Pathos, and Liberation*, p. 74.
41. Robert Beckford, *Dread and Pentecostal: A Political Theology for the Black Church in Britain* (London: SPCK, 2000).

with radical holistic change."[42] Like other liberation theologians, he argues
for using the exodus narrative as a model of resistance. But he supplements
this motif with the concept of diaspora because it reflects the situation of
cultural interaction, religious identity, history, and memory. Thus he starts
with diaspora as experienced by the African Caribbean community. Experience is central to his liberation theology, and he seeks to elucidate it in
terms of displacement, memory, lack of acceptance, and relationship to and
solidarity with the "homeland."

Building on black theology, as well as general liberationist scholarship,
he advances a liberation theological praxis with the goal of emancipation
for all members of society.[43] As such, liberation finds its fulfillment in the
concept of reconciliation, rather than in the production of a new group of
oppressors that displaces the previous one. Instead of perpetuating the cycle of oppression, the resolution of the unjust situation benefits everybody.
Methodologically, this process of theological engagement is achieved by
adopting the familiar practical-theological approach of an action-reflection
model. The process has three phases: experience, analysis, and action. In this
process cultural analysis is used alongside theological reflection drawing on
the Bible as a key source in order to renew action. He thereby advocates a
theology that is holistic, transformative, and grounded in hope for the black
Christian community. The sources of Scripture, experience, and the work
of the Holy Spirit are all present within this discussion, although the use of
pneumatology is probably less strongly represented than in the Hispanic
approaches noted above.

These liberationist contributions take seriously the experience of Pentecostal Christians and place it within a broader context of oppression and
marginalization. Very little has been written in the liberationist genre from
a P/C perspective, and therefore, these authors provide not just examples of
what Pentecostal liberation theology looks like, but also social critiques of
both American and British societies. Liberation is regarded as holistic, not
just social or political; it has an element of personal empowerment through
the work of the Holy Spirit. This is an important Pentecostal dimension,
since it is not simply about structures of injustice. These experiences of empowerment are rooted in particularity and solidarity. This is both a strength
and a weakness, as it provides strong sociocultural support in the context of
alienation, but may also add to the sense of otherness, such that the dichot-

42. Beckford, *Dread and Pentecostal*, p. 6.
43. Beckford, *Dread and Pentecostal*, p. 145.

omous social categorization of "them and us" is further accentuated. There is always the danger, despite protests to the contrary, that the dichotomy of "them and us" (oppressor and oppressed) is simply inverted rather than reconciled. It is also important that the biblical narratives in use are not just the typical exodus ones. The Pentecostal emphasis is naturally on the day of Pentecost and how that can be aligned with a new exodus typology driven by the universality of the Holy Spirit.[44] However, a deeper and wider engagement with biblical texts in broader canonical contexts might have nuanced this position. Unfortunately, the use of Scripture is restricted, and this inhibits the dialectic between context and biblical texts. Ultimately, reconciliation both with God and across humanity is the eschatological telos, and this goal is reflected in these theologies to some extent, even if it is not limited to them.

In summary, the three liberationist perspectives described above certainly contain discussions of the use of Scripture, experience, and pneumatology. The engagement with biblical passages varies; sometimes they are used as thematic pegs rather than in a detailed discussion. Experience is commonly experience of oppression due to forms of inequality, and it is holistic rather than focused on what we might call "religious experience." Pneumatology is played unevenly in these texts, and while it is certainly linked to Pentecostal experiential markers such as baptism in the Spirit, as well as the spirituality of the poor, it could have been developed more fully. Other versions of Pentecostal liberation theology may well address some of these concerns in the future.

## 1.4 Empirical Theology

The third strand of practical theology in the academy, a less developed but nevertheless important aspect of practical theology within P/C scholarship, is what has been called "empirical theology." I shall focus on my own experience of research within this tradition of inquiry in order to set the scene for how this current work fits within my own research trajectory.[45] In this

---

44. Peter Cotterell, *Mission and Meaninglessness: The Good News in a World of Suffering and Disorder* (London: SPCK, 1990), argues that the exodus narrative is about the glory of God and true worship rather than liberation (p. 257). However, I think there could be a case made to link them, in the light of the new exodus typology associated with Pentecost and Pentecost's association with doxology (see below).

45. I shall note other contributors below, but, because this book develops my own per-

context, I use the term "empirical theology" in the sense used by European scholars, which was established in 1988 with the publication of the *Journal of Empirical Theology,* edited by Johannes A. van der Ven. The founding of the International Society for Empirical Research in Theology in 2002 further advanced the paradigm, so that now it is firmly established within the discipline of practical theology. As a young research student working in the 1980s, I looked for methodological tools in the discipline of theology to study prophecy in P/C Christianity. I could not find anything suitable and was forced to improvise using sociology and theology. However, in the mid-1990s I discovered the *Journal of Empirical Theology* and began to publish some of my own empirical work.[46] The methodological text of van der Ven was used critically, and his hermeneutical commitments based on Jürgen Habermas were exchanged for different ones.[47]

In my study of glossolalia I aimed to explore the nature and significance of the phenomenon using empirical methods, both qualitative and quantitative, from within a theological framework.[48] This framework was informed by the lifeworld-system dialectic derived from Thiselton (who borrowed the idea from Habermas), in which the horizon of Scripture informed the system or theoretical perspective and the lifeworld or contemporary reality was researched using empirical methods.[49] The use of Scripture and contemporary inquiry was further informed by the work of N. T. Wright.[50] He suggested that the way Scripture can function normatively is shaped by its own narrative expressed via its canonical structure, and that the church seeks to live in

---

spective methodologically, it seems appropriate to locate myself within the typology and give an autobiographical account in this context. I trust that this lack of modesty does not offend too many people!

46. Mark J. Cartledge, "Charismatic Prophecy," *Journal of Empirical Theology* 8, no. 1 (1995): 71-88.

47. Van der Ven, *Practical Theology;* Mark J. Cartledge, "Empirical Theology: Towards an Evangelical-Charismatic Hermeneutic," *Journal of Pentecostal Theology* 9 (1996): 115-26; Mark J. Cartledge, "Practical Theology and Empirical Identity," *European Journal of Theology* 7, no. 1 (1998): 37-44; Mark J. Cartledge, "Empirical Theology: Inter- or Intra-Disciplinary?" *Journal of Beliefs and Values* 20, no. 1 (1999): 98-104.

48. Mark J. Cartledge, "The Symbolism of Charismatic Glossolalia," *Journal of Empirical Theology* 12, no. 1 (1999): 37-51; Mark J. Cartledge, *Charismatic Glossolalia: An Empirical Theological Study,* New Critical Thinking in Theology and Biblical Studies Series (Aldershot: Ashgate, 2002).

49. Thiselton, *New Horizons in Hermeneutics,* p. 388.

50. N. T. Wright, *The New Testament and the People of God* (London: SPCK, 1992), pp. 139-43.

ways *consistent* with the narrative that also open up *innovation* in different social and historical contexts. To provide a pneumatological basis for this consistency/innovation dynamic, I suggested using the Paraclete sayings in John's Gospel. For example, discipleship leads to obedience to the teaching of Christ (consistency), and love is expressed in new ways (innovation), as well as there being new ways of obeying Christ (innovation) with stability and security (consistency) (John 14:16-17). The teaching of the Spirit suggests consistency with the previous teaching of Christ, while the act of reminding the disciples suggests consistency but also the possibility of innovation since knowledge of the past may well inspire new events in the life of the church (John 14:26). The Spirit guides into all truth and conveys revelation in harmony with existing revelation, and is consistent as well as innovative in opening up new possibilities and understandings (John 16:12-15). Using this reading of the Paraclete sayings, I attempted to provide a pneumatological twist to an existing evangelical hermeneutic and methodology in order to make the approach more appropriate to the subjects of my research, namely, P/C Christians. Thus, the practical-theological framework used Scripture, hermeneutics, and empirical research methods to access the experiences, beliefs, and values of contemporary P/C Christians. As such it marked the beginning of a methodological journey for me.

My second book allowed me to develop my thinking in relation to practical theology and empirical methods. *Practical Theology: Charismatic and Empirical Perspectives* is the first book attempting to situate the empirical-theological paradigm within a P/C theological framework.[51] Instead of using cyclical approaches to research, for example, the pastoral cycle or empirical-theological cycle, I suggested that underlying these cycles is a more fundamental oscillation or dialectic. Following on from earlier work, I conceptualized two sets of dialectics at work. The first is between a theoretical system (represented by existing theological sources of Scripture and tradition, as well as social science theory) and the lifeworld or concrete empirical reality. The process of research is a movement between the two in order to follow a process of investigation leading to insights and new ideas as well as practices. The second dialectic is between practical theology and P/C spirituality. Here the theologian moves through the different stages of the spirituality cycle

---

51. Mark J. Cartledge, *Practical Theology: Charismatic and Empirical Perspectives,* Studies in Pentecostal and Charismatic Issues (Carlisle: Paternoster, 2003); cf. the earlier essay, Mark J. Cartledge, "Practical Theology and Charismatic Spirituality: Dialectics in the Spirit," *Journal of Pentecostal Theology* 10, no. 2 (2002): 107-24.

of search-encounter-transformation, such that the research process is also correlated with the spirituality process itself. It is as part of this spirituality process that the theologian asks: "(1) what is the Holy Spirit doing in this context? (2) how does this activity relate to the work of the Holy Spirit revealed in Scripture? and (3) what is the Spirit saying to the church (Revelation 2.11)?"[52] It is here that the research process is linked to the life of the church. In particular, it argues for the need to investigate the testimonies that are contained in the ecclesial narratives. Drawing on the work of Andrew T. Lincoln and his analysis of John's Gospel,[53] I suggested that the role of testimony is an important aspect of P/C theology and a legitimate mode of theological discourse that deserves to be explored empirically.

Further methodological thinking has allowed me to consider the role of the affections or emotions as part of the direct object of practical theology.[54] This is because beliefs and practices are intimately connected to feelings and desires, even when that connection is not fully acknowledged. Therefore the "affective" also provides material for theological investigation and reflection. Drawing on the work of Robert C. Roberts, I understand the affections as providing particular sensitivities or ways of seeing ourselves and the world that may have been previously hidden from us.[55] They can be based in an overarching concern such as the kingdom of God or the Christian narrative of salvation. In other words, they can be "conscious construals of particular situations that provide a link between relatively stable religious beliefs and appropriate practice."[56] This discussion between spirituality and the theology of practice connects quite naturally with Pentecostal discussions of the affections and their role within experience. For Steven Land, affections are shaped by the Christian story and communal narratives and practices, thus providing abiding dispositions rather than fleeting feelings and moods. Land identifies key affections that lead to particular actions; thus gratitude is expressed with worship practices, compassion is expressed in prayer and social action, and courage is expressed in witness to the transforming power of

52. Cartledge, *Practical Theology*, p. 30.

53. Andrew T. Lincoln, *Truth on Trial: The Lawsuit Motif in the Fourth Gospel* (Peabody, Mass.: Hendrickson, 2000).

54. Mark J. Cartledge, "Affective Theological Praxis: Understanding the Direct Object of Practical Theology," *International Journal of Practical Theology* 8, no. 1 (2004): 34-52.

55. Robert C. Roberts, *Spirituality and Human Emotion* (Grand Rapids: Eerdmans, 1982).

56. Amy Plantinga Pauw, "Attending to the Gaps between Beliefs and Practices," in *Practicing Theology: Beliefs and Practices in the Christian Life*, ed. Miroslav Volf and Dorothy Bass (Grand Rapids: Eerdmans, 2002), pp. 33-48 (p. 46).

Christ. From this Pentecostal perspective, Land argues that theology should be concerned with orthopathy (right affections), not just orthodoxy (right beliefs) and orthopraxy (right action or behavior).[57]

Land's Pentecostal contribution suggested to me that the direct object of practical-theological inquiry can be reconceptualized. The object of practical-theological inquiry is people engaged in some form of activity or located in some kind of scenario. Drawing on the work of van der Ven, I agreed that God is not the direct object of inquiry, since theology is a reflection on faith expressed in belief and practices. God cannot be researched directly because he is a transcendent reality. God is the direct object of faith, whereas the beliefs and practices of religious people are the direct object of theology, and thus God as a transcendent reality is the indirect object of theology. This means that the reception of God's self-revelation by a person can become the object of research, "especially in the religious experience in which he [*sic*] experiences reality as religious."[58] This reception of a religious experience is also accompanied by a response toward God in prayer and worship as well as a reaction toward others in theological speech, action, and ministry. It is in these dimensions that God is indirectly accessible to theological research. Thus affections and experience combine to become mediators of the Holy Spirit among communities and individuals. This led me to explore concrete expressions of church.

In my research I have been interested in case studies of churches, or congregational studies. I have been interested in the narratives that people tell regarding their faith, as well as the use of symbols and practices. I have always wanted to give due respect to this grassroots level of theological discourse, and this desire resonates with the ordinary theology project. So when I decided to conduct a study of an urban, multicultural Pentecostal church in Birmingham, UK, it seemed natural to want to pay particular attention to the local narratives, at personal and corporate levels.[59] This interest in narrative connects to the Pentecostal practice of testimony, which functions at a variety of levels, from personal conversation and group discussions to congregational practice and literary expression in denominational magazines. I

57. Steven J. Land, *Pentecostal Spirituality: A Passion for the Kingdom* (Sheffield: Sheffield Academic Press, 1993).

58. Van der Ven, *Practical Theology*, p. 103.

59. Mark J. Cartledge, "Pentecostal Experience: An Example of Practical-Theological Rescripting," *Journal of the European Pentecostal Association* 28, no. 1 (2008): 21-33; Mark J. Cartledge, *Testimony in the Spirit: Rescripting Ordinary Pentecostal Theology* (Farnham: Ashgate, 2010), pp. 16-18.

also wanted to connect this local or ordinary study to traditions larger than individual congregations, so I have consciously engaged with a discussion of early British Pentecostal theology as well as the classical Assemblies of God Pentecostal theology to which the congregation is affiliated. Furthermore, I wanted to engage in a conversation with the broader academy of P/C theology, with a little assist from others (e.g., social science). Therefore, I saw myself as working at a number of different levels of discourse (ordinary, ecclesial, and academic).

For my discussion of religious experience, I used Caroline Franks Davis's philosophical typology to categorize experience among members of this church. She identifies six categories of experiences: (1) interpretive, (2) quasi-sensory, (3) revelatory, (4) regenerative, (5) numinous, and (6) mystical.[60] While this fairly abstract typology was useful as a starting point, the categories clearly overlapped, and thereby the distinctions it sought to advance were to some extent compromised. It also assumed a rather limited definition of religious experience as a mental event, which, upon inquiry, did not capture the fully social and embodied kinds of experiences narrated by P/C Christians. Thus, its descriptive power was diminished in my view.

My central concept was the notion of "rescripting," which I borrowed from the sociologist David Martin.[61] I chose this concept because I was impressed by the way he applied the notion sensitively to Pentecostal adherents. Whereas he was suggesting that sociologists take care and theorize with due caution after having heard the notional script, I was more interested in using the theological narratives, in dialogue with selected social science perspectives. I came to the view that a respectful yet critical approach to Pentecostal ordinary theology was the way forward. Treating the narratives metaphorically as scripts allowed me to suggest ways in which the main thrusts of these narratives might be revised that were both in continuity and in discontinuity with ordinary theology. I did not think, nor do I now think, that ordinary theology should be allowed to dictate theological terms. But neither do I think that academic discourse should set the agenda exclusively, so that the ordinary is used as a kind of adornment, an illustration of a previously defined concept. I do believe that experientialist religious discourse should be respected as containing genuine theology. But an attitude

60. Cartledge, *Testimony in the Spirit*, p. 89; Caroline Franks Davis, *The Evidential Force of Religious Experience* (Oxford: Clarendon, 1999).

61. David Martin, "Undermining Old Paradigms: Rescripting Pentecostal Accounts," *PentecoStudies: Online Journal for the Interdisciplinary Study of Pentecostal and Charismatic Movements* 5, no. 1 (2006): 18-38.

of respect does not preclude theological evaluation or comment, which is what I attempted to offer.

So from these various narratives, analyses, and reflections, I developed what I regarded as a concrete ecclesiology. Ecclesiological categories derived from the congregational, denominational, and academic material were briefly expanded to suggest the contours of a P/C ecclesiology. Recent discussions of it have revolved around an existing theological scheme, notably the fivefold gospel of the Wesleyan Pentecostal tradition, which is christocentric: Jesus is the savior, sanctifier, Spirit baptizer, healer, and soon to be coming king. Although this framework has provided some useful reflections, the downside from the perspective of ordinary theology is that it starts with an a priori set of categories within which concrete particularities are expected to fit. From my own research of the particularities of a case study, I wanted to draw out themes that were embedded in the ordinary theology of the members of the congregation I was studying and had much wider resonance theologically within Pentecostalism and the broader Christian tradition. In dialogue with scholarship, and in particular biblical metaphors, I suggested a different fivefold description that I think is representative of P/C spirituality more broadly. It is worth describing the key features at this juncture.

(1) The metaphor of temple is used as a location for where God's Spirit dwells *(temple of praise)*. First Corinthians 3:16 correlates well with the day of Pentecost in which the people of praise declare the wonders of God in acts of glossolalia (Acts 2:11). Praise is the primary action of the living temple, the church. Spirit-inspired praise is constitutive of the church: the church is a people of praise. For Pentecostals identity is formed in the context of worship, as the Spirit of God indwells the people and is experienced intensely through the activity of sung worship. (2) Prayer for the sick is central to Pentecostal spirituality (James 5:13), and again the location of worship and prayer is often the setting in which healing is sought *(house of healing)*. The church can be regarded as similar to a household (Eph. 2:19), which is the basic unit of social care and responsibility. Belief in the healing power of God is not just a therapeutic emphasis (which it is), but it is also a therapeutic model of salvation. At the heart of Pentecostal soteriology is a belief in Christ the healer, the doctor in the house who has provided the answer to sin-sickness, alienation, and ultimately death. The healing model of the atonement dominates Pentecostal theology; the traditional evangelical forensic metaphors are regarded as secondary. (3) The human body *(members of ministry)* is also used as a metaphor for the church (1 Cor. 12:12-13). The one Spirit baptizes the many into the one body of Christ. Each member needs

the others for the body to function in a healthy way, and each member is a minister in the Spirit for the common good. If you like, the church is the charismatic fellowship of the Spirit, as members use their charismata for the benefit of all. The charismata are an essential feature of the church and represent the egalitarian character of Spirit-endowed ministry — "the Spirit has been poured out on all flesh." (4) The global nature of Pentecostalism and the multicultural nature of this congregation model hospitality at the heart of the ecclesial community *(community of hospitality)*. People from very different backgrounds are accepted and integrated into the one community. This feature reflects characteristics of the early church, which devoted itself to *koinonia* (Acts 2:47). This participation in fellowship was open and inviting, as new members were added to their number. It is a reflection of God's own hospitality, sharing the love of the triune life. This *koinonia* can also be seen to represent hospitality to other Christian traditions, as insights from other traditions can be integrated into P/C ecclesiology, without the loss of its distinctive identity. This might occur through the recognition of the baptismal practices of other Christians, for example (which incidentally was not always obvious in this congregation; e.g., my own baptism was not recognized as valid — being infant baptism). (5) Pentecostals are probably the most hopeful people I know. The early British Pentecostals expected Jesus to return in 1914! Whatever the eschatological failing of this group of people, their beliefs energized hope and active discipleship. Perhaps there is some resonance with the Gospel account of the road to Emmaus (Luke 24:13-35), which provides an example of how discipleship is a journey of discovery and of hope *(pilgrims of hope)*. Only at the end of the journey is Jesus revealed as the resurrected Christ. The presence of the Spirit in the eschatological community mediates this presence of the resurrected Christ. Following these resurrection encounters, and in anticipation of the new creation, the disciples are sent out on the road of mission (Acts 1:8): to proclaim the gospel and to interpret what they themselves have seen and heard (Acts 2:14-41). It is a *via salutis* — a way of salvation, a journey of salvation. It is framed eschatologically as the church experiences the now and not-yet of the kingdom of God.

In this description, well-known biblical metaphors are used to develop a contribution to ecclesiology. However, the original categories are found within the concrete particularities of the case study. The use of biblical metaphors and an interaction with Pentecostal and charismatic theology allow the suggested model to be generalized in ways that might appeal beyond the boundaries of this particular group of people. The use of Scripture expands the discourse and connects with ecclesiology from other traditions. Other studies can be said to fall within this genre even if they do not use the denotation "empirical theology"; they use empirical research methods in relation to theological accounts of contemporary beliefs and practices. Most of the material is qualitative in nature,[62] but William K. Kay, in particular, has researched Pentecostal Christians using quantitative methods.[63]

Permit me to offer a self-critical reflection based on the description of my work stated above.[64] I have clearly placed myself historically with the empirical strand of practical theology, although my work does not fall within this paradigm exclusively. This means that religious experience (expressed via beliefs, values, and practices) accessed via empirical research methods has been at the heart of what I have done. It has been informed by a discussion of the affections at one point, but I would concede that this dimension has not been subsequently developed in any great detail. I have attempted to place my approach within a hermeneutical framework that is shaped by a model derived from biblical pneumatology (John), thus aligning both Scripture and the work of the Holy Spirit. I would concede, however, that an extensive, detailed, and systematic exegetical engagement with Scripture has not been developed as fully as it might have been. Instead, I have been at the vanguard of the turn to testimony as a form of legitimate theological discourse, and I have used it critically by transposing it into a theological key and conceiving it in terms of different levels of discourse. This is an aspect of my theology that invites further development in dialogue with the use of testimony in conversation with narrative theology. Toward the end of my book *Testimony in the Spirit*, I offer a proposal sketching out the contours of a P/C ecclesiology that is derived from the congregational experience of the Holy Spirit as well as using biblical metaphors (as noted above). Again,

---

62. E.g., Stephen E. Parker, *Led by the Spirit: Toward a Practical Theology of Pentecostal Discernment and Decision Making* (Sheffield: Sheffield Academic Press, 1996); James H. S. Steven, *Worship in the Spirit: Charismatic Worship in the Church of England* (Carlisle: Paternoster, 2002); Cory E. Labanow, *Evangelicalism and the Emerging Church: A Congregational Study of a Vineyard Church* (Farnham: Ashgate, 2009); and David Morgan, *Priesthood, Prophethood, and Spirit-Led Community: A Practical-Prophetic Pentecostal Ecclesiology* (Saarbrücken: Lap Lambert Academic Publishing, 2010).

63. William K. Kay, *Pentecostals in Britain* (Carlisle: Paternoster, 2000); William K. Kay, *Apostolic Networks in Britain: New Ways of Being Church* (Milton Keynes: Paternoster, 2007).

64. For critical observations on the use of empirical research methods in practical theology, see Stephen Pattison, *The Challenge of Practical Theology: Selected Essays* (London: Jessica Kingsley, 2007), pp. 275-81, and Heather Walton, "Seeking Wisdom in Practical Theology: *Phronesis*, Poetics and Everyday Life," *Practical Theology* 7, no. 1 (2014): 5-18 (pp. 6-9).

this ecclesiology invites further exploration, and I have begun to suggest different dimensions to what a P/C or renewalist ecclesiology might begin to look like.[65] This present book develops my approach to practical theology and locates me specifically within a P/C perspective once again, and seeks to address some of my own weaknesses.

In summary, I have given an autobiographical, if brief, account of my research journey at the interface of practical theology, empirical research methods, and P/C theology. I have sought to place the research of P/C Christians within the methodological framework of empirical theology as a strand of practical theology. In so doing, I have critiqued existing hermeneutical perspectives explicitly from a P/C perspective in order to provide an alternative standpoint from which to research this tradition of Christianity. This standpoint is in sympathy with the basic spirituality and worldview assumptions of this form of Christianity, while at the same time being critical of specific forms of its expression. Throughout my work I have attempted to bring Scripture, Christian tradition, and claims or expressions of experience of the Holy Spirit into dialogue in order to renew theological praxis.

## 1.5 Conclusion

This chapter aimed to illustrate the kinds of approaches to practical theology that can be found among P/C theologians. It placed examples of these contributions within a threefold classification: (1) formation, worship, and ministry; (2) liberationist theology; and (3) empirical theology, following a useful classification suggested by the president of the International Academy of Practical Theology, Ruard Ganzevoort, in 2005. This typology is regarded as heuristic because it enables the contours of a field to be outlined. I considered each of the three categories in terms of three interrelated themes: the use of Scripture, the role of experience, and the role of the Holy Spirit in the expression of the theology. I chose these themes because of their importance for P/C theology generally and their promise for practical theology.

The formation and ministry strand of the P/C approach to practical theology provides a clear coordination of these three themes. It contains a strongly normative stance, whereby the ministry of Jesus and the early church is understood to stand in direct continuity with the church today

---

65. Mark J. Cartledge, "Renewal Ecclesiology in Empirical Perspective," *Pneuma* 36, no. 1 (2014): 5-24.

because of the ongoing work of the Holy Spirit in the life and experience of Pentecostal believers today. The liberationist strand understandably looks at experience through the lens of oppression and views specifically religious experience as a means of empowering the oppressed through the work of the Holy Spirit. Given the focus on injustice and the experience of specific communities, it could be said that the discussion of the Holy Spirit in relation to specific biblical texts is not fully developed. My own work in empirical theology has attempted to bring Scripture, experience of the Holy Spirit, and broader theological sources into conversation. It has taken seriously the ordinary theology of believers but has, nevertheless, sought to rescript it in order to make it theoretically developed and relevant to theological constituencies outside of P/C Christianity. These three strands do have different approaches and slightly different emphases: internal community life and witness, liberation of oppressed groups and justice, and theological accounts informed by empirical research methods. This means that the outcomes and import of these contributions will be different as well. Nevertheless, they do suggest an interesting agenda for research.

How are these different contributions to the internal conversations within P/C theology, especially concerning the three themes of Scripture, experience, and the Holy Spirit, used within the wider academy of practical theology? Only a limited number of scholars from the P/C community engage with the wider practical-theological academy, and virtually no one from practical theology appears to engage with P/C theology explicitly. Therefore, it is both important and timely to develop this conversation further. The following chapter looks at how practical theologians have engaged with these three important themes in order to elucidate how P/C scholarship might address the practical-theological academy.

# 2 Scripture, Experience, and the Holy Spirit in Practical Theology

## 2.1 Introduction

Christian theologians have from earliest times reflected upon and used the Scriptures, both Jewish and Christian, to develop an understanding of identity in the face of God's self-revealing presence as well as historical and social contingencies. This has been achieved in community as individuals have interacted with one another and prayed together, participating in ecclesial life and witness. It has also been transported into intellectual domains overlapping with and sometimes distinct from the church, most notably the academy. In this context the relationship between ecclesial life and intellectual academic pursuits has been a matter of push and pull, depending on local circumstance and politics. Over time theology has developed in many different ways and into a number of distinct subdisciplines. This fragmentation and specialization has been charted quite successfully by a number of writers in the field.[1]

With the emergence of practical theology as a distinct form of theology focused around issues of contemporary beliefs and value-laden practices, a number of slightly different if overlapping typologies about how the Bible is used have been stated. For example, Stephen Pattison suggests that the way the Bible has been used by pastoral care and counseling theorists can be described as (1) fundamentalist (e.g., Jay E. Adams); (2) tokenist or in-

---

1. E.g., Edward Farley, *Theologia: The Fragmentation and Unity of Theological Education* (Philadelphia: Fortress, 1983).

discriminate in use of texts (e.g., Howard Clinebell); (3) imagist/suggestive, that is, applying biblical themes or images (e.g., Alastair Campbell); (4) informative via different literary genres such as lament (e.g., Donald Capps); and (5) thematic analysis (e.g., William Oglesby).[2] The student textbook by Elaine Graham, Heather Walton, and Frances Ward offers the most inclusive typology for theological reflection to date.[3] Two of their seven types focus on the use of the Bible in particular. The first is "speaking in parables," which uses the parabolic nature of Jesus' ministry, and the second is "telling God's story: canonical narrative theology," which is associated with theologians such as Karl Barth, George Lindbeck, Hans Frei, Stanley Hauerwas, and Gerard Loughlin.

Paul Ballard has recently described how the Bible has been used within the discourse of practical theology. He observes that its use has proven both "elusive and problematic."[4] He suggests a number of reasons for this state of play: different traditions of interpretation, a gap between the Bible and theology created by the fragmentation of modern theology, and a multitude of hermeneutical approaches. Indeed, practical theology has its own problems because it is such a broad field of interest. On the basis of his analysis of how the Bible has actually been used, he articulates four ways in which the Bible can and should "play a role."[5] First, the Bible can be used as a resource for pastoral care that *illuminates contemporary experience.* According to the traditions in which the Bible is used, it can be applied normatively, in critical dialogue, or indirectly. Second, practical theology can work from the Bible as it is used in worship and spirituality. Here the Bible is central to the activity of liturgy and leads to its appropriation in *confessional approaches,* via the reader's pragmatic intention, by recovering "precritical approaches," and in prayer and preaching. Third, the Bible can be used as a *depository of wisdom* for use in theological reflection and contextual theology, for example, in critical correlation or pastoral cycle models. The desire is for practical wisdom that relies on biblical scholarship from within the community of

2. Stephen Pattison, *A Critique of Pastoral Care,* 3rd ed. (London: SCM, 2000; orig. 1988).

3. Elaine Graham, Heather Walton, and Frances Ward, *Theological Reflection: Methods* (London: SCM, 2005). Also see the earlier action-reflection text by Laurie Green, *Let's Do Theology: A Pastoral Cycle Resource Book* (London: Mowbray, 1990), pp. 82-90.

4. Paul Ballard, "The Use of Scripture," in *The Wiley-Blackwell Companion to Practical Theology,* ed. Bonnie J. Miller-McLemore (Oxford: Wiley-Blackwell, 2012), pp. 163-72 (p. 163); see also Paul Ballard, "The Bible in Theological Reflection: Indications from the History of Scripture," *Practical Theology* 4, no. 1 (2011): 35-47.

5. Ballard, "The Use of Scripture," p. 163.

faith using creative imagination. Fourth, practical theology is interested in discovering how the Bible is received and used by people using *empirical research* methods.

This analysis offers a useful summary of the practical-theological domain and provides a point of departure. However, a glance at a range of academic practical theology texts suggests that more needs to be said about how professional practical theologians go about their task before we can better understand the manner in which the Bible is used and indeed the nature of the problem. In other words, we need to appreciate the distinct academic practice in which the Scriptures are used. *How do academic practical theologians actually use Scripture in their theology?* To elucidate these points, I shall look at key contributions in textbooks and monographs as well as edited collections. I am concerned here with the *explicit* use of Scripture in theological reflection and construction. I shall then consider the Bible in Pastoral Practice project before reflecting critically on academic practice. Finally, I shall suggest five features that may constitute a practical-theological approach to reading Scripture, as a possible way forward.

Following this discussion of Scripture, I shall attend to my other key themes, namely, pneumatology and experience, especially religious experience. I shall treat these themes together because they are often intertwined in the literature. My intention is to describe the contours of the ideas that are present. It will become very obvious that these themes are considerably less well represented in the literature compared to Scripture and its use. Nevertheless, there are some examples of how they have been treated, and these provide material with which to engage and to elucidate the nature of the problem before us.

## 2.2 Scripture and Practical Theology

### 2.2.1 Identifying a Typology

One survey of the literature from the 1980s to the present day included authors mostly from Europe and North America. Attention was paid to the work of scholars associated with the British and Irish Association of Practical Theology as well as the International Academy of Practical Theology, which is the world-leading academy in the field. Different patterns can be detected in the literature analyzed, which can be viewed as constituting a typology of usage.[6] This typology varies from the ones mentioned above, although there is some overlap. Its significance lies in its portrait of *academic practice,* which has not been mapped with this level of detail before.

First, some authors use an overtly prior conceptual and hermeneutical framework derived from theory outside of theology in order to filter the reading of empirical, theological, and biblical material. This can be called an *a priori conceptual grid.* For example, Don Browning, in his classic text *A Fundamental Practical Theology,* argues that practical theology should listen to the Scriptures and the classic Greek texts that influenced Israel and her leaders. The "thick descriptions" emerging from the descriptive theological phase should guide the interpretation of classic texts, and five dimensions should be allowed to guide the biblical interpretation.[7] These five dimensions are regarded as validity criteria by which practical theology is constructed. The dimensions are (1) visional (including metaphysical claims), (2) obligational (normative ethical claims), (3) anthropological (human nature and needs), (4) environment-social (social-systemic and ecological constraints), and (5) rule-role (the concrete patterns of our actual praxis). These five dimensions should be used to describe the theory-laden practices and to assess Christian witness. A few specific biblical texts are used, but these are filtered via the a priori critical framework of the five dimensions. Johannes A. van der Ven provides a hermeneutical motif for assessing theological validity within the context of discussing Jürgen Habermas's communicative action theory and the normative principles of equality, freedom, universality, and solidarity.[8] He links the eschatological *basileia* symbol of Jesus' own praxis based on the Gospel accounts to the creation and exodus narratives. The symbol forms the metaethical basis for assessing communicative praxis. Similarly, Edmund Arens offers a christocentric approach to Habermas's communication action theory.[9] The biblical foundations for this position focus on the use of Gospel texts and the *basileia* symbol in the ministry of Jesus. But this key feature is very specific and defined in relation to a non-

---

6. Also, see the typology of student theological reflection by Roger Walton, "Using the Bible and Christian Tradition in Theological Reflection," *British Journal of Theological Education* 13, no. 2 (2000): 133-51.

7. Don Browning, *A Fundamental Practical Theology: Descriptive and Strategic Proposals* (Minneapolis: Fortress, 1996; orig. 1991), pp. 105-6, 139-40, who says: "The five dimensions can guide biblical interpretation" (p. 140).

8. Johannes A. van der Ven, *Practical Theology: An Empirical Approach* (Kampen: Kok Pharos, 1993), esp. pp. 69-70.

9. Edmund Arens, *Christopraxis: A Theology of Action* (Minneapolis: Fortress, 1995).

theological hermeneutical theory, which provides a filter through which the motif is used.

Second, some authors cite biblical texts without any obvious coherence to their usage. This can be called the *proof-text approach* (somewhat similar to the tokenist approach noted above). For example, the contextual theology of Stephen B. Bevans can be classified as a form of practical theology.[10] In this model biblical texts are dropped in or scattered in (what appears to be) a random manner throughout the book in order to support the ideas expressed. A similar approach is offered by Paul Ballard and John Pritchard.[11] They focus mostly on specific texts without analyzing the discourse in which these texts are set.[12] This practice is repeated by Henry S. Wilson et al.[13] Similarly, the text by van der Ven on reflective ministry simply suggests that the church should have a vision as the people of God, based on selected texts.[14] Janet H. Wootton's discussion of worship and feminist theology offers specific themes, but the level of engagement with the biblical texts gives it the feel of a set of proof texts used to reference a conversation.[15] The discussion by Clemens Sedmak of local theology uses texts as, what I would call, "mini-launchpads" for thematic discussion,[16] which is similar to the approach of Emmanuel Lartey.[17] Terry Veling is probably the most extensive example of someone whose mind is saturated with knowledge of biblical texts, so that when he writes on a subject he simply cites text after text in a kind of peppering process.[18] It is by far the most extensive example of proof texting that I found in the literature. Stephen Pattison does not really engage in biblical studies, although some proof texts are applied to the discussion of

10. Stephen B. Bevans, *Models of Contextual Theology* (Maryknoll, N.Y.: Orbis, 2002; orig. 1992).

11. Paul Ballard and John Pritchard, *Practical Theology in Action: Christian Thinking in the Service of Church and Society* (London: SPCK, 1996), esp. p. 117.

12. E.g., Ballard and Pritchard, *Practical Theology in Action*, pp. 155, 160, 162, 165.

13. Henry S. Wilson et al., *Pastoral Theology from a Global Perspective* (Maryknoll, N.Y.: Orbis, 1996).

14. Johannes A. Van der Ven, *Education for Reflective Ministry* (Louvain: Peeters, 1998).

15. Janet H. Wootton, *Introducing a Practical Feminist Theology of Worship* (Sheffield: Sheffield Academic Press, 2000).

16. Clemens Sedmak, *Doing Local Theology: A Guide for Artisans of a New Humanity* (Maryknoll, N.Y.: Orbis, 2002).

17. Emmanuel Y. Lartey, *In Living Colour: An Intercultural Approach to Pastoral Care and Counselling* (London: Jessica Kingsley, 2003).

18. Terry A. Veling, *Practical Theology: "On Earth as It Is in Heaven"* (Maryknoll, N.Y.: Orbis, 2005).

spirituality, as well as to his (perhaps controversial) discussion of the shadow side of Jesus.[19]

Third, authors use selected key passages in a strategic manner, even if their analysis of these texts might be viewed as rather limited.[20] This can be called *strategic selection.* For example, Patricia O'Connell Killen and John de Beer use Acts 9:1-17 and the experience of Paul's conversion to critique the notion of certitude in theology.[21] They use this text as a motif to justify the standpoint of exploration and openness in theological reflection. From this basic posture, lectionary passages can be discussed and reflected upon. Gerben Heitink offers some, if limited, engagement with biblical texts by considering praxis in the New Testament and the pneumatological basis for practical-theological hermeneutics.[22] Similarly, Duncan B. Forrester discusses the compassion of Jesus, the love of God, and the *habitus* of truth from John's Gospel (3:21) before addressing issues concerning worship.[23] Dale P. Andrews's work from the perspective of the African American context focuses on biblical themes but privileges the Hebrew prophetic tradition, especially the eighth-century prophets.[24] F. Gerrit Immink uses texts in a limited manner, but he nevertheless offers some biblical context and deals with broad themes such as justification, salvation, and eschatology.[25] Thomas John Hastings produces a fairly detailed treatment of Romans 12:1-12 as a paradigm for a missional-ecumenical approach before (ironically) ignoring it throughout the rest of his book, even though he discusses Pauline theological anthropology later on in some detail.[26] Richard R. Osmer suggests

---

19. Stephen Pattison, *The Challenge of Practical Theology: Selected Essays* (London: Jessica Kingsley, 2007).

20. Helen Cameron et al., *Talking about God in Practice: Theological Action Research in Practical Theology* (London: SCM, 2010), allow for an engagement with Scripture as part of the normative theology, but the examples contain little evidence of its use.

21. Patricia O'Connell Killen and John de Beer, *The Art of Theological Reflection* (New York: Crossroad, 2000; orig. 1994).

22. Gerben Heitink, *Practical Theology: History, Theory, Action Domains* (Grand Rapids: Eerdmans, 1999).

23. Duncan B. Forrester, *Truthful Action: Explorations in Practical Theology* (Edinburgh: T. & T. Clark, 2000).

24. Dale P. Andrews, *Practical Theology for Black Churches: Bridging Black Theology and African American Folk Religion* (Louisville: Westminster John Knox, 2002).

25. F. Gerrit Immink, *Faith: A Practical Theological Reconstruction* (Grand Rapids: Eerdmans, 2005).

26. Thomas John Hastings, *Practical Theology and the One Body of Christ: Toward a Missional-Ecumenical Model* (Grand Rapids: Eerdmans, 2007).

a model of practical theology that includes four tasks: descriptive, inter-pretative, normative, and pragmatic.[27] Each task is given a basis in biblical texts, focusing on the themes of wisdom, prophetic discernment, and servant leadership. Finally, James Newton Poling discusses themes of creation (Gen. 1–2), conversation (Psalms), including lament (Pss. 137:8; 39:4-13; 30:11-12; 66:17), as well as the persons of King David and Jesus Christ, before framing these themes within process theology.[28] Each chapter follows key doctrinal themes and is introduced by reference to strategic biblical texts interpreted in relation to process theology and the testimony of the survivors of abuse and violence.

Fourth, some practical theologians offer more sustained treatment of a biblical passage or tradition. This can be called a *sustained engagement*. What is found in this category is some level of exegetical treatment of a number of texts. For example, Ellen T. Charry assesses the contribution that Paul's letters make to pastoral theology as well as the significance of the Sermon on the Mount as authoritative teaching.[29] R. John Elford, in his attempt to provide a theological account of pastoral care, analyzes dif-ferent biblical traditions before suggesting how they might be retrieved.[30] The work of Ray S. Anderson is unusual in that it focuses on the reading of Scripture as a major task of practical theology in the context of reading human texts.[31] His book frames this reading in Trinitarian theology and contains four chapters based on biblical texts treated in a sustained manner. However, his later pastoral theology tends toward the thematic use of proof texts to support his theological points.[32] A slightly different, if nevertheless serious, use of Scripture is found in the work of David Lyall, who engages with the challenge of postmodernism and offers a narrative approach to biblical hermeneutics in the service of pastoral care.[33] Key New Testament

---

27. Richard R. Osmer, *Practical Theology: An Introduction* (Grand Rapids: Eerdmans, 2008).

28. James Newton Poling, *Rethinking Faith: A Constructive Practical Theology* (Minne-apolis: Fortress, 2011).

29. Ellen T. Charry, *By the Renewing of Your Minds: The Pastoral Function of Christian Doctrine* (Oxford: Oxford University Press, 1997).

30. R. John Elford, *The Pastoral Nature of Theology: An Upholding Presence* (London: Cassell, 1999).

31. Ray S. Anderson, *The Shape of Practical Theology: Empowering Ministry with Theolog-ical Praxis* (Downers Grove, Ill.: IVP, 2001).

32. Ray S. Anderson, *Spiritual Caregiving as Secular Sacrament: A Practical Theology for Professional Caregivers* (London: Jessica Kingsley, 2003).

33. David Lyall, *Integrity of Pastoral Care* (London: SPCK, 2001).

themes are used to frame pastoral practice theologically; these themes in-clude incarnation, crucifixion, resurrection, pneumatology, eschatology, and ecclesiology. The work of John Inge on the subject of place and space begins with a sustained engagement of the theme in both Old Testament and New Testament texts.[34] Finally, Helen Cameron et al. suggest how a thematic approach can be used by paying attention to broader issues in biblical hermeneutics.[35]

Fifth, one gets a sense that a number of practical theologians see the Bible as simply a huge problem for contemporary theology. They say it needs to be read in the light of some critical perspective; in other words, a *critical reading* should be provided. This may be due to the reception of historical-critical scholarship or ideological criticism of one kind or another. In some cases perceived problematic texts are highlighted for critique. For example, Zoë Bennett provides a feminist approach to the Bible in practical theology because she deals with issues of violence and abusive language, as well as what she regards as problematic texts.[36] The use of the Bible basically re-volves around how these texts, and the issues they raise for women, might be interpreted in the light of a feminist standpoint. She acknowledges that for women the Bible has been a source of subordination as well as liberation. Therefore, it continues to be a site of struggle for interpreters who wish to remain in critical solidarity with the Christian faith.[37] In her most recent study, suggesting how the Bible might be used in practical theology as public theology, she enters the hermeneutical circle at the point of struggle. Indeed, she asks whether the Bible itself is a site of struggle.[38] For Bennett the reading of Scripture is rooted in two things: (1) the person's own existing relationship to the Bible and to the individuals and communities who have mediated it to the person; and (2) the fact that experience is not an imported category but rather is essential to the origins of Scripture itself.[39]

34. John Inge, *A Christian Theology of Place* (Farnham: Ashgate, 2003).

35. Helen Cameron et al., *Theological Reflection for Human Flourishing: Pastoral Practice and Public Theology* (London: SCM, 2012), pp. 74-93.

36. Zoë Bennett Moore, *Introducing Feminist Perspectives on Pastoral Theology* (Sheffield: Sheffield Academic Press, 2002). She subsequently changed her name back to Bennett, which I used for the sake of consistency.

37. Her approach is developed differently in C. Rowland and Z. Bennett, "'Action Is the Life of All': The Bible and Practical Theology," *Contact: Practical Theology and Pastoral Care* 150 (2006): 8-17.

38. Zoë Bennett, *Using the Bible in Practical Theology: Historical and Contemporary Perspectives* (Farnham: Ashgate, 2013), pp. 10, 13.

39. Bennett, *Using the Bible*, pp. 18, 48. In her most recent work there is a shift away from

Sixth, some authors simply do not use the Bible in any obvious way. This can be called the *excluded approach*. For example, Elaine Graham refers to reading the Bible in new ways but does not specify these ways, and subsequently cites another author on the "exorcism of patriarchal texts."[40] Jeff Astley offers a few biblical references concerning the nature of learning, teaching, and communication without further explanation.[41] Marcel Viau, John Swinton and Harriet Mowat, John Reader, and Bonnie Miller-McLemore offer no engagement with biblical texts,[42] while Pete Ward refers to a couple of biblical texts with regard to worship and leaves it at that.[43] This classification relates only to the texts cited; the same authors may well use Scripture in different ways in their other writing.

Most edited collections in practical theology have extremely limited engagement with biblical texts. One of the earliest collections of essays edited by Paul Ballard contains an essay discussing the objections to theological reflection on practice and cites three biblical proof texts. None of the other essays contain any biblical references.[44] This pattern, in which most chapters do not contain any biblical engagement, while one or two chapters do (but in a fairly superficial manner), is all too common. It can be seen in a number of edited collections.[45] Since most of these edited collections are publications

---

an exclusively critical reading to one that seeks to balance different aspects such as comparison, analogy, and risk (pp. 49-50).

40. E. Graham, *Transforming Practice: Pastoral Theology in an Age of Uncertainty* (London: Mowbray, 1996), pp. 190-91.

41. Jeff Astley, *Ordinary Theology: Looking, Listening, and Learning in Theology* (Farnham: Ashgate, 2002).

42. Marcel Viau, *Practical Theology: A New Approach* (Leiden: Brill, 1999); John Swinton and Harriet Mowat, *Practical Theology and Qualitative Research* (London: SCM, 2006); John Reader, *Reconstructing Practical Theology: The Impact of Globalization* (Farnham: Ashgate, 2008); Bonnie J. Miller-McLemore, *Christian Theology in Practice: Discovering a Discipline* (Grand Rapids: Eerdmans, 2012).

43. Pete Ward, *Participation and Mediation: A Practical Theology for the Liquid Church* (London: SCM, 2008).

44. Paul Ballard, ed., *The Foundations of Pastoral Studies and Practical Theology* (Cardiff: Cardiff University Press, 1986).

45. Denise M. Ackermann and Riet Bons-Storm, eds., *Liberating Faith Practices: Feminist Practical Theologies in Context* (Leuven: Peeters, 1998); Paul Ballard and Pamela Couture, eds., *Globalisation and Difference: Practical Theology in a World Context* (Cardiff: Cardiff Academic Press, 1999); Johannes A. van der Ven and Friedrich Schweitzer, eds., *Practical Theology — International Perspectives* (Berlin: Peter Lang, 1999); James Woodward and Stephen Pattison, eds., *The Blackwell Reader in Pastoral and Practical Theology* (Oxford: Blackwell, 2000); Paul Ballard and Pamela Couture, eds., *Creativity, Imagination, and Criticism: The Expressive Dimension in*

of conference papers, this means that by and large papers engaging with the Bible are not presented at major international conferences.

### 2.2.2 *The Bible in Pastoral Practice Project*

In 2005 an edited collection of essays was published as the fruit of a collaborative project between the Bible Society and the Department of Religious and Theological Studies at Cardiff University. The project was interested in exploring the way that the Bible was being used in pastoral practice but also how it might continue to be used by pastoral workers, given the findings of empirical research, and how its use might be improved for the sake of better pastoral practice. It produced one key collection of essays edited by Paul Ballard and Stephen Holmes, and a couple of more practically oriented works aimed at practitioners, one of which was a workbook for Christian ministry edited by Stephen Pattison, Margaret Cooling, and Trevor Cooling.[46] For the purposes of this exercise, I shall focus on the edited collection of essays.

The collection seeks to address the "chasm" that has opened up between academics working in the fields of biblical studies and practical theology. This chasm came about partly because of the fragmentation of theological discourse within training contexts, and partly because of the emergence of the social sciences in the caring professions, which led to a marginalization of religious discourse. Very often the use of the Bible at the ordinary church level is simplistic and naïve, or it is marginalized from pastoral conversations when no obvious link can be made and it appears irrelevant. However,

---

*Practical Theology* (Cardiff: Cardiff Academic Press, 2001); Chris A. M. Hermans and Mary E. Moore, eds., *Hermeneutics and Empirical Research in Practical Theology: The Contribution of Empirical Theology by Johannes A. van der Ven* (Leiden: Brill, 2004); Elaine Graham and Anna Rowlands, eds., *Pathways to the Public Square* (Berlin: LIT Verlag, 2005); Hans-Georg Ziebertz and Friedrich Schweitzer, eds., *Dreaming the Land: Theologies of Resistance and Hope* (Berlin: LIT Verlag, 2007); Wilhelm Gräb and Lars Charbonnier, eds., *Secularization Theories, Religious Identity, and Practical Theology* (Berlin: LIT Verlag, 2008); Edward Foley, ed., *Religion, Diversity, and Conflict* (Berlin: LIT Verlag, 2010); Bonnie J. Miller-McLemore, ed., *The Wiley-Blackwell Companion to Practical Theology* (London: Blackwell, 2012); and Ruard R. Ganzvoort, Rein Brouwer, and Bonnie Miller-McLemore, eds., *City of Desires — a Place for God? Practical Theological Perspectives* (Berlin: LIT Verlag, 2013).

46. Paul Ballard and Stephen Holmes, eds., *The Bible in Pastoral Practice: Readings in the Place and Function of Scripture in the Church* (London: Darton, Longman and Todd, 2005), and Stephen Pattison, Margaret Cooling, and Trevor Cooling, *Using the Bible in Christian Ministry: A Workbook* (London: Darton, Longman and Todd, 2007).

there are signs that the detachment of biblical studies from use of the Bible within church life is beginning to be addressed with increasing attention to the study of the reception of biblical texts via reader response criticism. Given the complex and ever changing context in which the church finds itself, there is a constant challenge to appreciate just how the Bible might provide theological illumination and insight. Quite rightly, the editors ask: "How can a collection of ancient texts speak cogently to the twenty-first century?"[47] It is this question that drives the project and around which it is organized.

The book delineates the three very broad areas of history and tradition, contemporary biblical scholarship, and contemporary pastoral practice. Part 1 contains examples of the use of biblical texts (or what were to become biblical texts) in pastoral practice in the early second century (Polycarp and Dionysius of Corinth), the fourth and fifth centuries (Augustine), the Eastern Orthodox tradition, the fourteenth and fifteenth centuries (Margery Kempe), the sixteenth to eighteenth centuries (Luther, Perkins, Baxter, and Pietism), and the nineteenth and twentieth centuries (Schleiermacher, Newman, and Barth). In part 2, essays grapple with the problem posed for the use of Scripture within pastoral practice as exposed by modern historical-critical scholarship as well as the possible responses. These responses include the acceptance of historical-critical insights about the text; the use of philosophical and narrative hermeneutics, including the so-called theological interpretation of the Scripture; the postliberal framework associated with the performance of the biblical texts; and the use of contextual and liberationist reading strategies focusing on cultural issues. Finally, part 3 considers very different kinds of pastoral practice. These include pastoral care and narrative, the church and ethics, worship and pastoral care, preaching, evangelical spirituality, Ignatian spiritual exercises, music, and the arts. All the essays are insightful, but very few actually engage the body of literature cited above from the field of practical theology. Indeed, the attention to pastoral practice, while understandable and useful, tends to lead to a fairly dispersed set of case studies. Thus, there is something of a disconnection with the body of knowledge within the discipline of practical theology. Where there are some fruitful connections is with the discussion of how systematic theology uses Scripture within its own theological constructions, the so-called theological reading of Scripture.

47. Ballard and Holmes, *Bible in Pastoral Practice*, p. xvi.

### 2.2.3 Reflection on Academic Practice

I surveyed the practical theology literature to discover how academics use Scripture in their approaches and in their theological construction. The survey has not been exhaustive, however. Rather, it has been representative and illustrative of the discipline. It now remains for me to offer critical reflection on the practice of using Scripture.

It can be seen from the typology that there is diversity in the use of Scripture. I have identified six basic approaches: (1) a priori conceptual grid, (2) proof-text, (3) strategic selection, (4) sustained engagement, (5) critical reading, and (6) excluded. The majority of authors in academic practical theology either use Scripture in a limited manner or not at all. This does not mean that the discourse constructed is not theological; it is just not explicitly engaged with Scripture. There are some — admittedly, a minority — who do use Scripture to inform their methodology and their theological construction, but they achieve this somewhat variably and with limited interaction with biblical studies scholarship. Clearly, the more normative question as to whether contemporary practical theology *should* use Scripture explicitly needs to be asked. Of course, the answer will vary for a number of reasons. Let me elaborate on two of them, which are interrelated.

First, there are theological reasons why some academic practical theologians do not use Scripture either explicitly or extensively. For some the Bible contains texts that are so problematic that the theologians do not know how to use them. The option of ignoring the Scriptures altogether seems a very obvious one. Also, when there is such a vast array of theological sources outside the Bible, the academic is not short of possible dialogue partners. It would be reasonably fair to say that liberal theologians are more likely to use Scripture in a marginal, limited, or strategic manner. The more sustained treatment of biblical texts has often been by those who are less liberal in their own theological presuppositions. There is a legitimate suspicion of "applied theology," as if every piece of theology can be treated like a three-point sermon, complete with joke, cheesy illustrations, and the inevitable poem or extract from C. S. Lewis. But in reality, for many Christians, Scripture does permeate their existence through daily prayer and weekly worship. They cannot escape this theologically defined worldview in which biblical texts, ideas, and stories are embedded. In many cases, Scripture does provide points of departure for theological thinking and action, even if it is intertwined in experience or religious practice. If this appears to be the case, why is there such a disjunction at the academic level? It is also the case historically that

Scripture has been given normative status in the church and its life, but this position is represented weakly at best in this survey.

Second, there are academic reasons why the use of Scripture has been marginalized. There has been an extensive development of theology alongside the social sciences, such that the discourse produced has moved in a nontheological direction. Very often the discussion of a given subject is more informed by social science than by theology. The use of empirical research means that often the focus is on examining data of various kinds, and biblical texts rarely inform the framing of discussions, usually because the theories or concepts in use are unconnected to biblical ideas, themes, or texts. When theology emerges within this discourse, the theology used tends to draw more from systematic and broader theological domains than from Scripture. Of course, this does not mean it is not theology or that it is not valuable. In many cases it is sophisticated and insightful, but it is simply not informed by biblical texts in any obvious or explicit manner, which is my point. The edited collections of published conference papers inevitably reflect the conference theme, and quite rightly, many such themes are based on contemporary issues and questions. In addition, not everything can be achieved in a single conference, book, or project. Take, for example, the Bible in Pastoral Practice project, which is admirable in many ways. Yet, most of the contributors to the volume are not practical theologians, and, apart from a few places, the texts do not engage practical-theological scholarship at all. Consequently, it is not clear that it has had any real impact on the use of Scripture in academic practical theology.

It is probably fair to say that this portrait identifies something of a problem about how the Bible is used (or not used) in academic practical theology today. Of course, all typologies have their limitations and are constructed from a given perspective. And I am not saying that Scripture has to be used in the same way or that there is no room for creativity of engagement. I am also not saying that the understanding or use of Scripture is uncontested in an academic sense. There are numerous disputes about historical and grammatical points, and about which hermeneutical strategies are preferred and which aspects of Scripture should be regarded as normative for Christians today. *But what I am saying is that the practical-theological academy, for the most part, is content to sit loose to an engagement with Scripture.* Unlike systematic theology, which appears to have recovered its appropriation of Scripture through "theological" interpretations, practical theology seems either reluctant to use Scripture or under the spell of social science.

### 2.2.4 Excursus: Toward a Practical-Theological Reading of Scripture

Although this study is not a focused exposition of hermeneutics, inevitably it is concerned with hermeneutics and reflexivity toward reading strategies. In the context of a study in practical theology, and to propose a possible way forward given the previous analysis, I suggest that a distinctly "practical-theological" reading of Scripture is desirable and possible. I am conscious that this approach may seem similar to the "theological" reading of Scripture, where exegesis is specifically related to doctrinal issues and biblical texts are "read" with predefined or particular theological questions in mind.[48] I believe that conversation feeds into this one; nevertheless, the starting points and outcomes for practical theology are quite different. This is because practical theology is primarily concerned with contemporary beliefs and practice, not necessarily historical or doctrinal disputes, and the reading audience and performing communities can be varied indeed. I suggest that there can be at least five dimensions to a practical-theological reading of Scripture; some of these are discipline-specific, and others are in common with more general theological hermeneutics but nevertheless are given a practical-theological "twist."

First, a practical-theological reading of Scripture will be *hermeneutically reflexive*. We all read Scripture from somewhere, and we all have some prior relationship with Scripture that informs our approach either explicitly or implicitly. Therefore, given the debates within theology and biblical studies concerning commitments, strategies, and approaches to the biblical texts, it is essential for practical theologians to be "up front" about starting points and commitments. As part of this reflexivity, it is important to own the broader theological traditions that inform our readings, together with interests and commitments. This will include not just theological commitments but also other theoretical commitments, as well as contextual conditions under which we work and are accountable.

Second, a practical-theological reading of Scripture will pay attention to the *explicit or implicit praxis of communities and individuals* described or inferred in the text. Together with the explicit theological beliefs and values surrounding them, it will inquire as to the nature and importance of the action. What kind of praxis is described or prescribed or simply assumed?

---

48. See Stephen E. Fowl, ed., *The Theological Interpretation of Scripture: Classic and Contemporary Readings* (Oxford: Blackwell, 1997), and Francis Watson, *Text, Church, and World: Biblical Interpretation in Theological Perspective* (Edinburgh: T. & T. Clark, 1994).

How does it relate to the stated theological beliefs and unstated theological assumptions, as far as these can be detected? What was the significance of such praxis for those communities of faith as far as they can be identified?

Third, and allied to the above point, a practical-theological reading of Scripture will also pay attention to *agency and the relationship between the different agents* in the biblical texts. This will include both human and divine agency as described in the texts. Who are the major and minor agents, and who is excluded from the description? Where do these agents come from, and what is their purpose? What is the relationship between the different agents? How is the divine-human relationship portrayed, and what is its significance? Specifically, how might this reading inform a contemporary understanding of the divine-human interaction in the church and the world?

Fourth, a practical-theological reading of Scripture will treat the text as *holistic* and seek to trace trajectories across different genres where possible. This does not mean ignoring or suppressing specific voices; it means allowing each voice to be heard on its own terms, that all may be heard, even when it is understood that there are different emphases among the voices. It will acknowledge and explore plurality, but also identify harmony and unity. In this way, it holds together differences that are present in the texts and allows these differences to inform the overall reading. To use the analogy of a gospel choir from John Christopher Thomas, even the dissonant "blue notes" are part of the overall sound and need to be heard as part of the total musical experience.[49] By analogy, this holistic reading will interpret texts in broader contexts, whether specific to the book, genre, Testament, or canon as a whole.

Fifth, a practical-theological reading of Scripture will consciously bring *contemporary questions and issues emerging from lived reality* to the text. These questions will be shaped and informed by disciplined attentiveness to the contemporary situation, such that a dialectical relationship is initiated. Contemporary questions will be intentionally brought to the text in order to receive insight and illumination and to inform the theological reflection. This will mean both exegetical and theological rigor in the interpretation of texts and sociocultural sophistication in the mapping and reading of the contemporary situation. Both are required to complete the hermeneutical circle and allow the spiral to continue with energy and renewed praxis.

---

49. John Christopher Thomas, "'What the Spirit Is Saying to the Church' — the Testimony of a Pentecostal in New Testament Studies," in *Spirit and Scripture: Examining a Pneumatic Hermeneutic,* ed. Kevin Spawn and Archie T. Wright (Edinburgh: T. & T. Clark, 2012), pp. 115-29 (p. 125).

## 2.3 Experience and Pneumatology in Practical Theology

Practical theology has made much of the notion of "experience," but it has made very little of the person and work of the Holy Spirit. In general discussions of "experience" in theology, it is regarded as a slippery term with roots in the Latin term *experientia,* meaning "that which arises out of traveling through life." It can refer to the accumulation of wisdom and knowledge through practice of a profession, such as when we say a person is an "experienced doctor" or an "experienced lawyer." It can also refer to the inner mental life of individuals, although I regard this definition as excessively narrow and cognitive.[50] In theology, it has been regarded as either a source for theology or something that is interpreted by a theological framework. It would seem that within practical theology, "experience" is predominantly, although not exclusively, understood in the former rather than the latter sense. In this section, I begin with a description of the various contributions to "experience" before identifying a small number of contributors who have mentioned or engaged with pneumatology. Most of the discussions of experience fall within discussions of practical theology and its methodology.

### 2.3.1 *The Nature of Experience*

In the practical-theological literature, I identified two main themes emerging in relation to experience, namely, methodology, especially theological reflection, and personal and interpersonal relations, including with the wider world. Of course, it is clear that these themes interact with each other. I shall consider them in turn.

First, experience as a concept is often placed within a discussion of methodology. In most practical theology textbooks, "experience" is regarded as a starting point for theological reflection, usually using some form of the pastoral cycle.[51] Very often what is meant by experience is some form of pastoral experience or critical incident for which theological reflection is needed to make sense of it. Often it is simply defined as "the present situation" or "the more-or-less routine existence in a given context."[52] It is regarded as the "place"

---

50. Alister E. McGrath, "Theology and Experience: Reflections on Cognitive and Experiential Approaches to Theology," *European Journal of Theology* 2, no. 1 (1993): 65-74 (p. 65).
51. See, for example, Green, *Let's Do Theology,* pp. 42-56.
52. Ballard and Pritchard, *Practical Theology in Action,* p. 77.

where the gospel message is embodied and performed.[53] In a discussion of the empirical-theological cycle, van der Ven aims to clarify what he means by experience. He argues that experience for the purposes of empirical-theological research includes four phases: (1) perception, that is, the influence of the environment on a person and the person's awareness of that influence; (2) experimentation — the action of the person on his or her environment whereby sets of actions are chosen and tested to see if there is a difference in outcome; (3) examination of the outcome in order to understand the effects and in what ways the environment has been changed due to a certain course of action; and (4) assessment, that is, the way the whole effort to understand the value and meaning of the experiments is circumscribed. These phases are placed within an interactionist framework, which conceives of human beings in constant interaction with their environments, so that the influence is dialectical.[54]

Don Browning's classic text relates experience to the notion of praxis as value-laden practices. He argues that within practical theology ways must be found to include the analysis of personal experience by those who participate in action, and this will include personal histories. Drawing upon Tracy's revised critical correlation model,[55] he sees practical theology as dependent on two fundamental sources: Christian texts, and common human experience and language; these mutually interpret each other to produce a theoretical interpretation of contemporary praxis. To develop Tracy's model, Browning proposes not merely two poles in the dialectic, but indeed three: (1) interpretation of practices, including inner motivations and social-cultural histories of the agents; (2) interpretation of relevant cultural patterns and practices; and (3) interpretation of cultural and religious symbols that give meaning to individual and institutional action.[56] Thus "experience" is informed and shaped by all three hermeneutical perspectives.

Patricia O'Connell Killen and John de Beer's discussion of theological reflection assumes that experience is placed in a genuine conversation with a lived theological tradition. They give the following definition of experience:

> Experience is what happens to us; what occurs in which we are active or passive participants. Experience has an inner dimension — the feelings, thoughts, attitudes, and hopes that we carry into and out of any situation.

---

53. Swinton and Mowat, *Practical Theology,* p. 5.
54. Van der Ven, *Practical Theology,* pp. 112-13.
55. David Tracy, *Blessed Rage for Order* (Chicago: University of Chicago Press, 1996).
56. Browning, *A Fundamental Practical Theology,* pp. 60-61.

This inner dimension involves our response to and what we make of and do with what occurs. It accents how we experience events and situations. Experience also has an outer dimension involving people, places, projects, and objects that surround us and with which we interact. The outer dimension accents what we experience.[57]

Theological reflection on experience begins when we reenter the experience by describing the inner and outer aspects accurately. Often this is presented in the shape of a narrative, and this allows the content to resonate with the narratives of others. These concrete descriptions connect to the five senses and allow the narrator to experience the first experience a second time. This is because all "events involve interaction with ourselves and the world around us. Experience is the flow of interaction between a person and all the other people, places, events, material conditions, and cultural factors that constitute that person's identity, context, and world. Experience is a river in which we swim like a fish."[58]

Second, the dimension of the personal interaction with others is central to the notion of experience. This has been picked up by a number of scholars. Stephen Bevans argues that contextual theology should include the experience of personal life (individual or corporate), which enables a person or group of people to experience God, or inhibits them from doing so. These experiences are only possible within the context of a given culture and social location. All experience involves social exchange, and this is inevitably compressed in a globalized world. There are a number of models of contextualization, but one model focuses on religious experience as a starting point. The transcendental model of contextualization starts with the person's own religious experience, which is inevitably shaped by context and community. This is because "theology is conceived as the process of 'bringing to speech' who I am or who we are — as a person or persons of faith who are in every possible respect a product of a historical, geographical, social and cultural environment."[59] Bevans observes that the transcendental model presupposes that authentic religious experience is essential and is able to speak to other individuals. Godself is truly revealed within human experience as an event, and the human mind operates identically across different cultures and periods of history because the basic cognitive processes are the same.

---

57. Killen and de Beer, *Art of Theological Reflection*, p. 21.
58. Killen and de Beer, *Art of Theological Reflection*, p. 54.
59. Bevans, *Models of Contextual Theology*, p. 104.

Chris Schlauch approaches experience via the discourse of pastoral psychology.[60] Experience is identified as belonging to the dynamic through which humans relate to themselves, others, and their environment. Experience is regarded primarily as the process of registering information, which is followed by understanding or reflection upon that information and subsequent action or meaningful behavior. These dimensions are in fact concurrent and interactive rather than sequential. The registering of information can be sensate or verbal, or indeed both: we say what we see simultaneously. Sometimes this information can be received rather passively, as in, for example, background music. At times information is uncovered through very active inquiry, while at other times receptivity to information falls somewhere between being active and passive. However, to experience something is also to select aspects of that something because some aspects are attended to while others are not. This is because the selection is made through specific categories, including the unknown (it is placed in the category called "unknown"). This is because previous encounters with the same object are remembered that "prime" the subsequent perceptions of the same object or similar objects. In particular, specific words can enable the reception of some aspects rather than others, even if the use of words is a matter of convention within a particular language. These words can be developed and changed over time as the experience is constructed and reconstructed for different purposes.

Marcel Viau places his discussion of the concept of experience within the early American pragmatist philosophical tradition, and in particular the influence of William James.[61] From this perspective, experience cannot be limited to mental processes but is part of the wider world and gives rise to concepts that allow it to be described.[62] However, experience is "had" rather than "known," and it is part of a continuous stream that does not stop but includes the person having it. It forms part of a larger set of life experiences, which, for the religious person, includes experiences of faith before these experiences are reflected upon and articulated. These religious experiences, however, cannot be disentangled from other interactions experienced by the person because they are all connected in some way. For Viau, this means that

60. Chris Schlauch, "Sketching the Contours of a Pastoral Theological Perspective: Suffering, Healing and Reconstructing Experience," in *The Blackwell Reader in Pastoral and Practical Theology*, ed. James Woodward and Stephen Pattison (Oxford: Blackwell, 2000), pp. 207-22 (esp. pp. 214-17).

61. Viau, *Practical Theology*, pp. 20-38.

62. Viau, *Practical Theology*, p. 23.

God as the object of faith cannot be understood apart from the assistance of experience.[63]

However, in all the examples cited, it is uncommon to find discussions of so-called religious experience. This is because experience as a category is treated holistically rather than being dissected into the religious and the nonreligious. This may, of course, be an advantage rather than a disadvantage, but it does mean that the category can be ignored or overlooked. It has been suggested that human experience in a more general sense is the "place" where the gospel is grounded and an important locus for the work of the Spirit.[64] But how this occurs is never really discussed in any detail; it is simply noted occasionally. Indeed, very few authors actually discuss pneumatology with any degree of detail, but those who do are discussed below.

### 2.3.2 Reflection on Experience

From the descriptions above, it would seem that there are a number of working understandings of what "experience" means in practical theology. It can refer to a specific incident or event, which is regarded as critical or significant for some reason and becomes the focus of analysis and reflection. It can refer to "going through life" or ministry experience in some general fashion, usually in the sense of what is passively experienced, that is, what happens to us. Allied to this second sense is an assumption that there is something we can call "common human experience," which has a universal quality to it, even though it can be expressed in distinct practices and have different motivations and sociocultural histories. Given these different aspects, what can be said as critical reflection on the descriptions above?

Experience has been analyzed in terms of distinct phases. That is, normally individuals are expected to work their way through a process that we call experience in these terms. Although this may be analytically interesting and useful, it gives the impression that somehow we can divide experience into neat, sequential, universal processes. It is doubtful whether experience per se can always be interpreted in this manner. Experience is a difficult "thing" to capture, and this approach can feel artificial. Similarly, the idea that we can always focus a discussion of experience on the human mind seems rather restrictive. Obviously the mind is an important aspect of what

63. Viau, *Practical Theology*, p. 25.
64. Swinton and Mowat, *Practical Theology*, pp. 5-6.

is going on in an experience of some kind, but experience cannot be reduced purely to an individual mental event. Experience is social, or relates to a social context, and it is more than merely a mental process because it involves somatic dimensions as well. But the assumption that human minds, because they have the same biological foundation in the brain, function in the same manner across different cultures and periods of history is reductionist to say the least. No doubt there are common biological processes, but cognition is much more complicated than that.[65]

Indeed, the notion that we can talk about a "common human experience" does need careful consideration. No doubt there is some continuity between individuals since experience is mediated via social contexts, languages, and worldviews. However, if one allows that experience is always shaped by cognitive grids, and that these cognitive grids are shaped not only by common worldviews but also by individual beliefs and values, then we have both continuity and discontinuity between people even from tightly knit social groups and affiliations. Indeed, it could be argued that experience as shaped by cognitive grids is also implicitly theological. That is, specific beliefs and values, even materialist ones, are also theological, such that some experiences would be regarded as impossible, for example, God interacting with the created order in some manner. This means that at the very least we need to be careful in our appropriation of some "common" universal experience in our thinking. This discussion also raises an interesting possibility: What might a practical-theological analysis of religious experience look like? How might it differ from philosophical and social-scientific approaches and perspectives?[66]

In the light of this discussion, it can be argued that practical theologians need to pay greater attention to religious experience in general and its theological character in particular. This is because it is essential to the spirituality that informs and permeates religious life. Experience has been used in a general sense of referring to the whole of life or as providing an incident or crisis upon which to reflect theologically. However, very often

65. See the discussion of cognitive neuroscience and religious experience by Fraser Watts, *Theology and Psychology* (Aldershot: Ashgate, 2002), pp. 77-88.

66. A glance at the literature dealing with religious experience suggests that there is a focus on mental events and states, with the common language referring to self-consciousness, feelings, affections, states of mind, and cognition. See, for example, Wayne Proudfoot, *Religious Experience* (Berkeley: University of California Press, 1985); Caroline Franks Davis, *The Evidential Force of Religious Experience* (Oxford: Clarendon, 1999); Matthew C. Braggs, *Religious Experience, Justification, and History* (Cambridge: Cambridge University Press, 1999).

the theological narratives of those having religious experience are given only cursory attention, if any at all. Since practical theologians are often interested in the values motivating identity and action, it makes perfect sense to give the religious experiences associated with these values much more focused attention. Very often some allusion to this dimension is somewhere in the background of the discussions, but, given the argument of this book, that there is a deficit of this feature in contemporary practical theology, it deserves to be identified, appreciated, and considered in much more detail than it currently is. The reason for this focus is also allied to the notion of pneumatology, to which we now turn.

### 2.3.3 The Role of Pneumatology

The majority of books on practical theology simply ignore pneumatology altogether. There is a theistic or christocentric assumption in the theological discourse rather than a fully explicit Trinitarian framework. This means that pneumatology is largely excluded. However, in reviewing the literature, we do find some examples of pneumatology. They come mainly from evangelical, P/C, or Reformed theology.

Ray Anderson's model of practical theology is probably the only one (with the exception of my own) that explicitly links the praxis of the Holy Spirit to the experience of ministry in the church.[67] Anderson begins by suggesting that theological reflection must be done in the context of the Spirit's ministry in the world, in other words, by attending to the praxis of the Spirit. He uses the example of Peter's vision and call to visit the household of Cornelius in Acts 10 and 11 to illustrate his point, as the Spirit uses a "visual parable" to indicate the new thing that God is doing among the Gentiles. Luke narrates that as Peter was speaking to the household, the Holy Spirit came upon all who were listening, so that Peter felt compelled to baptize the whole household immediately (Acts 10:23-48). For Peter, this meant a paradigm shift in his theology as a result of the praxis of the Spirit, informed by both the vision and the context of the situation.

Anderson argues that the Spirit comes to the church from the future rather than the past, and that the presence of the Spirit anticipates the return of Jesus Christ. It is the first installment or pledge of the eschaton (Eph. 1:13-14). This is because the "resurrection of the same Christ and the resurrec-

---

67. Anderson, *Shape of Practical Theology*, esp. pp. 102-12.

tion of the dead constitute the normative praxis of the Spirit."[68] The praxis of the Spirit is understood in the light of God's desire for the end and the fulfillment of the cosmos, not merely a replication of the first century and the early church. This is seen on the day of Pentecost, when Peter declared that the last days had arrived and the Spirit had been poured out on all flesh (Acts 2:17-18). It is eschatological preference instead of historical precedence, but it is based on some biblical antecedent. Instead of looking back to what the church was like, it looks forward to what the church will be like at the end of time. Anderson cites Paul as an exemplar of this eschatological hermeneutic. "Paul allowed for the eschatological preference of the Holy Spirit where it could be implemented without causing disorder and confusion in the church. Giving way to expediency where it was necessary for the ministry in special situations apparently was not considered by Paul to establish a principle and precedent for all time. To make what was merely expedient normative would have supplanted the eschatological freedom of the Spirit of Jesus to prepare the church for the last century."[69] Following Pentecost, the praxis of the Spirit was determinative for the religious experience of the church in an active rather than merely passive sense. This contribution is significant because it places the role of pneumatology centrally within the methodology of practical theology.

Anderson's contribution is important to this present work because its positive pneumatology is placed within an eschatological framework and brings the future into the present situation. However, I think more could have been said about the "now and not yet" of the eschatological tension that accompanies this pneumatological turn, even if it is recognized to some extent. Nevertheless, he aligns Christian experience in practical theology with the person and work of the Spirit, which is a critical move. In many ways, this approach complements my own, which has sought to frame pneumatology and experience within the discourse of spirituality, seeing them as essential components.

Andrew Purves aims to rescue practical theology, and in particular pastoral theology, from its lack of explicit doctrinal content and advocates a christological foundation from a Reformed perspective as a remedy.[70] In elucidating this christological foundation, Purves discusses the ministry of

---

68. Anderson, *Shape of Practical Theology,* p. 106.

69. Anderson, *Shape of Practical Theology,* pp. 107-8.

70. Andrew Purves, *Reconstructing Pastoral Theology: A Christological Foundation* (Louisville: Westminster John Knox, 2004). Page references to this work have been placed in the text.

the triune God and the work of the Holy Spirit. He bases his reflection on the Pauline benediction: "May the grace of the Lord Jesus Christ, and the love of God, and the fellowship of the Holy Spirit be with you all" (2 Cor. 13:13 NIV). For Purves, following Paul, grace is tied to Christ and is the nature of God's operation by which we are restored to communion with God. The same love of God that flows between the persons of the Trinity in the unity of the Spirit is the ground of God's ministry to the world in and through Christ. His ministry is the incarnation of God's love. In this ministry of love, "the Holy Spirit is the personal presence of God by whom God brings us into communion with himself through relationship with Jesus Christ" (p. 39). The communion with the Holy Spirit means being in communion with the Father by means of the Spirit-led union with Christ. The communion is *of* the Holy Spirit and *in Christ.* The Holy Spirit unites the Christian to Christ and constitutes "a participation in Christ's righteousness, holiness, and mission through the bond of the Holy Spirit" (p. 40). It is *participatio Christi* rather than simply *imitatio Christi,* drawing on the Calvinist (and Pauline) tradition of "mystical union." This communion with Christ and the Father in the Spirit also enables Christians to have communion with each other in the church, the body of Christ, and thus to share in his mission and ministry to the world, as sent by the Father. "The ministry of Christ, sent from the Father, becomes, through the bond of the Holy Spirit that unites us to Christ, the evangelical and missionary ministry of the church" (p. 42).

This aspect of union with Christ forms the basis of pastoral theology and ministry. From this fundamental conviction flow five propositions: (1) the union with Christ is the main work of the Holy Spirit, which is a unilateral work that grafts us into him; (2) this gift of union is bestowed through the "ordinary means of grace," that is, the Word of God (preached) and the sacraments (duly administered); (3) through this union Christians share in Christ's righteousness as well as knowledge of and love for the Father; (4) this work of the Holy Spirit in joining Christians to Christ creates the church (the body of Christ) and the orders of ministry (a corporate priesthood serving Christ as prophet, priest, and king); and (5) via this union with Christ Christians participate in the mission of the Father (p. 83). These propositions are subsequently elaborated in terms of participating in "*God*-actualized" rather than "*self*-actualized" ministry practices (p. 152). These include: (1) the ministry of the Word of God, spoken (preaching and pastoral care), heard, and responded to (in faith and worship); (2) the ministry of the grace of God (forgiveness of sins, communion with God, vocation); (3) the ministry of the presence of God (comforting, appealing to Christ, supporting, exhorting and encouraging, enabling power through weakness), which is the ministry of the Paraclete; and (4) the ministry of the reign of God (hope, community, and works of liberation) (pp. 155-232). Thus, in the Reformed tradition, the work of the Holy Spirit is always united to the work of Christ within the context of Trinitarian-ecclesial relations.

Purves provides a Reformed account of the role of the Spirit as the means of the individual's union with Christ. This is an important strand of thought that is often neglected. However, the central weakness of this tradition is that it often subordinates pneumatology to Christology, and in many respects Purves perpetuates this move. Indeed, one of the tensions that inheritors of the Reformed tradition face is how pneumatology informs and shapes other theological loci when, historically at least, it has been made subordinate to Christology and the ministry of the Word. I might add that the Catholic tradition (broadly conceived) provides some parallel to this feature, but in relation to the ministry of the church and its sacraments.

James Poling discusses pneumatology in the context of ecclesiology, and in particular the marks of the church.[71] Framing his understanding within process theology, he describes the Holy Spirit as the person of the Trinity who is "a sign of the grace-filled generosity of God who relates to us in love rather than jealousy and judgment" and who "provides the basis for relational hope."[72] This leads Poling to offer five marks of faithful churches that are empowered by the Holy Spirit. They are: (1) inclusive relationality, in which people from all backgrounds and circumstances are welcome; (2) empowering justice, that is, the use of power for the sake of a just distribution of resources; (3) nonviolent resistance to evil, which includes resistance to violence not only against humans but also against the ecosystem; (4) multiplicity and unity, rooted in the primordial and consequent natures of God (these terms refer to an internal process theology debate); and (5) ambiguity and goodness, since God is also part of this ambiguity.

For Poling, pneumatology becomes a kind of justification for a different agenda, namely, providing relational hope. Without doubt pneumatology does provide relationality with God and indeed hope, but one gets the sense that it is so malleable that it can be shaped however he wants it to be because it lacks sufficient grounding in either Scripture or tradition. This is also one of the problems with pneumatology: it can be shaped and reshaped by other theological loci, such that, once again, it is pushed and pulled into different

---

71. Poling, *Rethinking Faith*, pp. 77-92.
72. Poling, *Rethinking Faith*, pp. 80-81.

theological molds. Nevertheless, the relationship between pneumatology and ecclesiology is an important one that will be developed later on in this study. At this stage it is worth stating that practical theologians have often critiqued the role of the church because of the reaction to the so-called clerical paradigm (often associated with the formation strand noted in chap. 1). They have often been society-focused rather than church-focused, and this is not necessarily a negative point per se. However, one of the consequences of this disposition is that practical theologians have tended to ignore or downplay ecclesiology, which has also meant a marginalization of pneumatology. By way of contrast, later on in this study I shall argue that ecclesiology needs pneumatology and pneumatology needs ecclesiology because the Holy Spirit constitutes the church and without the presence of the Holy Spirit there would be no church.

Finally, the most recent "state of the art" collection of essays designed to map the field of practical theology is edited by Miller-McLemore.[73] It contains fifty-six chapters, the majority of which do not refer to the person and work of the Holy Spirit or indeed the doctrine of the Trinity because the dominant discourse simply uses the terms "God" and "Jesus." However, one interesting exception is the essay by Elizabeth Conde-Frazier on participant action research.[74] She suggests that in this kind of research there is a relationship between God's *kairos* and the work of the Spirit. "[W]e understand the African meaning of *kairos* as the place where the Spirit of God is mediating and intervening in life and we participate in this action. Participatory action research fits within these different nuances of *kairos* and challenges us to enliven our spiritual practices as teachers and scholars and to discover a new partnership with the Spirit of life."[75] She suggests that the leading of the Spirit moves church communities toward praxis, that is, reflective practice in light of their interpretation of Scripture through their experiences and insights. This means that "the Holy Spirit is a prerequisite for this kind of research. It allows for the hermeneutical shift necessary to shape a ministry and a practical theology that responds to daily life. It is through pneumatological dependency that the possibility for new theological discourse is opened and leaders discover new truths and ways of being faithful."[76]

Conde-Frazier's discussion is very interesting because she understands

---

73. Miller-McLemore, *The Wiley-Blackwell Companion to Practical Theology*.
74. Elizabeth Conde-Frazier, "Participant Action Research," in *The Wiley-Blackwell Companion to Practical Theology*, pp. 234-43.
75. Conde-Frazier, "Participation Action Research," p. 241.
76. Conde-Frazier, "Participation Action Research," p. 242.

the work of the Spirit as mediating and intervening within human action. It also points to another tension, namely, the one between mediation and conflation. The mediation of the work of the Spirit through human agency and action always runs the danger of conflating the divine with the human. The divine accommodation toward mediation runs the risk of domestication and indeed manipulation. This important issue will be noted later in this study.

## 2.4 Conclusion

This chapter continues the context-setting work of chapter 1 by asking how Scripture is used in the academic practice of practical theology. The analysis of the literature revealed a typology of usage, which is both illuminating and disturbing. It revealed more about the nature of the problem. Except for a few individuals, practical theologians are very limited in their use of Scripture. Indeed, the major international academy displays extremely weak engagement with Scripture, as demonstrated by its publications. I speculated on the reasons for this state of play before suggesting that one way forward would be to construct a practical-theological approach to the interpretation of Scripture. This approach takes its cue from the so-called theological interpretation of Scripture but adds a distinctly praxis dimension to the theological lenses.

Further analysis of the practical-theological literature was conducted around experience and the role of the Holy Spirit. A parallel discussion of these two concepts is a useful way of considering their relationship and whether pneumatology is implicit in the category of experience or vice versa. Again, while there is a reasonable amount of material on the subject of experience, religious experience in particular was found to be underdeveloped. Similarly, the role of pneumatology in practical theology is virtually nonexistent. Only a few studies employ pneumatology in an explicit and strategic manner within the theological analysis and construction. These contributions were discussed, and Ray Anderson stood out as the most useful dialogue partner and contributor to this present study.

There is a clear problem within the academic study of practical theology because of its lack of attention to the relationship between Scripture, experience, and pneumatology. This lack of attention leads to a very clear deficit in practical-theological discourse, and this deficit is detrimental to the development of the discipline. Scripture is used in a limited manner; experience is addressed in a general sense or via specific incidents rather than being placed within spirituality; and pneumatology is largely absent — and where it is discussed, its intersection with Scripture and religious experience is extremely limited. Given the nature of this Pentecostal Manifesto book series, this lacuna in the practical theology literature offers an opportunity to investigate just how a pneumatology informed by P/C perspectives can address this weakness and make an interjection. Admittedly, it is only one form of interjection among many possible interjections, but P/C theology does have the capacity to make a distinctive contribution to practical theology in this way. Therefore, in the chapters that follow, this study aims (1) to draw upon P/C pneumatology and in particular the concept of mediation; (2) to engage in a selected dialogue with broader sources in pneumatology; and (3) to analyze aspects of what might be called "pneumatological mediation" in the key biblical material of Luke-Acts. In other words, a specific Pentecostal and pneumatological contribution will be made using theological and biblical sources.

# 3 The Mediation of the Holy Spirit

## 3.1 Introduction

In the previous chapters I have given an overview of practical theology from two perspectives. In chapter 1 I surveyed the way in which P/C theologians engage with practical theology. For the most part, Pentecostals have addressed formational issues from the context of training leaders for church ministry. They provided some interaction with the liberationist tradition, and I suggested that my own work represented a P/C approach to empirical research within a practical-theological framework. In chapter 2, and in contrast to Pentecostal formational approaches, I surveyed the way practical theologians have used the Bible and discovered that there is a considerable amount of literature that does not engage with the biblical texts in any meaningful way. I discerned six approaches to the use of the Bible in practical theology: (1) an a priori conceptual grid, used to "read" and indeed "filter" selected biblical texts; (2) a proof-text approach, which drops biblical texts into the discourse in a peppering fashion to support the discussion but without any reference to their context or wider biblical meaning; (3) a strategic selection that uses a key biblical passage in order to offer a model or a paradigm for contemporary practice; (4) a sustained engagement that seeks to offer detailed exegetical treatment such that a biblical passage or tradition is given more rigorous treatment and integrated into the overall theological argument; (5) a critical reading that uses historical-critical or ideological-critical approaches to the text; and (6) an exclusionary approach that ignores the Bible, so that it is hardly cited at all and makes no contribution to the theological construction. Overall, what appear to predominate are either liberationist approaches or empirical approaches, which are used to explore or test social science theory about religious beliefs and practices but make little if any attempt to engage with Scripture academically. However, these two emphases appear to be quite distinct and largely disconnected.

Chapter 2 also noted that a survey of pneumatology in practical theology revealed a further lacuna in the literature. Given that practical theology has very often started with or focused on experience, it is surprising just how few texts actually engage with the notion of religious experience and the possibility that pneumatology might emerge as part of that discussion. The concept of "experience" is treated in much more general terms. In fact, there is a general lack of treatment of pneumatology, although why this is the case may be debated. It appears that more general theological constructions dominate and simply refer to God or Christ. As noted above, this study uses insights from the P/C tradition of scholarship to address what is regarded as a deficit in the use of Scripture, in attention to the nature of religious experience, and in the role of pneumatology. My own work has addressed aspects of pneumatology in relation to P/C theology, and some of this earlier work can be seen as background to this current proposal.[1] However, the main person to address pneumatology as part of the methodology of practical theology, conceived as ministerial theology, is Ray S. Anderson.[2]

Anderson offers an evangelical interpretation of Don Browning's methodology, but he does so with a commitment to biblical categories, including pneumatology. "Practical theology is essentially a hermeneutical theology. That is to say, theological reflection that begins in the context and crisis of ministry seeks to read the texts of Scripture in light of the texts of lives that manifest the work of Christ through the Holy Spirit as the truth and will of God."[3] Anderson uses the idea of "praxis," by which he means an action that takes into account its telos or goal, that is, what it aims to achieve. In the context of the New Testament, this telos can be regarded as synonymous

---

1. Mark J. Cartledge, "Empirical Theology: Towards an Evangelical-Charismatic Hermeneutic," *Journal of Pentecostal Theology* 9 (1996): 115-26; "Practical Theology and Charismatic Spirituality: Dialectics in the Spirit," *Journal of Pentecostal Theology* 10, no. 2 (2002): 93-109; *Practical Theology: Charismatic and Empirical Perspectives* (Carlisle: Paternoster, 2003); *Testimony in the Spirit: Rescripting Ordinary Pentecostal Theology* (Farnham: Ashgate, 2010).

2. Ray S. Anderson, *The Shape of Practical Theology: Empowering Ministry with Theological Praxis* (Downers Grove, Ill.: IVP, 2001).

3. Anderson, *Shape of Practical Theology,* p. 37.

with the idea of the eschaton.[4] The "praxis of the Spirit," or end-time action of the Spirit, is not discerned by either cultural relevance or practical expediency; rather, the work of the risen Christ mediated via the Holy Spirit becomes normative for the church, wherein the word of Christ in Scripture is bound to the work of Christ through the Spirit today. For Anderson, the Trinity provides the framework for understanding this relationship, and it is illustrated by the event of Pentecost. That is, "practical theology is grounded in the intratrinitarian ministry of the Father towards the world, the Son's ministry to the Father on behalf of the world and the Spirit's empowering of the disciples for ministry."[5] Anderson has provided a very useful text with which to engage, and his work offers the nearest paradigm to what I am intending to achieve. But Anderson does not provide a detailed explanation of how the narrative of Pentecost is able to inform our understanding of the praxis of the Spirit as it is mediated in the early church and thereby inform an approach to practical theology. Pentecost is mentioned, but in a fairly superficial manner; therefore, given the P/C perspective of this work, this weakness will be addressed in some detail in chapter 4.

Given this "state of the art," the question driving this inquiry can now be stated: *How might a distinctively Pentecostal and pneumatological contribution be constructed that intervenes in the contemporary discourse of academic practical theology?* The aim of this chapter is to begin to answer this question by sketching out the contours of what might be considered such a contribution using the notion of pneumatological *mediation*.

## 3.2 Mediation, Pentecostal Experience, and the Holy Spirit

P/C Christians, far more than other kinds of Christians, appear to want to claim direct and unmediated experience of God, via their encounters with the Holy Spirit. This is especially obvious when one reviews the ordinary discourse of adherents and sees the language of "supernatural" and "miracle," as if the operations of the Spirit of God were always distinct from, being over and above, the created order. Even theologians speak of experience of the Holy Spirit as direct and unmediated, as if in some sense admitting that mediation means that the dynamic impact of the "presence" of the Spirit is

4. Anderson, *Shape of Practical Theology*, p. 103; although often "praxis" refers simply to "value-laden practices."

5. Anderson, *Shape of Practical Theology*, p. 40.

reduced or denied.[6] But the question could be raised: In what sense is the Spirit ever experienced directly at all? Even a "direct" voice from heaven would be mediated in some sense via sound waves and eardrums, and an "inner" voice is processed via the brain.[7] So, what exactly is being claimed here? Why is it problematic to admit to mediation? What is lost by such a move? Of course, there are parallels to the use of the Bible, and the view that we all can have direct access to the "Word of God" for ourselves, without the mediation of priests or pastors, although they are often the main interpreters and thus mediators of the sacred text. Most recent Pentecostal hermeneutical accounts have attempted to understand how the community of the church functions to mediate in a double sense: it mediates both the text of Scripture and the experience of the Holy Spirit via testimonies to the said experience.[8] But I wonder whether this model provides an adequate account of the mediation of the Holy Spirit. Methodologically, why should Acts 15, for example, be normative as opposed to, say, Acts 2; or indeed, why should any biblical text be normative over and against others? Is there another way of looking at the early church narratives that might suggest a

6. Amos Yong, *Discerning the Spirit(s): A Pentecostal-Charismatic Contribution to Christian Theology of Religions* (Sheffield: Sheffield Academic Press, 2000), p. 114, was one of the first Pentecostals to "shy away" from such claims.

7. See the discussion of the issue by Simeon Zahl, *Pneumatology and Theology of the Cross in the Preaching of Christoph Friedrich Blumhardt: The Holy Spirit between Wittenberg and Azusa Street* (London: T. & T. Clark, 2010), p. 92. My point is that a priori cognition is used as a means by which the Spirit's prompting is received such that it is filtered psychologically. However, I realize that, strictly speaking, no "third party" is involved unless one is tempted to use some form of segregated approach to theological anthropology (e.g., mind, body, spirit), which I am not doing in this context.

8. For example, see Steven J. Land, "A Passion for the Kingdom: Revisioning Pentecostal Spirituality," *Journal of Pentecostal Theology* 1 (1992): 19-46; Rickie D. Moore, "Canon and Charisma in the Book of Deuteronomy," *Journal of Pentecostal Theology* 1 (1992): 75-92; Clark H. Pinnock, "The Work of the Holy Spirit in Hermeneutics," *Journal of Pentecostal Theology* 2 (1993): 3-23; John Christopher Thomas, "Women, Pentecostals and the Bible: An Experiment in Pentecostal Hermeneutics," *Journal of Pentecostal Theology* 5 (1994): 41-56, in relation to the inclusion of the Gentiles in Acts 15, who argues that the Spirit's witness within the community influenced the choice and use of Scripture. This witness of the Spirit was and is made known through testimonies within the community (p. 52). Kenneth J. Archer, "Pentecostal Hermeneutics: Retrospect and Prospect," *Journal of Pentecostal Theology* 8 (1996): 63-81; Scott A. Ellington, "Pentecostalism and the Authority of Scripture," *Journal of Pentecostal Theology* 9 (1996): 16-38; Francis Martin, "Spirit and Flesh in the Doing of Theology," *Journal of Pentecostal Theology* 18 (2001): 5-31; L. William Oliverio Jr., *Theological Hermeneutics in the Classical Pentecostal Tradition: A Typological Account* (Leiden: Brill, 2012), pp. 224-32.

different approach? In particular, from a P/C theological perspective, does Acts 2 provide a different narrative account of *how* the Spirit "comes" to us? By what means, or I might say, "intermediary" means, do we experience the Spirit, and what is the significance of the experience for practical theology? I want to begin to answer these questions by looking at the praxis of the Spirit in Acts 2:1-39, which is informed by the notion of mediation. But first I need to discuss the nature of mediation and Pentecostal religious experience more generally.

### 3.2.1 Mediation

Mediation can be defined as the action whereby two distinct elements are brought together by an intermediary or third party. The term "mediation" is often used when two estranged parties are brought back into a reconciled relationship. The person who facilitates such reconciliation is often called a "mediator" or "go-between." Writing with respect to God and creation, Colin Gunton states that mediation theologically conceived "denotes the way we understand one form of action — God's action — to take shape in and in relation to that which is not God; the way, that is, by which the actions of one who is creator take form in a world that is of an entirely different order from God because he made it to be so."[9] In biblical terms, Christ is referred to as the mediator of the new/renewed covenant between God and humanity (1 Tim. 2:5), but he is also the one who comes into the world to re-create it.[10] However, it is possible to refer to the Holy Spirit as fulfilling this role in a complementary if distinct manner as well. Mediation in this study focuses on the way in which the Spirit is related to humanity in the Pentecost event and the means by which that intermediary role makes a relationship between God and humanity possible.

I assume that the Holy Spirit is present in the created order, but is distinct from it. The Holy Spirit cannot be collapsed into the category of creation, for the Holy Spirit is divine and not a creature even if there is a close connection to creation.[11] As Eugene Rogers argues, "[t]o reduce the Spirit to matter breaks the rule of Christian speech that God is not to be *identified*

9. Colin Gunton, *The Christian Faith: An Introduction to Christian Doctrine* (Oxford: Blackwell, 2002), p. 5.

10. Gunton, *The Christian Faith*, p. 67.

11. Unlike Mark I. Wallace, *Fragments of the Spirit: Nature, Violence, and the Renewal of Creation* (Harrisburg, Pa.: Trinity, 2002), who collapses the distinction.

with the world; to divorce the Spirit from matter breaks the rule of Christian speech that God is not to be identified by simple *contrast* with the world."[12] I assume that there is an inextricable connection between the work of Christ and the work of the Spirit, so that what we call the "coming of the Spirit" is in fact an *intensification* of the Spirit's work in creation but directed toward the eschatological goal of salvation in, with, and through Christ.[13] Mediation, therefore, means mediation in the context of the *via salutis,* the way of salvation, which maintains the tension between transcendence and immanence without collapsing one into the other, as noted by Rogers. This means that the Spirit as intermediary mediates the presence of the triune God such that God is recognized to be present within intermediate aspects of creaturely reality for the purpose of salvation. In other words, I am considering an intermediary agent, the Holy Spirit, as well as a set of intermediary material, processes, events, or moments, what we may call the creaturely and created means. This conceptualization means that both divine and creaturely mediation are required.

### 3.2.2 Pentecostal Experience and Mediation

In this section, I shall identify what I regard as the central aspects of mediation as they emerge from the literature before discussing key theological ideas through which the concept of mediation is given greater elucidation.

This is a subject that has been hinted at within P/C theology but rarely tackled head-on, that is, until the publication of Peter D. Neumann's doctoral thesis.[14] He argues that there is a growing appreciation of mediation in the experience of God. He describes how correlationist and noncorrelationist theologies have approached the experience of God in terms of mediation. In correlation theology, the two poles of Christian tradition and the contemporary context are linked by human experience. In a sense, this experience precedes the doctrinal tradition and shapes an understanding of the world. On this account, experience is not the source of an apprehension of God

12. Eugene Rogers, *After the Spirit: A Constructive Pneumatology from Resources outside of the Modern West* (Grand Rapids: Eerdmans, 2005), p. 58.

13. Also see the brief discussion of intensification of the Holy Spirit by James K. A. Smith, "The Spirit, Religions, and the World as Sacrament: A Response to Amos Yong's Pneumatological Assist," *Journal of Pentecostal Theology* 15, no. 2 (2007): 251-61 (esp. pp. 256-58).

14. Peter D. Neumann, *Pentecostal Experience: An Ecumenical Encounter,* Princeton Theological Monograph Series 187 (Eugene, Ore.: Pickwick, 2012).

but the medium through which God is encountered. There is an assumption of continuity between Christian experience and human experience in general, which is characteristic of theological modernity. Noncorrelationist approaches, by contrast, emphasize the discontinuity between common human experience and experience in the Christian tradition. In the contemporary setting, this suspicion of common universalizing experience looks more like a postmodern suspicion of the modernist enterprise. From this perspective, experience is viewed as a rupture with its context, as being in discontinuity with any notions of the universal, and therefore a focusing on the particular.[15] Karl Barth is hailed as the great exemplar of a noncorrelationist with his view that all experience is embedded in some form of belief system. This mantle has been taken forward by the postliberal tradition and its emphasis on the mediation of religious experience via cultural-linguistic systems, which serve to determine the nature of religious experience.[16] However, even here some noncorrelationists fear that the system will constrain the interruption of revelation and give humans "mastery" of God.[17]

From a P/C perspective, Neumann discusses a way forward posited by the philosopher James K. A. Smith.[18] Smith admits that all experience of God is mediated within cultural and linguistic horizons, and that God does concede to these horizons because he created them in the first place, but that he does so "on his own terms." Experience of God is always an encounter such that the finite human horizon cannot "contain" God, who remains other. Therefore, mediated experiences of God do not objectify God, such that the perceiver can in any sense claim to have "captured" the divine without remainder. Experience therefore functions more like a "testimony" to an encounter in which the transcendent one becomes immanent, at least for the duration and purpose of the encounter.[19] This means that the encounter is particular rather than general and cannot be simply equated with common religious experience across time and place. Rather, it is mediated via the particularities of faith commitments, belief systems, and religious practices.

---

15. Neumann, *Pentecostal Experience*, p. 28.

16. George Lindbeck, *The Nature of Christian Theology: Religion and Theology in a Postliberal Age* (London: SPCK, 1984).

17. Neumann, *Pentecostal Experience*, p. 29.

18. James K. A. Smith, "Faith and the Conditions of Possibility of Experience: A Response to Kevin Hart," in *The Experience of God: A Postmodern Response*, ed. Kevin Hart and Barbara Eileen Wall (New York: Fordham University Press, 2005), pp. 89-91.

19. See also the broader discussion in terms of epistemology by James K. A. Smith, *Thinking in Tongues* (Grand Rapids: Eerdmans, 2010), esp. pp. 62-71.

Intertwined within the experience is a set of already functioning interpretive grids that give shape to that which is mediated. Drawing on Dale M. Schlitt, Neumann uses the phrase "mediated immediacy" to capture this dynamic, which preserves divine transcendence and allows for its mediation via immanence.[20] Although not a Pentecostal, the Roman Catholic theologian Sebastian Madathummuriyil qualifies the notion of mediation from a Trinitarian perspective.[21]

> For in mediating the immediacy of God's presence in the person of Jesus Christ, the Spirit is united to Christ as the Spirit of Christ. In mediating God's presence through the words and actions of Jesus of Nazareth the Spirit is not simply a "mediator," a third party who stands in isolation outside of the "mediation," but rather he is the mediation of the mediator, because in mediating Christ, the Spirit is co-present as the Spirit of Christ. Therefore, there is an intrinsic unity and distinctiveness as far as personhood and the missions of the Son and the Spirit are concerned. For this reason, the understanding of the role of the Spirit as "mediated immediacy" helps us to understand the mutuality of the Son and the Spirit in the economy of salvation and in the understanding of the Church and the sacraments.[22]

This means that the Spirit mediates Christ to the church and unites the church to Christ. The role of the Spirit is not as "mediator" but rather as the "mediation of the mediator, because the Holy Spirit is the Spirit of Christ whom he shares with us."[23] In this way the Spirit functions as a kind of "point of entry," whereby the Father enters history and humankind enters the mystery of the Father through Christ. For Madathummuriyil, it is in the Spirit that the church becomes the sacrament of Christ and thus by its sacramental life mediates the salvation offered through Christ. The Spirit plays a mediatorial role in the liturgy so that Christ is present to Christians and vice versa but fundamentally as the "mediation" rather than the "mediator."[24] One does not need to accept Roman Catholic sacramental theology

20. Neumann, *Pentecostal Experience*, p. 31; Dale M. Schlitt, *Theology and the Experience of God* (New York: Peter Lang, 2001), pp. 35-36.

21. Sebastian Madathummuriyil, "The Holy Spirit as Person and Mediation: A Pneumatological Approach to Church and Sacraments," *Questions Liturgiques* 88 (2007): 177-202.

22. Madathummuriyil, "Holy Spirit as Person," pp. 194-95.

23. Madathummuriyil, "Holy Spirit as Person," p. 196.

24. Madathummuriyil, "Holy Spirit as Person," p. 198.

to appreciate the basic thrust of this case: the Spirit and Christ are mediated in a complementary fashion since their missions are complementary.

Scholarship in P/C theology has considered Spirit baptism the archetypal Pentecostal religious experience and uses it to discuss experience more generally. It is regarded as a crisis type of experience characterized by the divine interruption of human life, and it contributes to its transformation. This transformation is not just experiential but is also cognitive, such that interpretive frameworks of thought can be changed in different degrees, from minor modifications to quite radical shifts, depending on the original starting point. Therefore, the power of the mediated experience can influence the previous categories of thought and reshape them in the light of said experience. This mediation can be extended to general worship experiences in which there is a heightened "sense" of the divine, which is attributed to the Holy Spirit and again suggests an invasive quality to it.[25] In this case, there is often an emphasis on the transcendent quality of the worship, which is experienced immanently so that the dominant apprehension is one of "otherness" among the worshiping congregation. As Daniel E. Albrecht states with regard to the mystical encounter in worship, "[t]his encounter is mediated by the sense of immediate divine presence."[26]

Whether the focus is on Spirit reception as a key experience or on congregational worshiping practices, a number of features are common to P/C understandings of pneumatological mediation. It is clear that the Holy Spirit is mediated via both internal and external aspects. This means there is an emotional or affective pole, such that people "feel" certain kinds of things such as a sense of euphoria and joy but also grief and sadness, depending on different circumstances. There is also a ritual pole — a set of practices that are ritualized and into which people are socialized and participate as part of a social group. In worship, singing songs is a significant ritual, as well as listening to a preacher. The movement of individuals out of their seats to receive the laying on of hands or to pray for divine action of some kind is also a ritual that can be regulated considerably.

Worship is a congregational event, and description of the mediation of the Holy Spirit in this context is regarded as primarily communal rather than individual. The community share in and shape the experience together;

25. Neumann, *Pentecostal Experience*, pp. 112-14. He uses the supernatural versus natural distinction to frame the relationship between God and creation supported by the language of "intervention" rather than "interaction."

26. Daniel E. Albrecht, *Rites in the Spirit: A Ritual Approach to Pentecostal/Charismatic Spirituality* (Sheffield: Sheffield Academic Press, 1999), p. 239.

individuals do not experience the Spirit in isolation from the social dynamics of the corporate event. Ecclesial practices give a pattern to the experience of mediation as well as open up spaces for more spontaneous types of experiences, which nevertheless are understood as exhibiting certain recognizable forms. These corporate experiences of mediation are not just mental events, which are experienced in isolation. They are also embodied and relational.[27] The experience of sung worship, for example, takes on a particular intensity when certain types of songs are used, depending on the quality and style of the singers in a given location. Similarly, praying for healing often means that people are placed in close proximity to each other, standing close to each other as they lay hands on the person being prayed over. In this sense the mediation of the Spirit via worship rituals is holistic. Rituals influence all aspects of who the person is, as well as the whole context, and they function to mediate the Spirit's presence.

Inherent in these modes of mediation is an implicit sacramentality. That is, features within creation can provide signs that point toward God's salvific intentions. In the gospel, this general sense of symbolism is defined in terms of the person and work of Jesus Christ and the inauguration of the kingdom of God. For Pentecostals, the main signals of transcendence are located in signs and wonders, which are mediated via the intermediaries of people in a fourfold process: the God who sends, the Spirit who enables, the person who performs, and the person who benefits.[28] Therefore, the invocation of the Holy Spirit is less about sanctifying elements of bread and wine or water, as in Catholic traditions, and more about invoking the Spirit's intervention in healing and restoration. Of course, they are not mutually exclusive, but on the whole Pentecostal scholars have tended to reflect on mediation in terms of the miraculous dimensions of the church's life and witness. The exception to this way of thinking is found in the work of Chris E. W. Green, who has proposed a Pentecostal eucharistic theology that locates sacramental mediation of the Holy Spirit at its heart. "Plainly put, the church's Eucharist-event *is* an experience of Christ's personal presence, by the power of the Spirit immediately mediated and mediately immediate."[29] This is because all human experience is mediated in some way; therefore, the sacramental elements are themselves the material of such a pneumatological encounter.

27. Smith, *Thinking in Tongues*, p. 60.
28. William P. Atkinson, *Trinity after Pentecost* (Eugene, Ore.: Pickwick, 2013), p. 46.
29. Chris E. W. Green, *Toward a Pentecostal Theology of the Lord's Supper: Foretasting the Kingdom* (Cleveland, Tenn.: CPT Press, 2012), pp. 288-89.

Following on from this point, language itself can have a sacramental quality as words spoken can also evoke a set of expectations on what is occurring and what will occur as a result of the speech act in the context of a congregational setting.[30] In this sense, language as a speech act can perform what it says and signal the presence of the Spirit in the very act of speech itself. In terms of interpretive concepts, language also plays a second function in that it can attribute what is occurring in a given context to the work of the Holy Spirit. All experience of God is mediated within cultural and linguistic horizons, even if these horizons cannot capture in full every aspect of the experience and because God is always experienced partially because of his transcendence.[31] As Macchia argues, "religious experience is to be experience of God and not most fundamentally of our interpretive frameworks."[32] Despite this caution (as well as an acknowledgment of Macchia's Barthian tendencies), I would still wish to assert that the interpretative grid is always intertwined with the experience and functions to mediate that which is experienced, even as I agree with Macchia that God himself is free and not restricted by the interpretive frameworks. This means that certain theological metaphors can shape and be shaped by the pneumatological framework.[33] For example, the concept of "baptism," being immersed into something, both opens up certain possibilities experientially and restricts what can be said, and necessarily so. The idea of "infilling" is somewhat similar and yet different. One suggests being plunged into a liquid substance, whereas the other suggests the liquid substance being "poured into" the person or community. These examples are *analogical,* as everyday images are selected to express a transcendent interface with creation that is experienced in some sense as immanent. But, as noted above, in the very experience itself, metaphors and interpretive grids can be modified, recast, and even subsequently abandoned in the light of subsequent experience and theological reflection.

How certain things can be attributed to the Holy Spirit in relation to humanity is also explained by the concept of *concursus,* as recently discussed by

30. See the discussion of language and speech act theory by James K. A. Smith and David Hilborn in Mark J. Cartledge, ed., *Speaking in Tongues: Multidisciplinary Perspectives* (Milton Keynes: Paternoster, 2006).

31. Neumann, *Pentecostal Experience,* p. 31.

32. Frank D. Macchia, "Christian Experience and Authority in the World: A Pentecostal Viewpoint," *Ecumenical Trends* 31, no. 8 (2002): 10-14 (p. 12a).

33. See the discussion in terms of semiotics by Amos Yong, *Spirit-Word-Community: Theological Hermeneutics in Trinitarian Perspective* (Aldershot: Ashgate, 2002), pp. 206-15.

Joshua D. Reichard.[34] *Concursus* is normally associated with the doctrine of providence and refers to the ways in which God's actions and human actions interact or cooperate to produce results in the world.[35] These interactions are expressed in a variety of ways and are given a number of interpretations. From an analysis of the relevant literature, Reichard suggests that *concursus* can be identified in three ways. (1) The category of "prior *concursus*" refers to the Holy Spirit as the first cause that uses human action as a secondary cause. For Pentecostals, the experience of the Spirit's action that makes them feel as though control is lost falls into this category. An example of this is evidential tongues as associated with Spirit baptism. While there is mediation, the Spirit is perceived as the first cause and human experience the second cause. (2) The category of "sequenced *concursus*" refers to the prompting of the human will to act, but the Spirit does not act directly upon the person. The Spirit is active in persons but subsequently becomes manifest visibly through human action, for example, through ritual actions. (3) The category of "permissive *concursus*" refers to the Holy Spirit's permission for free human action to occur. This can be understood through the idea of blessing, whereby human action receives divine enabling. Reichard attempts to synthesize these three categories and create a distinct Pentecostal *concursus,* which he refers to as "appropriated power" within the divine-human relationship. It is an empowerment not only to act according to a "causal mechanism" but also to "act freely with spiritual power."[36] The foundation of such *concursus* is to be found within the doctrine of Spirit baptism, which releases empowerment through human cooperation and is manifest in charismata and signs and wonders. "Thus, Pentecostal *concursus* is best described as primarily concurrence with the power of the Spirit through human agency."[37]

Language is shaped by a number of factors within theology, not least the so-called sources of theology. I shall mention two in particular, Scripture and tradition. This is because reason is less a source in my view and more a way of analyzing, critiquing, testing, and shaping theological construction, given the different presuppositions, rationality, and style of the theologians concerned. Experience is potentially a source for theology (although often

---

34. Joshua D. Reichard, "Toward a Pentecostal Theology of *Concursus,*" *Journal of Pentecostal Theology* 22, no. 1 (2013): 95-114. For a discussion of *concursus* (coming together) and providence in Christian theology generally, see Mike Higton, *SCM Core Text: Christian Doctrine* (London: SCM, 2008), pp. 192-95.

35. Reichard, "Toward a Pentecostal Theology," p. 95.

36. Reichard, "Toward a Pentecostal Theology," p. 103.

37. Reichard, "Toward a Pentecostal Theology," p. 113.

contested on similar grounds to my comments about reason), but it is here the subject of our inquiry as it relates to the mediation of the Spirit. Indeed, mediation by its very nature is experiential, and so it is intrinsic to the object of this inquiry. Given the role of Scripture and tradition in the mediation of the Holy Spirit, it could be asked: What other theological loci are associated with pneumatology? The key loci can be identified as Christology, Trinity, soteriology, ecclesiology, and eschatology, which are all interconnected.

The person and work of the Holy Spirit must be understood as intrinsic to the eschatological in-breaking of the rule and reign of God. The very presence of the Spirit signals a new age, and this new age has a christological focus. "The Spirit embraces us or fills us with the divine presence in order to sanctify us and empower us to be living witnesses to Christ as the Son of God and the Spirit Baptizer."[38] Jesus Christ mediates the Spirit in relation to the church as this gift is given from the Father and enables believers to enjoy the communion between the Father and the Son.[39] This means that Christ establishes his church by means of his Spirit;[40] as the Spirit is outpoured at Pentecost, a *liminal event* is experienced that draws the disciples into union with Christ and begins to fulfill the eschatological work of redemption and the fulfillment of creation.[41] Here it could be suggested that Christ is executor of the work of the Spirit in fulfilling the purpose and destiny of the created order (Acts 2:33).

This christological point already displays a Trinitarian framework that gives shape to the mediated experience. Jesus Christ, by his Spirit, draws people into communion that exists between the Father and the Son and thus establishes a two-way movement: from the Father through the Son in the Spirit and from the Spirit through the Son to the Father.[42] This means that Christian experience is mediated by both the Son and the Holy Spirit,[43] suggesting a double mediation in the economy of salvation: the complementarity and interdependence of the Spirit and the Son. In the subsistence of the Holy Spirit the Godhead becomes a Trinitarian communion as the work of the Father and the work of the Son are directed toward the Holy Spirit.[44]

---

38. Frank D. Macchia, *Baptized in the Spirit: A Global Pentecostal Theology* (Grand Rapids: Zondervan, 2006), p. 159.

39. Macchia, *Baptized in the Spirit*, p. 160.

40. Steven M. Studebaker, *From Pentecost to the Triune God: A Pentecostal Trinitarian Theology* (Grand Rapids: Eerdmans, 2012), p. 88.

41. Studebaker, *From Pentecost*, p. 95.

42. Macchia, *Baptized in the Spirit*, p. 117.

43. Macchia, *Baptized in the Spirit*, p. 124.

44. Studebaker, *From Pentecost*, p. 95.

Thus the Holy Spirit participates in and facilitates the redemption of the created order via the eschatological event of Pentecost.

P/C worship experiences are first and foremost communal before they are individual, since they are shaped by narratives (biblical and historical), symbols (biblical and contextual), and practices (oral, kinesthetic, and musical) mediated via the ecclesial community.[45] Of course, these narratives, symbols, and practices change and develop over time, but the locus of these things, namely, the community of the church, is also the mediator of the Spirit, so that it becomes a "living tradition."[46] As a living tradition, the church is a "mother" to her people, nurturing them in the faith, preceding them and incorporating them at different times and in many places.[47] Therefore, the church can be described as a living temple of the Holy Spirit, built by its living stones and linked to its head, Jesus Christ. It mediates the presence of the triune God, who unites all in Christ. Without this presence the church would not exist ontologically as the church, since the Spirit constitutes the body of Christ and unites the church with her head, making the *totus Christus*.[48]

### 3.2.3 Observations, Comments, and Questions

This discussion raises some interesting and important questions. Neumann cites David Brown, and suggests that "language" might be given too much weight in the mediation of experience of God.[49] But we could ask: How can this be the case? Is not all expression of experience shaped by language, unless one opts for a noncognitive view of religious experience, which is less popular these days?[50] In what ways might "contextualization" limit the nature

45. See Mark J. Cartledge, *Encountering the Spirit: The Charismatic Tradition* (London: Darton, Longman and Todd, 2006), pp. 116-31.

46. Simon Chan, *Liturgical Theology: The Church as a Worshiping Community* (Downers Grove, Ill.: IVP, 2006), p. 35.

47. Chan, *Liturgical Theology*, p. 24.

48. Chan, *Liturgical Theology*, p. 32; for a more detailed account of ecclesiology, see Simon Chan, *Pentecostal Ecclesiology: An Essay on the Development of Doctrine* (Blandford Forum: Deo Publishing, 2011).

49. Neumann, *Pentecostal Experience*, p. 30; David Brown, "Experience Skewed," in *Transcending Boundaries in Philosophy and Theology: Meaning and Experience*, ed. Kevin J. Vanhoozer and Martin Warner (Aldershot: Ashgate, 2007), pp. 159-75 (pp. 172-73).

50. Caroline Franks Davis, *The Evidential Force of Religious Experience* (Oxford: Clarendon, 1999), pp. 5-10, 147.

of the mediation, as opposed to, say, facilitate such mediation? In terms of religious experience, "encounters" with the Spirit of God will always be particular, because that is their nature. But this does not eradicate the possibility of some kind of continuity between different rituals, even if the subjective qualities do differ between individuals; otherwise the anthropological notion of "portable practices" in the religious sphere would not have any currency.[51] This notion points to the possibility of some form of transcontextuality to religious practices, even if the interpretations of such practices (e.g., prayer for healing) do indeed vary considerably.

It is certainly the case that P/C Christians have emphasized the language of the "supernatural" or the "miraculous." There are, of course, many reasons for this rhetoric. It could be said that behind this language is an assumption that God is so transcendent (hence supernatural) that he can only establish a relationship via the mode of "intervention." There is a sense that the relationship is conceived in spatial terms, whereby God "up there" intervenes among us "down here." But the dominance of this spatial language can be challenged because if God is said to sustain the whole of the created order, so that creation would cease to exist were he to withdraw his presence, then one can argue for an already existing interactive presence of the Spirit in order to sustain creation. Only an *interactionist* model does justice to this existing relationship, and the language of invasion or intervention fails to capture the already existing relationship between God and his creation.[52]

It is not surprising that P/C scholars wish to put an accent on the communal nature of religious experience and the mediation of the Holy Spirit. This is to be expected. However, in what sense is this communal turn already present within the literature on pneumatological mediation? In particular, what kinds of sacramental theology are informed by pneumatology both within P/C Christianity and outside of it?

Furthermore, questions need to be raised regarding the mediation of Scripture and tradition. How are they mediated within ecclesial practices? One would expect a considerable amount of plurality here. So, how might we discern the appropriateness of this mediation? What kinds of criteria do we employ in the process of such discernment, and who is responsible for this discernment? Additionally, if "tradition" is a living entity, intrinsi-

---

51. Gertrud Hüwelmeier and Kristine Krause, introduction to *Traveling Spirits: Migrants, Markets, and Mobilities*, ed. Gertrud Hüwelmeier and Kristine Krause (London: Routledge, 2010), pp. 1-16.

52. See Cartledge, *Practical Theology*, pp. 25, 37 n. 64.

cally dynamic and transforming, what constraints might be placed upon its transformation? Are limitations ever to be placed on the evolution of tradition, and if so, who will place them? Similarly, if all experience of God is mediated by the created order (including the church), to what extent does the sinfulness of creation (including the church) inhibit the mediation of the Spirit? To what extent might we say that the Spirit is quenched? Yong, no doubt, would acknowledge that all knowledge of God is partial and fragmentary, being both cataphatic and apophatic.[53] How might the category of the eschaton be used to provide a framework for assessing the nature of mediated knowledge of the Holy Spirit? In other words, does the "now and not yet" of the kingdom of God influence in a legitimate manner the way we conceptualize the mediation of the Holy Spirit? Linked to this point is the idea of Studebaker, that we can conceive of the Spirit's mediation in terms of the metaphor of *liminality*. To what extent is this metaphor already located in the broader theology of mediation of the Holy Spirit?

The discussion by Reichard of *concursus* is a useful addition to conceptualizing mediation. He prefers the idea of "concurrent *concursus*" with regard to Spirit baptism because it affirms both the reception of spiritual power and human agency, which releases charismata and signs and wonders. It overcomes the rather mechanistic causation found in other versions and emphasizes the cooperation of human and divine agency. But it is doubtful that Spirit baptism provides a general model for interpreting all religious experience or indeed the ordinary, what we might call the "low-level," interaction between the divine and the human. This is a model for the spectacular, which may be potentially regular (or indeed more regular than non-Pentecostals would allow), but which nevertheless assumes that this is the ideal form of religious experience. For most Pentecostals, the experience is far more likely to be dominated by "sequenced *concursus*" or "permissive *concursus*" than by "appropriated power *concursus*." At the end of the day, a one-size-fits-all approach to *concursus* is unlikely to satisfy the range and diversity of religious experience from the mundane to the spectacular, with all the variety in between.

With these observations, comments, and questions in mind, I turn to the broader theology of pneumatological mediation in modern Protestant theology in order to develop the discussion above and to see in what way these observations and reflections are modified in light of a broader engagement with literature.

---

53. Yong, *Spirit-Word-Community*, p. 208.

## 3.3 Mediation and the Holy Spirit in Protestant Perspective

To appreciate the significance of the discussions in P/C theology, as well as my own analysis of the day of Pentecost narrative, we must relate them more broadly to the topic of mediation of the Holy Spirit in theology. A literature review of the contemporary discussion on the subject locates it largely within modern Protestant theology. I have followed the sources as they have been highlighted by the literature review and engaged with them in a more or less historical trajectory from positions representative of liberalism and existentialism to neo-orthodoxy and postliberalism. (It would be interesting to explore connections with other theological traditions, especially with Roman Catholicism and Eastern Orthodoxy. Unfortunately, the scope of this project makes this impossible.)

Not surprisingly, the mediation of the divine by means of the Holy Spirit has been associated with the liberal Protestant theologian Friedrich Schleiermacher. In his discussion of the work of the Holy Spirit, he theorized (1) that the Holy Spirit is the union of the "divine essence" with human nature; (2) that every regenerate person partakes of the Holy Spirit, so that there is no fellowship with Christ apart from the indwelling of the Holy Spirit; and (3) that the church is animated by the Holy Spirit, with each regenerate sinner being "an indispensable constituent of this fellowship."[54] For Schleiermacher, the Holy Spirit is the spiritual influence after Jesus' departure, giving coherence to the life of the church as a spiritual entity.[55] Metaphysical definitions of the Trinity are "ditched" in favor of "ethical" and "experiential" ones. As Gary Badcock observes about Schleiermacher's pneumatology, "even in Jesus' life the absolute God-consciousness was mediated by the Spirit of God, the Holy Spirit is the union of the 'divine essence' with human nature in the form of the common Spirit that exists among believers."[56] Additionally, Kevin Hector explains that in Schleiermacher's view,

---

54. Friedrich Schleiermacher, *The Christian Faith*, ed. H. R. Mackintosh and J. S. Stewart (London: T. & T. Clark, 2005; orig. 1830), pp. 569, 574, 578. However, the Holy Spirit does not merely animate a previously established institution. The Holy Spirit *constitutes* the church of believers. As Yves Congar, *I Believe in the Holy Spirit*, vol. 2, *He Is Lord and Giver of Life* (London: Geoffrey Chapman, 1983), p. 15, states: "The Spirit *acts* in order to enable men [*sic*] to enter that Body, but he is *given* to the Body and it is in that Body that we receive the gift of the Spirit."

55. Veli-Matti Kärkkäinen, *Pneumatology: The Holy Spirit in Ecumenical, International, and Contextual Perspective* (Grand Rapids: Baker Academic, 2002), pp. 62-63.

56. Gary D. Badcock, *Light of Truth and Fire of Love: A Theology of the Holy Spirit* (Grand Rapids: Eerdmans, 1997), p. 116.

redemption (that is, the development of God-consciousness) is mediated to us by the Spirit via the community of the church, and this mediation is God's own activity. This means that the new humanity in Christ is mediated to us through the church's socially constructed norms. Just as there is no gap between the divinity and humanity of Christ, there is no gap between the Spirit's activity and human activity, and the Spirit's personhood is not diminished by being "intersubjectively mediated."[57]

Schleiermacher's position that the Holy Spirit is mediated via corporate God-consciousness of the community may not be one that we find convincing, but it does emphasize the role of the community of the church, and on this matter at least there is some resonance with P/C scholarship. There may be some disagreement on where the emphasis is to be placed. P/C theologians would place it on the community, whereas Schleiermacher would accent the individual before the community. Of course, as noted above, Schleiermacher gives the impression that the Spirit *subsequently* animates the already existing community of the church, whereas P/C scholars are clear that the Spirit *constitutes* the church and that the church would not exist in any sense without the presence of the Spirit. The body of Christ is always united to its heavenly Head by means of the Holy Spirit, thus constituting the *totus Christus*.

In this line of liberal pneumatology, the work of Paul Tillich is most often identified with the notion of mediation because of his affiliation with the method of correlation in theology. He observes that the media of the divine presence are usually associated with the Word and the sacraments.[58] Tillich also wishes to extend the media to include personal and historical events. He suggests that words communicating the divine presence become the "Word," whereas material objects that become vehicles of the divine Spirit are sacramental materials. Thus, he defines a sacrament in the following manner: "The largest sense of the term denotes everything in which the Spiritual Presence has been experienced; in a narrower sense, it denotes particular objects and acts in which a Spiritual community experience the Spiritual presence; and in the narrowest sense it merely refers to some 'great' sacraments in the performance of which the Spirit Community actualizes itself."[59] This means for Tillich that the presence of God cannot be received without some sacramental element. This is because the sacramental material is not merely a sign but a

57. Kevin W. Hector, "The Mediation of Christ's Normative Spirit: A Constructive Reading of Schleiermacher's Pneumatology," *Modern Theology* 24, no. 1 (2008): 1-23 (p. 16).

58. Paul Tillich, *Systematic Theology*, vol. 3, *Life and the Spirit, History, and the Kingdom of God* (Chicago: University of Chicago Press, 1963), p. 120.

59. Tillich, *Systematic Theology*, 3:121.

symbol. The sacramental materials are intrinsically related to that which they represent: water, fire, oil, bread, and wine have inherent qualities that make them adequate for the symbolic function and make them irreplaceable. The Holy Spirit makes use of these natural elements in order to "enter" the human spirit. The symbol is neither a "thing" to be handled and controlled nor a mere sign pointing beyond itself. Rather, it "participates in the power of what it symbolizes, and therefore, it can be a medium of the Spirit."[60] Normally, such symbolism is related to the great moments in the human life cycle, but Tillich believes that each ecclesial community is free to appropriate symbols that enable it to experience the mediation of the Spirit, provided that they connect with new life in Christ and historical doctrinal symbols. On the day of Pentecost a number of elements mediated the presence of the Spirit: (1) the ecstatic character of the spiritual community; (2) the creation of faith that had been destroyed by the crucifixion; (3) the creation of love expressed in mutual service; (4) the creation of unity and the reunion of estranged humanity; and (5) the creation of universality via the missionary drive.[61]

Tillich's position on the broader nature of sacramentality is something that P/C scholarship is beginning to appreciate because of the role that embodied symbolic rituals play within the spirituality. The greater appreciation of ritual and symbol by the sector means that actions beyond the dominical sacraments are now considered "sacramental" in a broader sense, and thereby a means of potential mediatorial actions of the Holy Spirit. The freedom to appropriate words and actions outside the usual domain of the sacraments has already been engaged by P/C scholars, and this has been demonstrated in discussions of foot washing, glossolalia, and charismatic phenomena. However, the idea of levels of sacramentality is not something that P/C theologians have appropriated. Nevertheless, it does resonate with the notion of "intensity" in terms of the manifestation of the Spirit and might suggest a way of correlating (to use Tillich's term) pneumatological immanence with sacramentality broadly conceived.

The work of the existentialist theologian John Macquarrie also provides an interesting example of the theology of mediation. Hope Marie Hirshorn's doctoral thesis examines this theme in his writings and provides useful insight into the subject. She uses his work to construct a theology of mediation and illustrates how it is used in contemporary theology. She suggests that mediation is about God using the material world to convey the divine pres-

---

60. Tillich, *Systematic Theology,* 3:123.
61. Tillich, *Systematic Theology,* 3:151.

ence among embodied human beings without deviating from the natural order that God has created.[62] Central to this mediation is the incarnation: Jesus Christ is the mediator between God and humanity (1 Tim. 2:5-6a). As a corollary, the sacramental approach sees the infinite in the finite, the spiritual in the material, and the transcendent in the immanent.[63] Therefore, the sacred is discovered in the ordinary, in which God is the initiator and sovereignly uses the material world. Macquarrie's existential commitment means that he perceives theology primarily from the perspective of human experience.[64] From this Hirshorn argues that mediation is primarily christological and experiential. She states that "the term mediator is never applied to the Holy Spirit. 'The Greek word *mesites* [mediator] and its cognates are never used of the Spirit (cf. Rom 5.5; 8.26-27; John 12.16-17, 26 [*parakletos*].' While the work of the Holy Spirit functions in both directions from God to humanity and from humanity to God, this is not typically understood as mediation. The work of mediation flows from God the Father through God the Son and is a movement from God to humanity."[65]

The issue raised by Hirshorn regarding the Holy Spirit and mediation is important and needs to be addressed, not least because it could be understood to undermine this whole project. Traditionally, theology has conceived of mediation as solely the work of God in the world, and this is focused around the person and work of Christ. Jesus Christ is the mediator of the new/renewed covenant, as Moses was the mediator of the original/old covenant; however, the concept of mediation needs to be placed within both a Trinitarian framework and a pneumatological context. After the ascension of Christ and on the day of Pentecost, the Spirit mediates the presence of God to the people in an overwhelming manner. That is precisely the point of Pentecost: Christ receives the Holy Spirit again (Acts 2:33) in order to bestow the Spirit upon his people, whom he has brought back into union with the Father. The broader Trinitarian theological context and the actual narrative of mediation, as demonstrated

---

62. Hope Marie Hirshorn, "John Macquarrie's Theology of Mediation" (Ph.D. diss., Fordham University, 2011), p. 5.

63. Hirshorn, "John Macquarrie's Theology," p. 6.

64. John Macquarrie, *Principles of Christian Theology*, 2nd ed. (London: SCM, 1977): "it is experience of existing as a human being that constitutes a primary source for theology" (p. 6); and "the word and the sacraments are effectual only in so far as the person to whom they are directed relates to them in an *existential* manner" (p. 451).

65. Hirshorn, "John Macquarrie's Theology," p. 18. Interior quotation is from A. George Anderson, Francis Stafford, and Joseph A. Burgess, eds., *The One Mediator, the Saints, and Mary* (Minneapolis: Augsburg Fortress, 1992), p. 66.

above, should not be undermined by the lack of a specific word group. The *concept* of mediation and its association with the Spirit are very clearly present even if the actual word is not used in relation to the Holy Spirit in the New Testament. This is somewhat similar to the concept of Trinity, which can be argued to be present at an experiential and soteriological level even though the word itself is absent.[66] Hirshorn's lack of developed pneumatology and Trinitarian theology undermines her theology of mediation, and her decision to identify the presence of a "concept" with a specific "word" group is also problematic because concepts are expressed by a variety of words.[67]

Moving on to neo-orthodoxy, it has been suggested that Karl Barth's discussion of the work of the Holy Spirit is rather limited, and I would agree. Nevertheless, there is more to discover than one might first imagine, given his christological focus. For Barth, the Holy Spirit constitutes and guarantees the unity of the heavenly head, Christ, with his earthly body, the church community, thus constituting the *totus Christus*.[68] It is worth citing Barth in more detail on this point:

> The work of the Holy Spirit, however, is to bring and to hold together that which is different and therefore, as it would seem, necessarily and irresistibly disruptive in the relationship of Jesus Christ to His community, namely divine working, being and action on the one side and the human on the other, the creative freedom and act on the one side and the creaturely on the other, the eternal reality and possibility on the one side and the temporal on the other. His work is to bring and hold them together, not to identify, intermingle nor confound them, not to change the one into the other nor to merge the one into the other, but to co-ordinate them, to make them parallel, to bring them into harmony and therefore to bind them into a true unity.[69]

---

66. See, for example, the discussion by Gordon D. Fee, "Paul and the Trinity: The Experience of Christ and the Spirit for Paul's Understanding of God," in *The Trinity*, ed. Stephen T. Davis, Daniel Kendall, and Gerald O'Collins (Oxford: Oxford University Press, 2001), pp. 49-72.

67. See, for example, the discussion on the relationship between concepts and word groups in Peter Cotterell and Max Turner, *Linguistics and Biblical Interpretation* (London: SPCK, 1989), pp. 115-23.

68. Karl Barth, *Church Dogmatics* (hereafter *CD*) IV/3.2, trans. G. W. Bromiley, ed. G. W. Bromiley and T. F. Torrance (Edinburgh: T. & T. Clark, 2004 [orig. 1961]), p. 760; see the discussion in John Thompson, *The Holy Spirit in the Theology of Karl Barth* (Eugene, Ore.: Pickwick, 1991), pp. 96-107.

69. Barth, *CD* IV/3.2, p. 761.

Thus Barth's position could be regarded as one of "co-ordination," whereby the Spirit harmonizes the divine and the human, Christ and the church, God and creation.

Commenting on Barth's pneumatology, Rosato suggests that the Spirit's proper function is precisely to hold Christ and the Christian in tension, "inseparably connecting" them to each other.[70] Barth adopts a theological concept of mediation rather than a philosophical or hermeneutical one and rejects Schleiermacher's use of the human or communal consciousness of redemption. Barth argues that both God's revelation and human faith are mediated by the activity of the Holy Spirit, because God can only be known by God.[71] The Holy Spirit, while creating experience, can never be identified with it, because of his transcendence.[72] This is because the Holy Spirit is God's own "self-mediation" between the unique Christ event and its "universal import."[73] Rosato comments further:

> In order to give primacy to the mediating role of the Holy Spirit, Barth purposely downplays man's [sic] role in the process of divine-human mediation; not to do so is to sacrifice pneumatology to anthropology or to sacrifice Christ to a vague notion of the Spirit. Barth's own pneumatology is at its core a search for a theologically legitimate principle of mediation at the centre of Christian dogmatics — at the point where the transition is made between Christ and the Christian. Only the Holy Spirit, the divine mediator, can serve this function.[74]

Therefore, for Barth, God, in his third mode of existence, makes the actions of the Father and the Son historical realities. The Holy Spirit completes the self-revelation of God to humanity and creates eternal community between them, just as the Spirit perpetually creates community within the Godhead.[75]

---

70. Philip J. Rosato, *The Spirit as Lord: The Pneumatology of Karl Barth* (Edinburgh: T. & T. Clark, 1981), p. 16.

71. Kevin Hart, "The Experience of the Kingdom of God," in *The Experience of God*, pp. 71-86 (p. 75). Also see T. F. Torrance, *Theology in Reconstruction* (London: SCM, 1965), who states: "It behoves Jesus Christ to be God that he might give his Spirit to men [sic], for only God can give God. It behoves Christ also to be Man, that he might receive the Spirit of God in our human nature and mediate it to his brethren through himself" (p. 245).

72. Thompson, *The Holy Spirit*, pp. 28-29.

73. Rosato, *The Spirit as Lord*, p. 20.

74. Rosato, *The Spirit as Lord*, p. 21.

75. Rosato, *The Spirit as Lord*, p. 64. Barth's theology of mediation is also expressed in relation to the knowledge of God using the distinction of "primary" and "secondary" divine

It is interesting to consider the work of Thomas A. Smail at this point because he was influenced by both Barth and Charismatic Renewal.[76] In his first main book on the person and work of the Holy Spirit, he discusses the reception of the Holy Spirit in the light of Charismatic Renewal.[77] He observes that in Acts there is no "monotonous uniformity" of Spirit-generated experiences but rather a variety. Nevertheless, in all these experiences, the Holy Spirit brings Christ to us and us to Christ. Thus the Spirit mediates the Son and gives him earthly glory.[78] In his later writings Smail preferred to see the Holy Spirit as the Giving Gift.[79] The Father and Son are regarded as givers and the Spirit is regarded as gift. The Father and Son stand on one side of the relationship over and against humanity as givers, whereas the Holy Spirit stands with humanity as gift. The gift originally belonged on the divine side but has moved over to the humanity side of the relationship in the same way that a gift passes from donor to recipient. This gift is sheer grace without conditions, concerns the impartation of life that requires both the giver and the receiver in community, and is a deeply personal gift that expresses God's love. "When God in Christ gives us the Spirit, he gives us nothing less than himself. A gift is often an object that is passed from one hand to another. But here the Gift is a subject, living, acting, sovereign and free."[80] This gift is less like a fortune to spend, says Smail, and more like a friend to cultivate. He is in us but never becomes part of us so that we own him or can manipulate him. Rather, he stands with us on our side of the relationship, as the "go-between God," to cite the phrase of John V. Taylor.[81]

---

objectivity. The "givenness" of God to us in revelation is the means of his secondary objectivity and cannot be understood as being identical with God himself because of the introduction of creation into the secondary objectivity, which means that it has a sacramental quality to it. See *CD* II/1 (Edinburgh: T. & T. Clark, 1957), p. 16, and the commentary by Badcock, *Light of Truth*, pp. 225-27.

76. See Mark J. Cartledge, "*Theological Renewal* (1975-1983): An Editor's Agenda for Church and Academy," *Pneuma: The Journal of the Society for Pentecostal Studies* 30 (2008): 83-107.

77. Thomas A. Smail, *Reflected Glory: The Spirit in Christ and Christians* (Grand Rapids: Eerdmans, 1975).

78. Smail, *Reflected Glory*, pp. 42-44, 53-59.

79. Tom Smail, *The Giving Gift: The Holy Spirit in Person* (Lima, Ohio: Academic Renewal Press, 2002).

80. Smail, *The Giving Gift*, p. 21; also noted by John McIntyre, *The Shape of Pneumatology: Studies in the Doctrine of the Holy Spirit* (London: T. & T. Clark, 2004), p. 200, who calls it "bisociation," that is, the connection between two normally distinct entities.

81. John V. Taylor, *The Go-Between God* (London: SCM, 1972), where the Spirit is desig-

But he enables us to focus on the Father and the Son in the immediacy of the experience. It is only afterward, when we step back, that we see this has been made possible because of the hidden and mysterious action of the Spirit, who shines a light not on himself but on the other two persons of the Trinity. "The indwelling of the Father and the Son in us is the Holy Spirit, who is their personalized self-giving to us. The Spirit is the originating love of the Father and the responding love of the Son given to us in and of our response to what God has done in Christ."[82]

Barth's (and to some extent Smail's) account of pneumatology places the accent on the distinctions between the divine and the human sides of the relationship. The important point in these descriptions is the distinctions between the divine and the human that cannot be collapsed; this is crucial to any discussion because the temptation to collapse the categories is real indeed. This perspective would stress that the qualitative distance between the two cannot be blurred without serious loss of identity, in particular from the divine side. This is where the P/C language of intervention supports the distinction, even if it is unsatisfactory in other ways. The Holy Spirit is mediated by Christ, but the Spirit is also mediated by intermediaries within creation. Both aspects need to be maintained in tension and not resolved in favor of one or the other, because then there is a loss of transcendence or loss of immanence.[83] Perhaps controversially, it could be said that liberal theology lost transcendence (recovered by Barth), whereas neo-orthodox theology lost immanence (recovered by Moltmann). In any case, it alerts us to the problem of *conflation* once again, whereby divine agency is indistinguishable from human agency. This is a problem that is inevitably associated with mediation. The issue is whether this problem is recognized, appreciated, and thereby reflected upon critically in practice or not.[84]

Jürgen Moltmann's work on experience and mediation is also worth discussing, not least because his theology is both indebted to Barth and a reaction

---

nated the "ground of meeting" between humanity and God, as the "elemental energy" of the meeting (p. 18).

82. Smail, *The Giving Gift*, p. 162.

83. This concern probably lies behind Gunton's statement that the Father is "mediated in a twofold way, by his Son and Spirit, not *through* experience but *as they are* experienced." *The Christian Faith*, p. 181.

84. See the discussion of conflation in a different context by Martyn Percy, "Power in the Local Church: Locating the Implicit," in *Exploring Ordinary Theology: Everyday Christian Believing and the Church*, ed. Jeff Astley and Leslie J. Francis (Farnham: Ashgate, 2013), pp. 55-63 (p. 56).

to it. He is critical of Barth's position on the Holy Spirit and the categories of revelation, whereby the Father is the "revealer," the Son is the "revealed" (mediator), and the Spirit is the "revealedness" (that which is mediated). Moltmann suggests that in this conception the Spirit is simply the efficacy of the Son and the Father.[85] By contrast, he argues that when experience of the Holy Spirit leads us to talk about wind, fire, light, and so forth, we are in fact talking about kenotic forms of the Holy Spirit, forms in which the Spirit is emptying himself. They cannot be regarded as objectifications of the Spirit but kenotic forms based on the person of the Spirit who determines these forms. They come to us as experiences that are socially mediated because concepts and experiences are mutually informing.[86] In terms of charismatic experiences and their means of mediating the presence of God, Moltmann states:

> In the charismatic experience, God's Spirit is felt as a *vitalizing energy.* In the nearness of God we are happy, and life begins to vibrate. We experience ourselves in the vibrancies of the divine field of force. That is why charisma is also described as *dynamis* or *energeia.* From the earliest times, the charismatic experience of the Holy Spirit has been pictured as a flowing, an outpouring and a shining. If we take these experiences as starting point[s], we can say that the Holy Spirit appears as the well of life — the origin of the torrent of energy — the source of the light that gives the shining splendour.[87]

Moltmann continues by saying this presence is a reciprocal *perichoresis* between God and humanity: a communion of reciprocal indwelling such that the eternal Holy Spirit participates in our temporal life and we participate in the eternal life of God. Indeed, it could be argued that, for Moltmann, the work of mediation is intrinsic to the very personhood of the Holy Spirit, which he defines as "the loving, self-communicating, out-fanning and outpouring presence of the eternal divine life of the triune God."[88]

Moltmann's aim to move beyond Barth, at least to some extent, is an attempt to hold the tension between transcendence and immanence, even if his panentheism is unsatisfactory in some respects because it begins to resolve the tension in favor of immanence. His language of *kenosis* is, how-

---

85. Jürgen Moltmann, *The Spirit of Life: A Universal Affirmation* (London: SCM, 1992), pp. 290-91.

86. Moltmann, *The Spirit of Life,* p. 18.

87. Moltmann, *The Spirit of Life,* p. 195.

88. Moltmann, *The Spirit of Life,* p. 289.

ever, helpful because it offers a parallel to christological *kenosis* and gives greater attention to the possibility of intimacy with God in and through the Holy Spirit.[89] The perichoretic life of the divine Trinity is mediated by the reciprocal indwelling of the church in the Spirit and the Spirit in the church. This *communio* approach to ecclesiology is based in the mediation of the Holy Spirit, especially in eucharistic practices, but there is always the danger of pneumatological domestication, such that the church "controls" or "dispenses" the Spirit via its sacramental practices.

This leads to a consideration of a pneumatological reading of George Lindbeck by Jane Barton Moulaison,[90] even though Lindbeck could not be said to have made a significant contribution to pneumatology within his ecclesiology.[91] Moulaison begins by noting the feminist critiques of Lindbeck's work, which suggest that the disruptive capacity of the Holy Spirit undermines or at the very least qualifies the givenness of the church in Lindbeck's theology. She suggests that by "regarding the church as *the* locus of the Holy Spirit, George Lindbeck offers a premature sanctification of the church structures."[92] Inevitably this has consequences for those who remain outside the power structures of the church. The power of the Holy Spirit can be differentiated from the institutional power structures and provides a basis for a critical hermeneutics. She cites Reinhard Hütter's appropriation of the *communio* approach to ecclesiology, which emphasizes the pneumatological character of the church. "The work and witness of the church, according to Hütter, *are* the works of the Holy Spirit, who mediates between the Godhead and the church, allowing for the overflowing of perichoretic inter-triune relations within core church practices."[93] He suggests that the church is *enhypostatically* bound to the Godhead by the Spirit, so that the Spirit mediates between the two *koinoniai*. Importantly, the works of the church inhere in the salvific economy of the Spirit.[94] This does not mean

---

89. See the discussion of *kenosis* and pneumatology in Atkinson, *Trinity after Pentecost,* pp. 60-63.

90. Lindbeck, *The Nature of Christian Doctrine;* Jane Barton Moulaison, *Lord, Giver of Life: Toward a Pneumatological Complement to George Lindbeck's Theory of Doctrine* (Toronto: Canadian Corporation for Studies in Religion and Wilfrid Laurier University Press, 2007).

91. For example, George Lindbeck, *The Church in a Postliberal Age,* ed. James Buckley (Grand Rapids: Eerdmans, 2002).

92. Moulaison, *Lord, Giver of Life,* p. 45.

93. Moulaison, *Lord, Giver of Life,* p. 122; Reinhard Hütter, *Suffering Divine Things: Theology as Church Practice* (Grand Rapids: Eerdmans, 2000).

94. Hütter, *Suffering Divine Things,* p. 133.

that the church possesses them or that they merely coincide, but rather that
they constitute the "indispensable 'mediate forms' of its activity."[95] Moulaison is understandably wary of any domestication of the Spirit to the church
and consistently reminds her dialogue partners that the Spirit disrupts and
judges church life.[96] Ultimately, she understands the Spirit in terms of drawing people to the point where they can hear God's Word of address, which
is located in the cross, "a storied sense of reconciliation," whereby the Holy
Spirit draws us to the heart of the gospel. "[I]t is here that the supposed distance between humanity and God is more than merely mediated. God does
not simply condescend to our humanity: rather, God of His great love freely
and abundantly offers His very Self as the inner-triune life is enhypostasized
within our humanity."[97]

Moulaison's points are well taken. It would be unwise to privilege certain church structures by suggesting that they mediate the Holy Spirit more
authentically than others, although this is sometimes implied by certain
kinds of ecclesiology. It could be suggested that all ecclesial structures, at
least potentially, reflect both the weaknesses of humanity and the grace and
goodness of God. It is in the midst of this tension that God's presence by his
Spirit is mediated and can be discerned. However, as Moulaison reminds
us, the Spirit can never be reduced to ecclesial mediation, because once
again this would signal conflation and the collapse of the transcendent into
the immanent, as well as a kind of overrealized eschatology. Both have the
potential to distort and manipulate the freedom of the Holy Spirit in the
claims that are made.

Neumann and others use the phrase "mediated immediacy" in an attempt to maintain the tension between transcendence and immanence, as
well as the distinctions in the relations between the persons of the Trinity,
especially Christ and the Spirit. Madathummiyil emphasizes that the Spirit
is the mediation of the mediator, Christ, copresent as the Spirit of Christ and
not some distant third party. Therefore, a way of capturing this important
dynamic is required, one that maintains the three aspects of the mediator,
the mediation, and the receivers of both the mediator and the mediation.
However, discussions of mediation in the theological literature pay very little
attention to the actual biblical texts that describe most obviously the manner
in which the mediation of the Spirit occurs. Therefore, these key biblical texts

95. Hütter, *Suffering Divine Things*, p. 128.
96. Moulaison, *Lord, Giver of Life*, p. 126.
97. Moulaison, *Lord, Giver of Life*, p. 150.

invite exploration and discussion of this important concept. The discussion in this chapter has alerted us to the kinds of issues that surround the concept theologically. It remains for Scripture to be allowed to shape and inform the existing ideas that have been discerned from within the various traditions.

## 3.4 Conclusion

This chapter has discussed the key concept at the center of the thesis of this book, namely, pneumatological mediation. It has done so, first of all, by engaging with recent P/C scholarship. This scholarship explains mediation and pneumatology in relation to religious experience, and in particular Spirit baptism, in the context of P/C communities and their ecclesial practices. Although these experiences are specific, they can be used in a more general sense to speak about how the person and work of the Holy Spirit can be mediated. The outcome of this discussion is subsequently brought into conversation with key figures in the broader Protestant theological tradition. Thus the ways in which the idea of pneumatological mediation is expressed are given a Protestant ecumenical context. This enables the P/C theological conversation to be set alongside other historical and contemporary theological conversations, which allows resonances to be discerned.

As a preliminary answer to the first part of the research question set at the beginning of the chapter, it may be said that a distinct contribution is constructed from the notion of *pneumatological mediation.* This concept is informed by Pentecostal experience and associated empowerment, is shaped by specific theological loci, and is expressed in ecclesial practices, especially sacramental practices broadly conceived. These practices can be appreciated in terms of the providential notion of *concursus,* which accounts for the manner in which divine and human agency are understood to coordinate and function. This chapter sets the broader conceptual framework for the notion of pneumatological mediation, which will focus on the elucidation of key biblical texts in Luke-Acts, to which we now turn.

# 4 Pentecost and the Acts of the Apostles

## 4.1 Introduction

This chapter builds on my earlier discussion of the practical-theological use of Scripture, and in particular the possibility of advocating a practical-theological reading of Scripture. In chapter 2, I suggested five dimensions: (1) hermeneutical reflexivity; (2) attention to praxis, explicit or implicit; (3) awareness of agency, both human and divine; (4) treating the text holistically and contextually; and (5) bringing contemporary questions and issues to the text.

In the light of these dimensions, it is worth reflecting on them personally at this stage of the study. I am an ordained priest in the Church of England, and a critical participant, commentator, and theologian working from a P/C perspective, although sometimes this is less evident, depending on academic conventions and the nature of a given piece of work. At the time of writing, I am a professional theologian working in a secular university department in the UK (but by the time this book is published, I shall be working in a Christian university setting in the USA). Therefore, I straddle the confessional and academic divide in theology, belonging to both worlds simultaneously (although this relationship may be configured differently for me in the future). In this project I am using the resources of scholarship within P/C theology to address the wider academic discourse of practical theology. Therefore, I concentrate on the key biblical text for Pentecostals, namely, Acts 2.[1] I am concerned

---

1. Luke's two-volume work (Luke-Acts) has often been regarded as the "canon within the

with the praxis of the early church and the agency of both the Holy Spirit and the disciples using the concept of mediation as a theological lens of interpretation. My treatment of Acts 2 is given a broader context by addressing other Spirit reception texts in Acts, but stops short of addressing other New Testament texts because of the constraints of space. The contemporary questions concern the use of Scripture and the role of pneumatology in academic practical theology and how these might be addressed in a constructive fashion.

This chapter is probably the most densely argued chapter in the book. However, I would encourage readers to stay with the discussion of the biblical texts in order to fully appreciate how a detailed engagement with them can have significant benefits for practical theology, especially when the ecclesial life that we research is deeply informed by them at different levels and in various ways. Pentecostals in particular are apt to appeal to the primitive church for patterns for contemporary church life, and it is important that theologians are attentive and understand this kind of ordinary hermeneutic and bring academic theological hermeneutical lenses alongside it. Therefore, this chapter aims to do the following: (1) read the text of Acts 2, paying attention to mediation as a pneumatological lens; (2) review other Spirit reception texts throughout the book of Acts; (3) analyze the nature of pneumatological mediation in these specific texts; and (4) suggest how these findings might renew an agenda for practical theology more broadly.

The argument of this chapter is worth stating up front, so to speak. I wish to argue that in Scripture we have a model for understanding the relationship between religious experience and pneumatology, and that it is inextricably connected to ecclesiology. The personal presence of the Holy Spirit constitutes the *ecclesia* and mediates to it the presence of the other persons of the Trinity, thus uniting the Godhead to the church. The church also mediates the presence of the Holy Spirit both internally to its members and externally to others by intermediaries. These forms of mediation are intrinsic to the life and witness of the church.

---

canon" of Pentecostal theological hermeneutics. While this may be problematic at one level (it excludes other significant biblical texts), at another level it provides a focus for an inquiry such as this one.

## 4.2 The Day of Pentecost

The analysis of the day of Pentecost narrative has illuminated three features, which are considered in turn.

### 4.2.1 Mediation of the Holy Spirit[2]

First, the book of Acts considers experience of the Holy Spirit as a starting point: "But you will receive power when the Holy Spirit has come upon you" (Acts 1:8 NRSV). This statement is both a command and a promise. The disciples are to wait to receive power so that they might fulfill their vocation as witnesses to the risen Messiah.[3] It is the promise of the Father that the vocation of Christ and the vocation of the disciples become inextricably linked by means of the Holy Spirit, as the anointing upon Christ is to be transferred to the disciples and the *ecclesia* (1:4).[4] There are indeed obvious parallels between Christ's reception of the Spirit to fulfill his messianic ministry and the disciples' reception of the Spirit for their ministry of witness: both are praying, and the Spirit "descends" and looks *like* something physical.[5] But there is also contrast between Jesus' baptism and theirs. On the one hand Jesus was baptized by John the Baptist as his identification with Israel, which was preparatory; on the other hand Christ himself baptizes with the Spirit (2:33), which is a sign that the Messiah has indeed arrived and, with him, a new eschatological era.[6] The disciples witness not only to the Messiah but also to the kingdom of God. They are witnesses not to a doctrine but to a person and his reign via the Spirit in creation.[7]

---

2. It will become clear in this chapter that the phrase "the mediation of the Spirit" is both subjective genitive (the Spirit as subject mediates the persons of the Trinity) and objective genitive (the Spirit as object is mediated by Christ, creation, the church, and individuals). Obviously, the context in which the phrase is used determines in which sense it should be understood.

3. Craig S. Keener, *Acts: An Exegetical Commentary,* vol. 1 (Grand Rapids: Baker Academic, 2012), p. 675.

4. Clark H. Pinnock, *Flame of Love: A Theology of the Holy Spirit* (Downers Grove, Ill.: IVP, 1996), p. 113; cf. Wolfgang Vondey, *Heribert Mühlen: His Theology and Praxis — a New Profile for the Church* (Lanham, Md.: University Press of America, 2004), p. 115.

5. Keener, *Acts,* p. 679.

6. Darrell L. Bock, *Acts,* Baker Exegetical Commentary on the New Testament (Grand Rapids: Baker Academic, 2007), p. 57.

7. Justo L. Gonzalez, *Acts: The Gospel of the Spirit* (Maryknoll, N.Y.: Orbis, 2001), p. 20. There is a debate among Pentecostal and charismatic scholars about whether the Holy Spirit

There appear to be four discernible means through which the presence of the Holy Spirit is mediated to the disciples on the day of Pentecost. This event occurs during the Jewish Feast of Weeks, held on the fiftieth day after the first Sabbath of the Passover.[8] It was originally a harvest festival of firstfruits at which the first sheaf of the wheat harvest was dedicated to God (Exod. 23:16; 34:22; Lev. 23:15-21; Num. 28:26; Deut. 16:9-12). As such, it was an occasion when diaspora Jews would flock to Jerusalem to celebrate the goodness of God. One tradition has associated it with the giving of the Law on Sinai and the theophany associated with that event (Exod. 19:16-19), although this is disputed within scholarship because Luke does not clearly link it with Mount Sinai.[9] Scholars also suggest that the event is a reversal of Babel because the Spirit does not eliminate the differences in languages but appears to accentuate them. However, there is no explicit reference to Babel (Gen. 11:1-11), and Luke does not consider tongues a single language, so it must remain a background allusion.[10]

1. We read that the disciples were all together *(pantes homou epi to auto)* in one place (Acts 2:1); that is, 120 people were gathered in a single place in anticipation of the fulfillment of the promise made by Jesus in 1:8: that they would receive power when the Spirit came upon them, and they would be witnesses to him.[11] A community of people was located in close proximity in a single space. It is not clear where this "room" was located historically, or whether it was the same location as the upper room in which the Last Supper was eaten.[12] It might have been in the upper

is given primarily for witness (Shelton), or exclusively for witness (Menzies), or whether the giving of the Holy Spirit is primarily focused around a new exodus typology (Turner). Keener suggests that empowerment for mission logically precedes Israel's restoration; see *Acts,* p. 690. I suspect that the themes are sufficiently intertwined as to make the issue more a matter of tradition-specific emphasis: classical Pentecostal versus charismatic.

8. Ben Witherington III, *The Acts of the Apostles: A Socio-Rhetorical Commentary* (Grand Rapids: Eerdmans; Carlisle: Paternoster, 1998), p. 131; James D. G. Dunn, *The Acts of the Apostles* (Valley Forge, Pa.: Trinity, 1996), p. 23.

9. Keener, *Acts,* p. 787; Roger Stronstad, *The Prophethood of All Believers: A Study of Luke's Charismatic Theology* (Sheffield: Sheffield Academic Press, 1999), p. 57.

10. Frank D. Macchia, "Babel and the Tongues of Pentecost: Reversal or Fulfilment? A Theological Perspective," in *Speaking in Tongues: Multi-Disciplinary Perspectives,* ed. Mark J. Cartledge (Milton Keynes: Paternoster, 2006), pp. 34-51, has argued that Babel is an important resonance and sees Pentecost not so much as a reversal of Babel but more as a fulfillment of it.

11. Cf. Daniela C. Augustine, *Pentecost, Hospitality, and Transformation* (Cleveland, Tenn.: CPT Press, 2012), who observes that this unity among the disciples is a sign of the church (p. 17).

12. Witherington, *Acts,* p. 131.

city next to the temple.[13] Indeed, the location could have resembled a mansion excavated in Jerusalem that contained a meeting hall.[14] In any case, either this gathering would have been semipublic, because a crowd gathered to watch what was occurring, or it would have "spilled out" into more public space near the home.[15] We are told that the 120 disciples are sitting in a house when, with no announcement, the Holy Spirit "comes upon" them.[16] The impression is given that all those present (both men and women) experienced the Holy Spirit coming upon them.

The narrative suggests that the Spirit is given to the church corporately before it is given to individuals. *The Holy Spirit is mediated via the intermediary of the community.* This would have been even more the case in a Middle Eastern culture, where corporate identity is prior to individuality. Indeed, in many cultures around the world, identity — who we are and who we regard ourselves to be — is first and foremost shaped by the community to which we belong.[17] We belong to this community before we articulate its beliefs and values for ourselves.[18] Unfortunately, in the Western world, we have accentuated individualism to the extent that corporate identity is regarded as secondary in identity formation.[19] One of the insights that Pentecostal hermeneutics has recovered is the sense of community formation in beliefs and practices. There is a strong sense of connectedness in believing, which means that theology and its development are considered part and parcel of the action of the community, at least in an ideal sense, by Pentecostal theologians. How that works out on the ground among ordinary believers

13. Keener, *Acts,* p. 797.

14. Bock, *Acts,* p. 94. He adds that it is less likely that it was the temple because Luke appears to distinguish between the references to the temple and houses by the terms that he uses. He always uses *hieron* for temple and *oikos* for house.

15. David G. Peterson, *The Acts of the Apostles* (Grand Rapids: Eerdmans, 2009), p. 132.

16. Gonzalez, *Acts,* p. 34.

17. John McIntyre, *The Shape of Pneumatology: Studies in the Doctrine of the Holy Spirit* (Edinburgh: T. & T. Clark, 1997), p. 53.

18. Graham H. Twelftree, *People of the Spirit: Exploring Luke's View of the Church* (London: SPCK; Grand Rapids: Baker Academic, 2009), suggests that the church existed in nascent form prior to Pentecost, but at Pentecost it became the heir of the eschatological kingdom and the hope of Israel (p. 28).

19. Michael Welker, *God the Spirit* (Minneapolis: Fortress, 1994), illustrates this point by giving priority to the individual rather than the community. His language is important: "[O]ne's own particularity is experienced in the midst of a consciously perceived polyindividuality and polyconcreteness, in the midst of a diversity which, while foreign to the individual human person, through the Pentecost event allows and makes possible commonality and common experience and knowledge" (p. 233).

has only begun to be researched. Nevertheless, it is important for our proposal to identify the primary significance of communal identity in relation to the experience of the Holy Spirit. Many commentators on Pentecostal and charismatic Christianity have emphasized its individualistic and consumerist side, which no doubt exists, but this is in tension with the primary communal experiential dimension.

2. In verse 2 we read that the Spirit came *like (hōsper)* a violent wind from heaven and filled the house (cf. 1 Kings 19:11-12). Luke begins to use a series of analogies to describe what is happening (wind, fire, tongues).[20] It is the sound that fills the house, not the wind as such.[21] Obviously the notion of "coming from heaven" suggests a transcendent, and by implication divine, origin, but the statement also uses notions of space: from up there to down here. The Spirit comes to people from outside of them, and yet the Spirit is also immanent within them, breathing life and vitality into them. There are echoes of earlier biblical texts where the Spirit of God is related to the breath of life (Gen. 2:7), as well as theophanies where God's presence is understood to have come down from heaven, the place where God dwells in his majesty and splendor.[22] This analogy picks up these themes and points to an eschatological event that fulfills earlier promises and is a "firstfruit" of the future age that is already on its way.

In this text, we see that the Spirit's presence is *intensified* in space and time of the created order. There are moments of "encounter" and there are places of "encounter." That is, very often ordinary places become spaces of significance because of these moments of intensity in the presence of the Spirit.[23] There is nothing special about the place (if it can be assumed not to be the temple), and yet places where people gather to meet with each other and the Spirit in prayer can be said to contribute to the mediation of the Spirit's greater intensity. Of course, the times and places will vary according to the particularities of social, historical, and cultural conditions. This is inevitable, but it is often overlooked. People also experience the presence of the Spirit as a punctuated process. The punctuations are events of significance within the process, and they are specific to times and places. Indeed, the people

20. Witherington, *Acts*, p. 132.

21. Luke Timothy Johnson, *The Acts of the Apostles* (Collegeville, Minn.: Liturgical Press, 1992), p. 42; although the rush of wind was also associated with early Hebrew theophanies (2 Sam. 22:16; Job 37:10; Ezek. 13:13); see Twelftree, *People of the Spirit*, p. 71.

22. Keener, *Acts*, p. 800; Stronstad, *The Prophethood*, p. 55.

23. John Inge, *A Christian Theology of Place* (Farnham: Ashgate, 2003), p. 67: "the world in all its diverse aspects can be the place of God's own self-revelation to us."

did not simply experience the presence of the Holy Spirit. It seems that the "presence" filled the whole house; whatever that actually meant in terms of space, it is clear that ordinary space and the people who inhabited that space had a remarkable encounter with the divine. Therefore, it can be said that *the Holy Spirit is mediated via the intermediary of place and time in creation.*

3. They "saw" what are *likened (hōsei)* to "tongues of fire" separating *(diamerizō)* and resting on each of them (Acts 2:3).[24] In the context of the communal mediation of the Spirit's presence, there are also individual experiences. The "tongues of fire" rested on everyone but also on *each one,* symbolizing the way in which the one Spirit is mediated to and via individuals.[25] Fire was also a common theme in Jewish theophanies, and therefore it comes as no surprise that such a feature is present here.[26] Tongues of fire are simply received passively *(ōphthēsan),* as if to emphasize that this event is divinely orchestrated and cannot be otherwise.[27] Each individual experiences the same Spirit but differently, depending on a range of factors that are not Luke's focus and so are not commented upon by him, but from our perspective might include personality and disposition. We are not told how the experiences differed, presumably because the emphasis is on common experience (all people, Acts 2:17). Did they see these "tongues of fire" literally or imaginatively? I do not know the answer to this question.[28] Luke clearly wishes to emphasize the analogous quality of the event: these separations of the Spirit *appear as* tongues of fire on each person's head (just as the Spirit *appeared as* a dove at Jesus' baptism).[29] But I am not entirely sure that it

24. It has been suggested that the accompaniment of "tongues of fire" is "vaguely conjunctive" *(kai)* rather than "decidedly sequential"; see John R. Levison, *Filled with the Spirit* (Grand Rapids: Eerdmans, 2009), p. 328.

25. Levison, *Filled with the Spirit,* p. 329, suggests the following: "It is this association of filling and fire that contributes to a distinct impression of entry into an ecstatic state over which Jesus' followers had no control; for this association Luke situates the experience of Pentecost in a Greco-Roman literary context in which inspiration was depicted as a fiery experience, a context in which filling with *pneuma* was understood as an experience that ignited and inflamed a person possessed."

26. Keener, *Acts,* p. 804. Peterson, *Acts,* p. 133, situates this imagery against OT texts such as Exod. 3:2-5; 19:18; 24:17; 40:38, where fire symbolizes the presence of God.

27. Bock, *Acts,* p. 96.

28. Dunn, *Acts,* p. 25, argues that the language used by Luke indicates that the experience is visionary; also Twelftree, *People of the Spirit,* p. 71, who regards the occasion as a communal vision. However, I am unsure how precise we can be regarding the matter.

29. I am less convinced by the unsophisticated "trance" theory used by some commentators, not least because they have swallowed whole the rather dubious position of Felicitas Goodman, about which I have written myself. See, for example, Bruce J. Malina and John J.

matters in terms of mediation, because on the literal account external sight is used and on the imaginative account internal sight is used. Both internal and external forms of mediation could be individual experiences as well as corporate ones.

*The Holy Spirit is mediated via this intermediary context to individuals who in turn contribute to the social dynamic of the group.* This feature is an important balance to the corporate emphasis of point 1. It seems as though individuals are an important category within the context of group mediation because they interact within the dynamics of the group, even within the restoration of Israel and the constitution of the *ecclesia*. In the rest of the book of Acts we read about important individuals who are significant leaders in the witness to the message of the kingdom of God.[30] However, we also read of less well-known people who nevertheless are used by God within the community of the church. The Holy Spirit enables them to fulfill their natural capabilities and unique gifting, and does so in ways that do not homogenize their identities but rather allows for complementarity of identity and service. Of course, there is always some tension between the group and the individual as part of the group, but at least in this context the Spirit appears to affirm both as legitimate intermediaries of his action in the world.

4. All of them were "filled with the Holy Spirit" (Acts 2:4), that is, the indwelling of the Spirit. The verb is an aorist passive of *pimplēmi* ("they were filled"), but it seems as though Luke can use a variety of liquid-type metaphors to describe the Spirit coming upon people — filling, baptizing, and pouring — and can use them interchangeably, although he does not use the verb "to baptize" of subsequent infillings.[31] This intensity of the presence of the Spirit within all individuals in the group leads to a further aspect of mediation.[32] In the event of reception, there is a return movement back toward God in which the presence of the Spirit is revealed even more intensely

Pilch, *Social Scientific Commentary on the Book of Acts* (Minneapolis: Fortress, 2008), p. 28. See my "Interpreting Charismatic Experience: Hypnosis, Altered States of Consciousness and the Holy Spirit," *Journal of Pentecostal Theology* 13 (1998): 117-32 (pp. 127-29).

30. The reception of the Spirit by individuals can also be understood as an experience of the Trinity; see Augustine, *Pentecost, Hospitality, and Transformation*, p. 28.

31. Witherington, *Acts*, p. 133. It is possible that "infilling" is a stylistic variation on "being baptized"; see Anthony C. Thiselton, *The Holy Spirit — in Biblical Teaching, through the Centuries, and Today* (Grand Rapids: Eerdmans, 2013), p. 55.

32. Levison, *Filled with the Spirit*, p. 329, emphasizes the chaotic character of the event; also see Augustine, *Pentecost, Hospitality, and Transformation*, p. 18, who says: "The believers are positioned 'in' and united 'with' Christ as the Holy Spirit saturates them with the divine presence."

via doxological speech. In this text it is glossolalic speech (*heterais glōssais,* "other tongues," v. 4), which is further defined as speech declaring the wonders of God (*ta megaleia tou theou,* "the great deeds of God," v. 11), in other words, praise and worship, although the precise nature of these declarations is not spelled out in any detail.[33] It has been argued that this speech was solemn and not necessarily ecstatic since *apophthengomai* often suggests serious forms of plain speech.[34] This means that the very act of Spirit-inspired worship leads to a greater intensity of the Spirit's presence, which spills out in superabundance. In the overflow of this worship, doxological speech also "goes public"! Of course, this last point depends partly on the location of the meeting room and its interface with the public space inhabited by the crowd. But wherever the precise location of the "house," there is an interface between the worshiping *ecclesia* and wider society.[35] This means that *the Holy Spirit is mediated via the intermediary of doxological speech (glossolalia here) and worship.* Presumably God is primarily addressed by such speech, but clearly there is a secondary human audience as well (both inside and outside the community of the church).

Verses 5-7a suggest that doxology as an event brings the presence of the Spirit into public awareness. Worship is not merely a private matter but spills out into the public square. The private room cannot contain the presence of the Spirit. Doxological speech is heard from outside (v. 6), or at least from the periphery of the event, and thus (in a sense) mediation could be said to be extended. This speech was not essentially a proclamation of the gospel but rather a declaration of doxology, even if it carried missiological implications.[36] The disciples may have moved from the house to the open public space, but this is not made explicit by Luke.[37] In any event, people in the public square hear the doxological speech before they begin to process the meaning of the presence of the Spirit. In fact, public mediation can be bewildering, leading to amazement. Questions are asked by those witnessing this mediation because things do not fit their expectations of what should be occurring (vv. 7b-13). They hear the declarations of praise in their own languages (v. 8), but they do not understand what is happening. The hearers are a mixture of Jerusalem Jews and diaspora Jews attending the festival, and

33. Twelftree, *People of the Spirit,* p. 73.

34. Gonzalez, *Acts,* p. 35.

35. The change of scene to the public place is not clearly expressed, so Hans Conzelmann, *Acts of the Apostles* (Philadelphia: Fortress, 1987), p. 14.

36. Peterson, *Acts,* p. 137.

37. Gonzalez, *Acts,* p. 35.

the languages represent the then-known world.[38] The list of the nations in Genesis 10 probably informs this list (as it did most Jewish lists of the period), which means that there is some allusion to Babel, although, as noted above, the text does not *explicitly* refer to Genesis 11.[39] As a result of the ambiguity of the event (not the speech), the observers ask each other questions regarding the meaning of the doxology. They also mock the speakers and accuse them of drinking wine *(gleukos)*.[40] Amazement can also lead to confusion and cynicism.

In summary, the passage suggests that on the day of Pentecost the "presence" of the Holy Spirit was mediated via distinct intermediaries: the community and the particular space and time, which together mediate the presence of the Holy Spirit to the individuals, who in turn contribute to the community, and finally via the intermediary of doxological speech, addressed to God but heard in the *ecclesia* and in the public context and thus mediated to a wider human audience. It could be suggested that the first two intermediaries are primary and are inextricably connected. Can they, in effect, be defined in terms of the "community," as some Pentecostal models would suggest? I think this would be a reductionist move because specific times and places appear to influence how the Spirit is experienced. Theoretically, you could take people from the same ecclesial community to a different place and they could have a different set of pneumatic experiences than previously known (e.g., when visiting revivalist pilgrimage sites). I also think that individual differences in the context of group dynamics have a significant influence on how people experience the intensity of the Spirit's action. On this occasion glossolalic speech accompanied these other two intermediaries, but this was not always the case. Further events in Acts would tend to confirm this conclusion (it is not present in 8:17 and 9:18 but is present in 10:46 and 19:6). If glossolalic speech can be extended as a category to embrace worship more broadly, then this central communal practice becomes even more significant for a pneumatology of mediation. Therefore, we can identify four forms of mediation:

---

38. Witherington, *Acts,* p. 36.

39. Keener, *Acts,* p. 842.

40. There is some debate on whether sweet or new wine would have been available six months after the main grape harvest. See, for example, the discussion by Witherington, *Acts,* p. 137, and Keener, *Acts,* p. 859. The point, however, is fundamentally the same, whatever kind of wine is assumed: they are accused of being drunk! Levison, *Filled with the Spirit,* pp. 331-32, suggests that the "others" who "sneered" were a sizable group of observers, who might have considered there to be a parallel with the Bacchus ritual; thus there could have been a "thinly veiled charge" that they were acting like devotees of Bacchus.

(1) the creation mediates the Holy Spirit to the church; (2) the church mediates the Holy Spirit among its individual members; (3) the church mediates the Holy Spirit in doxological speech; and (4) the church mediates the Holy Spirit to the wider public of humanity outside the church via its overhearing of this doxological speech. This means that religious experience and pneumatology are inextricably connected both in the internal life of the church and in its witness to the world.


### 4.2.2 Scripture

A passage from Scripture is used to interpret the event of Pentecost: "This is what was spoken through the prophet Joel" (Acts 2:16 NRSV). Following the actual events of Pentecost, a theological interpretation and explanation is given by Peter. This addresses the need for practical theology to be further grounded in Scripture and tradition. It is in this account that three features can be discerned, enabling us to appreciate what is being mediated via the Spirit's presence.

1. Peter addresses the crowd (Acts 2:14-21) and offers an explanation to his Jewish audience based on Joel 2:28-32 (LXX 3:1-5).[41] He refutes the ambiguity suggested by the observers of the event and attempts to bring clarification and greater understanding to their initial perceptions. Although it is possible that Peter, as a representative, is defending the honor of the group and using forensic rhetoric to attack his opponents, theologically what is happening here goes beyond a shame/honor scenario.[42] The reception of the Spirit is the sine qua non of the Christian life.[43] The *pesher* (or interpretation) of Joel 2:28-32 is used to give meaning to the event within an eschatological and apocalyptic framework.[44] This event is a sign of the inauguration of the last days in which God will pour out his very presence upon all people.[45] There is no pneumatic differentiation between people, despite biological and social (sex,

---

41. For a discussion of the textual changes made by Luke, see Johnson, *Acts*, p. 49; also see Max Turner, *Power from on High: The Spirit in Israel's Restoration and Witness in Luke-Acts* (Sheffield: Sheffield Academic Press, 1996), pp. 269-70. The abbreviation LXX refers to the Septuagint.

42. Malina and Pilch, *Social Scientific Commentary*, p. 33; Witherington, *Acts*, p. 138.

43. Witherington, *Acts*, p. 140.

44. The Hebrew word *pesher* is translated "this means" or "the interpretation is" and is normally followed by a commentary on a biblical text.

45. Turner, *Power from on High*, states: "God's *Spirit* (even more strongly than the *Shi-*

age, social status) distinctions: this is a divine act of sociocultural leveling.[46] Despite existing norms within society, and indeed the church, this fundamental pneumatological egalitarianism functions as an eschatological critique of such conventions of social stratification. Indeed, this prophetic empowerment should characterize the whole church: all who are incorporated into the people of God are included in the band of prophets.[47] In the kingdom of God social distinctions are relativized in the egalitarianism of the Spirit: a new age has dawned.[48] The notion of "all flesh" *(pasan sarka)* implies that the promise is extended beyond the boundaries of Israel, even as Peter addresses the people of Israel in Jerusalem. There is an allusion to Isaiah 57:19, which also applies the prophecy to the Gentiles and supports the application of Joel beyond the boundaries of Israel.[49] Such a fundamental social reordering is seen as part of the end-time purposes of God. This restoration of the "spirit of prophecy" places the community of the church within a framework of promise that will be fulfilled at the consummation of the age. The reference to the apocalyptic signs in Joel suggests a resonance with the Jewish expectation of the Day of the Lord (Ezek. 13:5; Amos 5:18; Joel 1:15), such that this day was proleptic of that great and terrible day.[50] This means that for Luke the inauguration of the kingdom of God on earth can be tangibly witnessed in the event of Pentecost, and that it correlates with the notion of salvation: to be "saved" means to participate in this new exodus deliverance from bondage. It is a liberation that recalls the exodus event, but it is associated with the coming of the Holy Spirit to Israel and the nations. *Therefore it could be said that the Holy Spirit mediates the inaugurated eschatological reality of Christ's kingship.*

2. Peter further explains that the inauguration of the eschatological reign of God makes sense from a Jewish perspective when it is understood as part of the ministry of Jesus of Nazareth. He was the one whom God attested by means of mighty works, signs, and wonders *(dunamesi kai terasi kai sēmeiois)* (Acts 2:22), which suggests an allusion to Moses and his exodus signs of deliverance.[51] This Davidic deliverer fulfills the messianic expecta-

---

*kinah) was a way of speaking of the active* (usually self-revealing) *personal presence of the transcendent God himself*" (p. 277).

46. Gonzalez, *Acts,* p. 42.

47. Keener, *Acts,* p. 881.

48. F. F. Bruce, *The Book of the Acts,* rev. ed. (Grand Rapids: Eerdmans, 1988), refers to the fulfillment of Moses' expectation in Num. 11:29, p. 68.

49. Keener, *Acts,* p. 882.

50. Keener, *Acts,* p. 919.

51. Keener, *Acts,* p. 925.

tions of Israel, especially the resurrection from the dead and the exaltation to the right hand of the Father (vv. 22-36), which is the highest place of honor. The title "Lord," used as a divine title in the LXX, is transferred to Jesus (v. 25) as the vindicated and exalted Messiah (v. 35). From this position of authority, he receives the Spirit again (v. 33) in order that he might bestow the Spirit upon all people in a definitive act. This event, which they are witnessing with their own eyes, echoes the sign language of verse 22, but this time in relation to the reception of the Spirit among them.[52] The fact that the Spirit is being poured out by Jesus is evidence that he already reigns as risen, ascended, and glorified Messiah. "If Jesus as God's agent pours out God's Spirit, he fulfils an explicitly divine role."[53] Jesus is Lord of the Spirit. *This means that the exalted Christ is the mediator of the Holy Spirit from the Father to the church and the basis upon which all other forms of mediation are derived.*[54] This further reception of the Spirit upon his glorification suggests that the mediation of the Spirit must be understood as part of a christological and Trinitarian reality. In the context of Pentecost, the Trinitarian explanation is that the Father has given the Spirit to the Son (as the executor), who has given the Spirit to his people. There is both a Trinitarian context to the giving of the Spirit and a christological focus. The one they crucified has been exalted to the highest place. The one who endured the scandal of the cross has been vindicated. God has made him both Lord and Christ. The anointed one anoints his people with the presence of his Spirit. Therefore, the church continues in the anointing of the Messiah for the sake of the kingdom of God. *It also means that the Holy Spirit mediates the presence of Christ and the Father to the church.*

3. Verse 37 records that Peter's explanation and challenge to his audience had the desired effect: they were "cut to the heart" *(katenugēsan tē kardian),* suggesting profound pain,[55] and were led to ask the practical-theological question: What should we do? Peter's response was very clear: they should repent, be baptized in the name of Jesus Christ for the forgiveness of sins, and receive the gift of the Holy Spirit. This is because this

---

52. Keener, *Acts,* p. 955.

53. Keener, *Acts,* p. 957.

54. Turner, *Power from on High,* pp. 277-78, suggests that "Jesus does not merely mediate in the bestowing of God's Spirit as the eschatological gift; he actually also becomes the author of specific phenomena given to the disciples by the Spirit — he has 'poured out' the specific charismata the audience 'see' and 'hear.'" However, as I have argued with respect to the overall text, even this ownership is mediated by the Spirit as well as the created order.

55. Gonzalez, *Acts,* p. 43.

promise is for them, their children, and all who are far off. The Judaism of the day stressed repentance as a way of dealing with sin, and it stressed a change in religious commitment. The disciples of Jesus Christ were accepting a new king, and they were enacting that transition via the ritual of baptism linked to repentance. "In the name of Jesus" was not necessarily formulaic and therefore associated verbatim with the ritual of baptism, but it emphasized discipleship of Jesus and an association with his kingship and his kingdom.[56] This promise is not just for those present but extends to their households, the diaspora, and beyond to the world of the Gentiles, again alluding to Isaiah 57:19, "everyone whom the Lord our God calls to him" *(hosous an proskalesētai kurios ho theos hēmōn)* (Acts 2:39). In effect, Peter further clarifies the nature of this mediation with reference to the sacrament of baptism, which is part of the conversion-initiation process (vv. 37-39). An interpretation has been provided, and now further action is required by those who have heard the explanation. There is a close connection anticipated between repentance, the ritual of baptism, and the reception of the Spirit, which suggests that in the mystery of the sacramental process there is mediation of the Holy Spirit. In this conversion-initiation complex, what it means to be "saved" is mediated via the presence of the Spirit to those who respond. Therefore, it could be argued that the sacramental ritual provides another form of intermediary process for the presence of the Spirit to be mediated. It is thus a sign and symbol of life in the kingdom of God. *Therefore, the Holy Spirit mediates soteriological reality via the process of conversion-initiation.*

### 4.2.3 Ecclesial Community

The narrative suggests that the outcome of the Pentecost event is the establishment of a community of believers, which began with about three thousand people responding to Peter's explanation and experiencing conversion (v. 41). We are informed that members of the church devoted themselves to the apostles' teaching, fellowship, the breaking of bread, and prayer (v. 42). The apostolic teaching was probably an exposition of the Hebrew Scriptures, as would be found in the synagogues of the period.[57] The term *koinōnia* suggests a number of different nuances beyond the obvious translation "fel-

56. Keener, *Acts*, p. 982.
57. Keener, *Acts*, p. 1002.

lowship," including cooperation, common enterprise, company, partnership, solidarity, participation, and harmony.[58] Linked to *koinōnia,* the "breaking of bread" could possibly refer simply to ordinary household meals, but the resonance with the Last Supper and the Emmaus road experience suggests a connection with the presence of Jesus at these meals.[59] This community was characterized by many signs and wonders *(polla te terata kai sēmeia)* through the apostles (v. 43). There was a sharing of resources as members in need were assisted, which resonates with the teaching of Jesus on material wealth, as well as the notion that these people constitute a new family and are therefore worthy of receiving the benefits of one's household.[60] In addition, the church participated in daily temple worship, fellowship/eucharistic meals in homes, and experienced a steady numerical growth (v. 47). *What is implied in these practices is that the Holy Spirit mediates the inaugurated and salvific reign of Christ via community life that includes fellowship, teaching, prayer, sacraments, signs and wonders, sharing of resources, and worship.* What is interesting is that mediation includes both the patterned and routine aspects of church life and the more spectacular and dramatic aspects of signs and wonders. The Holy Spirit mediates the kingdom of God to the church via both means, and they do not stand in opposition to one another but rather complement each other as aspects of the same eschatological and soteriological reality.

In summary, we note three further, important aspects of mediation. (1) The exalted Christ is the mediator of the Holy Spirit to the church. This is properly foundational to all other forms of mediation, and without it Pentecost would not have happened. (2) In a reciprocal relationship, the Holy Spirit is also the mediator of Christ to the church, the meaning of which is filled out in terms of a wider reference to the presence of the Trinity, as well as salvation presented within an eschatological framework. (3) Within the life of the church certain ecclesial practices mediate the presence of the Holy Spirit to the community internally and also provide signs of salvation to the external world. Thus the presence of the Spirit constitutes the body of Christ and unites the body through its experiences of the Spirit to its heavenly head and the life of the Trinity.

---

58. Gonzalez, *Acts,* p. 50; Keener, *Acts,* p. 1002.
59. Witherington, *Acts,* p. 160; Bruce, *Acts,* p. 132.
60. Keener, *Acts,* p. 1022.

## 4.3 The Holy Spirit Reception Narratives in Acts

To appreciate the ways in which the Holy Spirit is mediated throughout the narratives of the Acts of the Apostles, I shall focus especially on those accounts that describe the circumstances in which the Holy Spirit is received. These narratives are well known in P/C theology, especially because they are used to support the doctrine of baptism in the Spirit. However, I shall "read" them in a different manner because I am less concerned with propagating that doctrine in this context and more concerned with understanding how these texts inform a theology of mediation of the Spirit.

### 4.3.1 Acts 8:5-25: The Samaritans

We read that the Samaritans had received the gospel message preached by Philip and many had been baptized (8:12). When the apostles heard this news they sent Peter and John to them (v. 14), presumably to investigate the matter and find out for themselves what had actually happened. Peter and John prayed for the converts, that they might receive the Holy Spirit *(hopōs labōsin pneuma hagion),* because they had not yet received the Spirit.[61] They had only been baptized in the name of Jesus (v. 16). The apostles laid their hands on them and they received the Holy Spirit, although the narrative does not give any details as to how the reception was signaled or symbolized.[62] But what is clear is that *the mediation of the Holy Spirit upon this group of people was via the intermediary of the laying on of hands and prayer of the apostles.*[63] The suggestion is that somehow the conversion-initiation was incomplete

61. Thiselton, *The Holy Spirit,* p. 56, tries to make the point (following Bruner) that in Acts people do not pray to receive the Holy Spirit for themselves, but clearly they pray that others receive him, as illustrated here. Surely it is only a small step from someone praying for another person or a group of people to a person praying the same prayer for himself or herself?

62. Dunn, *Acts,* p. 111, suggests that Luke knows of no "silent" comings of the Spirit; even so, he does not say anything here except that they received the Spirit. Bock, *Acts,* p. 330, discusses the possibility that it might have been an apostolic "confirmation" but dismisses the idea as implausible. This is because both Acts 8:38 and 10:44 indicate that the apostolic laying on of hands is not required (p. 332).

63. Again, Thiselton, *The Holy Spirit,* p. 65, takes issue with Macchia (*Baptized in the Spirit: A Global Pentecostal Theology* [Grand Rapids: Zondervan, 2006], p. 166) for making "the laying on of hands disproportionately important." I might suggest that this is because Macchia understands the nature of pneumatological mediation as a Pentecostal and Thiselton apparently does not!

because they had not received the Holy Spirit. To rectify this anomaly, the apostles intervened, laying on hands and praying.[64] Simon (the sorcerer), who had himself been baptized as a believer, asked for the same power that had been displayed through the ritual of prayer and the laying on of hands, which suggests that there had been some visible demonstration of "power" (the word used is *exousia*, normally translated "authority," which suggests legitimately sanctioned power). He attempts to buy this authority from the apostles, but Peter replies that the gift of God (*tēn dōrean tou theou*, v. 20) is not for sale.

### 4.3.2 Acts 9:1-19a: Saul's Conversion

The account of Saul's conversion in Acts 9 builds on the picture that emerges from Acts 8 in terms of the mediation of the Spirit. After the dramatic encounter with the risen Christ on the Damascus Road (9:3-8), he was led into Damascus, having lost his sight during the event. For three days he neither ate nor drank (v. 9). Ananias was told in a dream to visit Saul, and Saul himself had been told in a dream to expect Ananias to visit him in order that he might regain his sight (v. 12). Upon entering the house where Saul was residing, Ananias laid hands on him, telling Saul that he had been sent by the Lord so that Saul might regain his sight and be filled with the Holy Spirit (*kai plēsthē[i]s pneumatos hagiou*, v. 17).[65] The narrative records that at this moment something likes scales fell from Saul's eyes, and he regained his sight.[66] Immediately he was baptized. Again, *the Holy Spirit was mediated via the intermediary action of the laying on of hands, through which Saul received his sight and was filled with the Holy Spirit.* We are not told that Ananias actually prayed, but it is implied that the ritual of laying on of hands for the reception of the Holy Spirit included some form of prayer. The "something like scales," or "as scales" *(hōs lepides)*, is reminiscent of the language of Acts 2 and "as" tongues of fire, but here the removal of the blindness is couched in this language rather than the reception of the Spirit directly. Again, this suggests that the reception of the Spirit was initiated by a dramatic conversion-type event

64. Peterson, *Acts*, p. 286, contends that it can be assumed that when Luke refers to the laying on of hands, this includes prayer because it is explicitly stated elsewhere (6:6; 13:3; 28:8).

65. Bock, *Acts*, p. 362, observes that Ananias, as a nonapostle, is the "mediator of the restoration of Saul's sight and of the Spirit's infilling."

66. It has been suggested that this healing is reminiscent of the healing accounts in Tobit 3:17 and 11:10-12; see Dunn, *Acts*, p. 124, and Peterson, *Acts*, p. 310; Conzelmann, *Acts*, p. 72.

in Saul's life, followed by the use of dreams to communicate both to Ananias and Saul in preparation for the laying on of hands as the direct medium of Spirit reception for Saul, which was sealed in baptism.

### 4.3.3 Acts 10:23b-48: The Household of Cornelius

In this narrative Cornelius, a devout God-fearer, received a vision of an angel (10:3), who instructed him to send messengers to summon (*metapempsai*, v. 5) Peter from Joppa to come and visit him and his household. During the journey of the messengers, Peter had a vision in which all food was declared clean; this occurred three times (v. 16). As Peter was trying to make sense of the vision, the messengers arrived from Cornelius. We are told that at this moment the Spirit communicated with Peter concerning the three men who had just arrived, that he should not doubt but accompany them as they requested, because the Spirit had indeed sent them to him (*hoti egō apestalka autous*, v. 20).[67] They explained to Peter that an angel had appeared to Cornelius in a dream and had directed him to invite Peter to visit. The next day they traveled to Cornelius's house, where he and his relatives and near friends were waiting to receive Peter (v. 24). Peter confessed before them that as a Jew he should not have been visiting a Gentile household but that God had revealed to him a new definition of purity (v. 28). Cornelius recounted his experience of the angel, and Peter explained the message of Christ, that he is Lord of all (*houtos estin pantōn kurios*, v. 36), that God had anointed Jesus with the Holy Spirit and with power (*dunamis*, v. 38), and that he had healed the sick and delivered those oppressed by the devil. Jesus was crucified and then raised on the third day, and Peter was a witness to this fact (v. 41). Jesus had commanded the apostles to testify that he was now appointed as the judge of the living and the dead, just as the prophets had predicted, and therefore all who believed would have their sins forgiven (*aphesin*, v. 43). It was during this speech that the Holy Spirit "fell on" those in the household (*epepesen to pneuma to hagion epi pantas tous akouontas ton logon*, v. 44). This means that *the mediation of the Spirit was via the preaching of Peter*.[68] The Jewish believers were amazed because the gift of the Holy

---

67. Ling Cheng, *The Characterisation of God in Acts: The Indirect Portrayal of an Invisible Character* (Milton Keynes: Paternoster, 2011), pp. 24-25, argues that the Spirit's precise indication of the number of visitors, the nature of the vision, and the arrival of the visitors display the Spirit's omniscience and authority over the whole event.

68. Bock, *Acts,* p. 401, states: "God is working directly to make the point. There is no

Spirit had been poured out on the Gentiles (*hoti kai epi ta ethnē hē dōrea tou pneumatos to hagiou ekkechutai,* v. 45), for they heard them speaking in tongues (*lalountōn glōssais,* v. 45) and magnifying God (*megalunontōn ton theon,* v. 46). "The Spirit 'fell upon' them (as in 8.16); something 'hit' them; there was a visible impact of invisible power."[69] Peter subsequently asked if anyone could prohibit them from being baptized because they had already received (*elabon,* v. 47) the Holy Spirit. Subsequently, they were baptized in the name of Jesus (v. 48).

The first medium mentioned in this longer narrative is the use of visions or dreams in which divine agents are revealed and a message is communicated. A mixture of angels, the Lord Jesus Christ, and the Holy Spirit is mentioned in the narrative. The medium of the internal world of the mind is used to communicate to both Cornelius and Peter. Once this is acted upon, further means of revelation are experienced. Upon the visit of Peter to the household, the Holy Spirit is manifest upon the Gentile household while Peter is still speaking his message about Jesus. This comes as a surprise to Peter and his Jewish colleagues, and it is signaled, as on the day of Pentecost, by doxological speech (glossolalia). In this scene, the conversion-initiation process is completed by baptism. The medium of the Spirit appears to be the preaching of Peter. No hands are laid upon the Gentiles, no prayers are prayed over them. Instead the Spirit mediates via the spoken message of the gospel. In contrast to Peter's speech on the day of Pentecost, where he explains what is happening after the event, here, while he is explaining what has happened, he is surprised by the sovereign move of the Spirit upon the Gentile household independent of any ritual of laying on of hands that was beginning to emerge in the early church as deployed by Peter, John, and Ananias. The significance of this finding for mediation is the role that speech plays directly or indirectly in the reception of the Spirit.

### 4.3.4 Acts 15:1-29: The Jerusalem Council

Acts 15 recounts how Barnabas and Paul returned to Jerusalem to report back to the apostles all that had happened among the Gentile believers as

---

apostolic intermediary on earth who helps with the distribution." Also see Dunn, *Acts,* p. 145: "The coming of the Spirit awaits no human regulation or ordering." But, in my view, these statements underplay the role of Peter's preaching because it is *associated* in the narrative with the coming of the Spirit.

69. Dunn, *Acts,* p. 146.

a result of their ministry. There was a debate on whether Gentile converts should be expected to convert to Judaism and be circumcised and obey the Law in order to be Christian. Peter explained what happened when he spoke to the Gentile household of Cornelius, namely, that God, who knows the heart, had testified to them by giving them the Holy Spirit as he had done on the day of Pentecost (v. 8). Barnabas and Paul also recounted how God had done signs and wonders through them during their time among the Gentiles (*epoiēsen ho theos sēmeia kai terata en tois ethnesin di' autōn,* v. 12). James interpreted these testimonies as fulfilling the promise to rebuild David's household, and including the Gentiles, based on a reading of Amos 9:11-12, with the opening phrase from Jeremiah 12:15 and the closing one from Isaiah 45:21.[70] This decision to include the Gentiles within the renewed household of faith was attributed to the work of the Holy Spirit: it seemed good to the Holy Spirit and to us (*edoxen gar to[i] pneumatic to[i] hagio[i] kai hēmin,* v. 28). *This suggests that the mediation of the Spirit was via the intermediary of the council's deliberations, including reasoned discourse,*[71] *which were in turn based on testimonies to the Gentiles' experiences of signs and wonders and the interpretation of a Hebrew passage of Scripture.* Subsequently, instructions were written to the Gentile converts requiring them to abstain from certain immoral acts, food associated with idolatry, and the blood of strangled animals, thereby respecting some (if not all) aspects of Jewish purity laws (v. 29).[72] The important point that reflects on mediation is that the Holy Spirit is understood to be active in the signs and wonders through the ministry of Barnabas and Paul that brought the Gentiles to faith and through the deliberation of the Council, so that a decision was made to include the Gentiles in the household of faith. This expands the range of media explicitly identified by Luke in his day of Pentecost narrative.

---

70. Dunn, *Acts,* p. 203.

71. I recognize that this is implied in the text, but it does counter the assertion made by Thiselton, *The Holy Spirit,* p. 68, that those involved in contemporary P/C Christianity do not use reason and reflective processes alongside the inspiration of the Holy Spirit in their decision making.

72. Twelftree, *People of the Spirit,* p. 162, captures the dynamic of divine initiative followed by the human discernment via the congruence with Scripture, the leadership of James, and the participation of the community.

### 4.3.5 Acts 19:1-7: The Ephesian Disciples

The narrative describes how Paul came to the city of Ephesus and met twelve disciples of John the Baptist. He inquired whether they had received the Holy Spirit when they believed (*ei pneuma hagion elabete pisteusantes;* 19:2). They replied that they had not even heard that there was a "Holy Spirit," so he asked about their baptism.[73] They said they had received the baptism of John, which Paul defined as a baptism of repentance, and John preached that they should believe in the one coming after him, namely, Jesus (v. 4). So, they were baptized this time into *(eis)* the name of Jesus (v. 5). Paul laid his hands on them and the Holy Spirit came upon them (*ēlthe to pneuma to hagion ep'autous,* v. 6); and they spoke in tongues and prophesied (*elaloun te glōssais kai eprophēteuon,* v. 6).[74] Again, *the reception of the Spirit is mediated via the laying on of hands either subsequent to baptism or as part of the baptism ritual* (the narrative is not explicit on the point). As on the day of Pentecost, the reception of the Spirit was expressed via glossolalic and prophetic speech, although unlike at Pentecost, the nature of the speech (whether it was doxological or not) is not made explicit. However, it would be fair to assume some resonance between these texts on this matter.

In summary, the mediation of the Holy Spirit can be categorized in four distinct ways. (1) In response to various stages of conversion-initiation among the groups represented, the apostles lay hands on individuals and pray for the reception of the Holy Spirit. (2) While Peter preaches, the Holy Spirit comes upon his audience, inferring at the very least that his speech was an aspect of the mediation to the group. (3) Signs and wonders mediate the presence of the Holy Spirit to the Gentiles. (4) The Jerusalem Council's decision making mediates the presence of the Holy Spirit among its members by recalling the signs and wonders, by interpreting Scripture, and through its own communal reasoning processes. Thus the church can be seen to mediate the Holy Spirit to humanity in its acts of witness and via its own internal processes. This pneumatological mediation once again supports the notion that the Holy Spirit constitutes the church, because the church in its mission and internal life does not function without the Spirit's presence but is always united corporately to the divine life.

73. Bock, *Acts,* p. 599, suggests that this statement probably means that they had not heard that the Holy Spirit had been poured out on all flesh.

74. Paul is the medium of the bestowal of the Spirit on this occasion (Bock, *Acts,* p. 338), even if the correlation between the laying on of hands and reception of the Spirit is limited to one other occasion in the book of Acts, as noted by Peterson, *Acts,* p. 532.

## 4.4 The Mediation of the Holy Spirit

Given the above analysis and discussion, it is possible to represent the different forms of mediation with five propositions:

1. Christ mediates the Holy Spirit to the church (M1).
2. The Holy Spirit mediates Christ and the Father to the church (M2).
3. Creation mediates the Holy Spirit to the church (M3).
4. The church mediates the Holy Spirit internally (via individuals, groups, worship, and practices) (M4).
5. The church mediates the Holy Spirit externally (via individuals, groups, public worship, and practices) (M5).

The exalted Christ receives the Holy Spirit again and bestows the gift on the church, and with this gift comes not only one person but three, because these three are indeed one and all their operations are united *ad extra*. Thus the doctrine of the Trinity frames the christological point of mediation. In addition to the reciprocity between Christ and the Spirit, the Spirit also mediates the presence of Christ and the Father to the church. This fundamental dual mediation is essential to understanding the reign of Christ as exalted Messiah and Lord of the Spirit, as well as the inaugurated salvation made possible through the Spirit in the church. The context of this mediation of salvation is creation, since creation by the Spirit participates in its own renewal and mediates the presence of the Spirit to the church. The church is embedded in creation and is itself a creature united to its heavenly Lord through the Holy Spirit. Within this creaturely context, the church mediates the Spirit to individuals who are part of creation and members of the church, thus united to Christ. The church offers its worship in, with, and through the Holy Spirit, such that its very doxology is Spirit-inspired, and it simultaneously mediates the Spirit to creation and wider society. In doxology the Spirit enables the church to participate in heavenly as well as earthly reality, thus experiencing the triune life in its midst. The church mediates the Holy Spirit to humanity through its practices of laying on of hands and prayer, preaching, and signs and wonders. Through these means it enables individuals and groups to engage in conversion-initiation and become incorporated into its community. But the church also mediates the Holy Spirit internally to itself, both as a corporate body and to its individuals through its practices, such as fellowship, teaching, sacraments, resource sharing, testimonies, interpretation of Scripture, and decision making.

The diagram below illustrates the pivotal role that the Holy Spirit plays in uniting the triune God to the church in order to mediate salvation to the world and enable the church to participate in the life of the Trinity in worship and service. This diagram shows how the person of the Holy Spirit constitutes the nature of the church, and how without the presence of the Holy Spirit the church would not be united to Christ, as the body of Christ, nor experience fellowship with the Father. As subject the Holy Spirit mediates the presence of the Trinity. As object, the Holy Spirit is mediated within the created order and especially the church. The intermediary roles of the church and creation are also noted as significant features of pneumatological mediation.

*Post-Pentecost Mediation of the Holy Spirit*

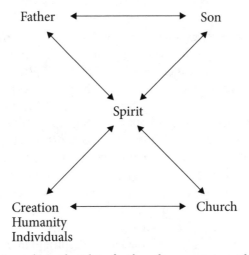

How might this analysis elucidate further the accounts outlined in chapter 3? I shall try to draw together the different contributions from across the traditions.

All the types of mediation identified by the five propositions can be found within the literature, although there are clearly very different emphases. Macchia emphasizes the mediation of the Spirit by Christ as the gift from the Father, but he also wishes to suggest a double movement whereby the Spirit also mediates Christ to the church (M1 and M2). Madathummuriyil goes further and suggests that the Spirit is not merely a third party that stands apart from the mediator, Christ, but is "the mediation of the mediator" as the "copresenting" Spirit of Christ.[75] This means that the double

75. See Sebastian Madathummuriyil, "The Holy Spirit as Person and Mediation: A

mediation of the Son and the Spirit in relation to the church is the divine foundation for mediation, upon which all other redemptive mediation is based. With Barth, Smail, and Chan, we can affirm that the church is united to Christ and is the *totus Christus,* which would be impossible except for the mediation, or coordination, of the Spirit (M2).[76] As Moltmann and Hütter argue, the presence and mediation of the Spirit are the basis of a reciprocal relationship via *perichoresis* between the triune God and humanity. Similarly, the presence of Christ in the Eucharist, as argued by Green, would be impossible except for the mediation of the Spirit (M2). With Smith we can agree that the Spirit is mediated through creation, and in particular cultural and linguistic horizons, in that God concedes to these means. But I would add that there are material aspects to these features that also need to be acknowledged and not merely subsumed without remainder under the category of the cultural (M3). In a sense, the church is a subset of the category of creation, and therefore the statements about the influence of culture and language also apply to the church; thus M3 is always properly basic to the mediation of the church. Yet there are ways in which the church functions uniquely as the mediator of the Spirit to individuals via particular experiences, suggested by Smith and Madathummuriyil in the phrase "mediated immediacy." Yet, as Smail and Hütter remind us, this does not mean that we corporately or individually "own" the Spirit, even after such a dramatic and transformative experience as Spirit baptism. Indeed, I would not wish to focus exclusively on Spirit baptism, as many Pentecostals inevitably do. I wish to frame religious experience within a broader conceptual framework that includes Spirit baptism but does not allow it to dominate the frame of reference. Clearly, many more things are occurring on the day of Pentecost than individuals being baptized in the Spirit (M4).

The mediation of the Spirit by the church in and through worship is implied in the work of Macchia and Chan (M4 and M5). In the context of a discussion of worship, Chan observes that the church is the living temple of God and suggests that the Spirit participates in and facilitates the human

---

Pneumatological Approach to Church and Sacraments," *Questions Liturgiques* 88 (2007): 194-95.

76. I would propose a similar distinction to Barth, although using different language; that is, I would distinguish between the primary mediation within the Godhead and the secondary mediation through creation and the church; see *Church Dogmatics* II/1 (Edinburgh: T. & T. Clark, 1957), p. 16. However, where I would fundamentally differ from Barth is in the role of the Holy Spirit in such mediation. Barth does not mention the Holy Spirit even once in this section, which seems a remarkable omission!

action of doxology to the Son and the Father, and that doxology is thus a mediation of the Spirit. In Acts 2:11, this doxological speech is glossolalia, although it does not need to be glossolalia to fulfill this function. But it is in relation to glossolalia that Pentecostal interpreters have often used Romans 8:26 to suggest that there is an alignment of the Holy Spirit with the human spirit in the cries of the heart, which suggests not only intercession but also doxology. The mediation of the Spirit in worship has not received a lot of attention in Pentecostal theology, but given its basis in the day of Pentecost narrative, it invites further reflection. Not least, because it is foundational to the nature of the church as participating in the life of God, and this mediation gives expression to an aspect of this participation.

The mediation of the Spirit by means of the church to external society is noted by some P/C scholars (M5), although this aspect of mediation is somewhat underplayed in favor of discussions of internal mediation within the church (see below). Often it is not appreciated as an aspect of mediation because of the focus on ecclesial and individual experiences. However, the range of activities associated with the reception of the Spirit in Acts, as noted above, suggests that ecclesial mediation of the Spirit to wider humanity via its missionary activities is an aspect that invites further investigation. Additionally, and following Hirshorn, I suggest that the mediation of the Spirit might just as well be understood through the mundane and the ordinary as through the spectacular, provided that it fulfills certain criteria, such as pointing to Christ and embodying an aspect of the gospel message in some sense.

P/C theologians have tended to focus on the mediation of the Spirit by the church to the church, that is, among its members, its congregations, denominations, and ecumenical relations (M4). This mediation finds some resonance with liberal and postliberal theology (e.g., Schleiermacher, Macquarrie, Lindbeck, Hütter), although expressed rather differently. It has also been discussed in terms of worship practices, language, and sacramentality, whether explicit or implicit, dominical or extended. Tillich's sacramentality finds resonance with Pentecostal spirituality here because of the use of sacramental materials that are linked to the elements of creation. However, this stands in tension with Madathummuriyil, who, from a Roman Catholic perspective, understands the church as the sacrament of Christ and identifies the primary location of mediation in the liturgy and the sacraments. Again, this invites further exploration from a P/C perspective but lies beyond the scope of this study.

The preliminary answer to the first part of the research question given at the end of chapter 3 can now be expanded. The mediation of the Holy Spirit can now be conceived in terms of five features, which of course intersect and intertwine. These features concern the relationship between primary (Trinity) and secondary (creation, church, and humanity) mediation. In turn, they reframe the nature of *pneumatological mediation* located in P/C theology as well as the broader theological literature. The accompanying analysis of these biblical texts also provides an agenda for interventions in practical theology, which answers the second part of the question in a provisional manner, to which we now turn.

## 4.5 An Agenda for Interventions in Practical Theology

A number of contributions can be regarded as providing an agenda for interventions in practical theology when the mediated nature and role of the Holy Spirit are brought into dialogue with practical-theological concerns. Given the argument derived from analysis of the biblical texts above, namely, that the Holy Spirit not only constituted the early church but continues to constitute the church in present-day reality,[77] one would expect to be able to discern the continual mediation of the Holy Spirit through the concrete ecclesial communities and intermediaries today. In the following section a number of interventions can be suggested in relation to both ecclesial practices and accompanying theological loci.

### 4.5.1 Ecclesial Practices

It makes perfect sense, from the findings of this study, to invest time and energy investigating church congregations. This means that the narratives, symbols, and praxis associated with such groups can inform not only ecclesiology but also pneumatology because of the mediation. This does not mean we can collapse the two categories, but it does mean they can be understood as distinct yet complementary. Furthermore, the social spaces in which congregations meet and the areas in which they are located are important features of ecclesial life and cannot be ignored.[78] This is because the

---

77. John D. Zizioulas, *Being as Communion: Studies in Personhood and the Church* (Crestwood, N.Y.: St. Vladimir's Seminary Press, 1985), pp. 132, 136, 140.

78. For example, see John Inge, *A Christian Theology of Place* (Aldershot: Ashgate, 2003). However, Inge completely ignores pneumatology.

experience of the Spirit does vary according to concrete contexts, and this should come as no real surprise. Of course, there will always be a dynamic between the social and the individual, and it should be obvious that the study of individual differences can provide insights into how the Holy Spirit is mediated via differently gifted persons. The research indicating that P/C Christianity is predominated by extroverted individuals suggests that the interplay between individual differences and social dynamics is important for understanding not only theological anthropology but also pneumatology.[79] *Therefore, empirical research among ecclesial communities is essential for understanding and addressing issues in contemporary church and society.*

Worship is central to P/C Christianity, and the mediated role of the Holy Spirit cannot be understood apart from the analysis of worship. Therefore, practical theology should be interested in the nature, function, and significance of worship among congregations, especially the relationship between narratives, symbols such as the sacraments, and praxis.[80] This is because "traditioning" or socialization is especially strong among Christian communities where there is a high level of participation among congregational members. This enables them to be shaped and reshaped according to pneumatologically mediated symbols and practices. Indeed, the (oral) liturgy provides a narrative and worldview and also offers a critique of the idolatry so prevalent in contemporary culture. Therefore, it could be seen as a discourse of resistance against secular, materialist Western cultural values. It has distinctly political ramifications as it provides an alternative polis that challenges the power structures in wider society.[81] Of course, there is a reaction to Spirit-inspired doxology, and Acts 2 gives insight into this reaction: confusion, cynicism, and mockery. Practical theology should not be dissuaded from its task, despite criticism from theological "purists," who consider theology an exercise in abstraction (from a particular mode of rationality), or from social scientists advocating methodological, if not formal, atheism (the collapse into the anthropological/sociological). Public conversations about the nature and influence of worship are central to the discourse of practical theology

79. For example, see Leslie J. Francis and William K. Kay, "The Personality Characteristics of Pentecostal Ministry Candidates," *Personality and Individual Differences* 18, no. 5 (1995): 581-94, and Leslie J. Francis and Susan H. Jones, "Personality and Charismatic Experience among Adult Christians," *Pastoral Psychology* 45, no. 6 (1997): 421-28.

80. For example, see my *Testimony in the Spirit: Rescripting Ordinary Pentecostal Theology* (Farnham: Ashgate, 2010), pp. 29-54.

81. See Amos Yong, *In the Days of Caesar: Pentecostalism and Political Theology* (Grand Rapids: Eerdmans, 2010), pp. 155-65.

and should not be marginalized. *Central to the study of congregations is the nature and impact of worship as it shapes and forms them and their relationships with wider society.*

The relationship between the church's worship and wider society is crucial. P/C worship often includes a journey of encounter. I have explored this feature in the study of spirituality and have argued that there is an ongoing process or cycle whereby individuals, congregations, and ecclesial communities are engaged in a search-encounter-transformation process.[82] At the center of this encounter is worship as an experience of intimacy with God such that individuals are transformed and empowered in their Christian discipleship. This "pull" into an intense and often dramatic set of experiences is followed by a "push" outward in missionary love and service. The dynamic experience of being loved by God and loving God in return produces what is often called "love energy,"[83] which leads to a propulsion out into loving service toward the wider community and society. Empowered individuals explore how to love one's neighbor as oneself, and this can be expressed in sacrificial acts of service for the sake of others.[84]

The other narratives in Acts suggest a distinctive role for interpersonal relationships between church leaders and audiences. In Acts 8, 9, and 19 a person ministered to another person by the laying on of hands and prayer. There is some form of symbolic physical contact through which the Holy Spirit is mediated.[85] This relationship of a leader to a church community has been at the forefront of traditional pastoral theology, especially conceived from the shepherding perspective and concentrated in clergy training. In

---

82. Mark J. Cartledge, *Encountering the Spirit: The Charismatic Tradition* (London: Darton, Longman and Todd, 2006), pp. 25-27.

83. This phrase originates with Pitirim A. Sorokin, *The Ways and Power of Love: Types, Factors, and Techniques of Moral Transformation* (Radnor, Pa.: Templeton Foundation Press, 2002; orig. 1954).

84. See, for example, Donald E. Miller and Tetsunao Yamamori, *Global Pentecostalism: The New Face of Christian Social Engagement* (Berkeley: University of California Press, 2007). Also see the range of literature on the notion of "godly love": Margaret M. Poloma and Ralph W. Hood, *Blood and Fire: Godly Love in a Pentecostal Emerging Church* (New York: New York University Press, 2008); Matthew Lee and Margaret M. Poloma, *Social Filters of Godly Love: A Sociological Study of the Great Commandment in the Pentecostal Context* (Lewiston, N.Y.: Edwin Mellen Press, 2009); and Margaret M. Poloma and John C. Green, *The Assemblies of God: Godly Love and the Revitalization of American Pentecostalism* (New York: New York University Press, 2010).

85. Eugene Rogers, *After the Spirit: A Constructive Pneumatology from Resources outside of the Modern West* (Grand Rapids: Eerdmans, 2005), pp. 59-60.

recent years the importance of this relationship has been diminished as the emphasis has been on the laity and the whole people of God, with a move away from the clerical paradigm. This move has to be contrasted with an emphasis in many sectors on the nature of leadership and the importance of leadership for the success of organizations. In terms of the mediation of the Holy Spirit, leadership plays a significant role in these texts. *The importance of leadership studies in the broadest sense cannot be underestimated and is an area for investment in practical theology.*

Acts 15 has a special place in the P/C discussion of theological method because it has been used as a model for describing the relationship between the text of Scripture, the role of the community, and the experience of the Holy Spirit. Although in this passage the power of the Holy Spirit is mediated through dramatic signs and wonders, the *will* of the Holy Spirit is mediated via the Council's reasoned deliberations. Of course, the text of Scripture, in this case Amos 9:11-12, is also mediated (by James), as is the account of the experiences of the Spirit among the Gentiles (by the testimonies of Barnabas and Paul). The P/C theological method correctly interprets the role of deliberation as a communitarian activity, but I would propose that it be appreciated as a *critical,* not merely consultative, process. Therefore in practical theology, the relationship between the Spirit in religious experience, the Spirit-guided interpretation of Scripture, and the Spirit in the deliberations of the faith community should be given a greater profile. *The interplay between Scripture, the experience of the Holy Spirit, the community decision-making processes, and especially the modes of rationality employed is essential to ecclesial life.*

### 4.5.2 Theological Loci

These narratives require that certain theological loci are brought into the foreground of practical theology. I mention only three briefly at this point.

The nature of human and creational reality should be framed in terms of *eschatology.* The kingdom of God has been inaugurated and will one day be consummated with the cosmic enthronement of the Lord Jesus Christ. Both Christ's lordship and his kingship are mediated by the presence of the Holy Spirit in real time now, but they give only a foretaste of that greater reality to come. As Daniela Augustine states, "The radical Christocentricity of the event of Pentecost which shapes and marks the ecclesia as the Body of Christ, is consistent with the work of the Spirit as the agent who mediates, articulates, and leads all redemptive history towards its eschatological fulfilment and summation in the risen Lord."[86] This framework provides an overarching metanarrative for appreciating issues in temporality, culture, and identity. Therefore, this present time should be neither absolutized nor denigrated. It should be understood as part of a greater trajectory that is determined not only by the past, but significantly by the future (Anderson's eschatological preference). Sadly, practical-theological discourse rarely, if ever, discusses the nature of inaugurated eschatology and its impact in shaping theological narratives of hope and destiny.[87]

In this explanation, *Trinity* and *Christology* are dominant theological categories. Pentecostal and charismatic Christians are unashamedly christocentric in their theological constructions, and to this has been added a Trinitarian framework by their academics (although Trinitarian grammar is certainly in need of development at the congregational level). This mediation of the Spirit brings both of these doctrines into focus as explanatory theological categories. However, in practical theology, these categories are rarely if ever used. Either a general theism predominates, whereby the name of God is used because it can be a container for a general kind of "divinity," or there are scattered references to Jesus Christ, usually with reference to Gospel passages only. This means that Christology is rarely developed as a central theological constructive category (an exception is Purves; see chap. 6). Furthermore, absence of a robust Trinitarian framework can lead to a restricted, limited, or weak Christology, which is often the case. Once again, such a Christology may serve the presuppositions of some scholars and certain scholarly communities, but it does not carry sufficient theological freight to connect to other forms of theological discourse or indeed serve the wider church.[88] The restoration of pneumatology does more than bring the Spirit back into the conversation; it inevitably restores a discussion of the doctrines of the Trinity and Christology as well.

86. Augustine, *Pentecost, Hospitality, and Transformation*, p. 19.

87. Very few practical theology texts actually deal with eschatology. For example, the edited collection of essays from the International Academy of Practical Theology conference in 2005 contains only one article that makes a brief connection (by Norbert Mette), even though the theme is based on vision and hope. See Hans-Georg Ziebertz and Friedrich Schweitzer, eds., *Dreaming the Land: Theologies of Resistance and Hope* (Berlin: LIT Verlag, 2007).

88. Ward's short section on the Trinity and Christ in his book does connect these categories, if briefly; soteriology is implicit in what appears to be an adoption of a more Eastern approach. See Pete Ward, *Participation and Mediation: A Practical Theology for the Liquid Church* (London: SCM, 2008), pp. 103-5.

Finally, practical theology should be concerned with *soteriology* — a central rather than a peripheral category for theological thought. The narratives above show it to be a key category of thought for Luke.[89] It refers to the in-breaking of the kingdom of God through the presence of the Holy Spirit, which brings liberation and transformation to the people of God and faces them outward toward the world.[90] David Bosch, discussing soteriology in Luke-Acts, says: "Salvation involves the reversal of all the evil consequences of sin, against both God and neighbor. . . . Liberation *from* is also liberation *to*, else it is not an expression of salvation. And liberation *to* always involves love to God *and* neighbour."[91] However, it is rare for practical theologians to engage in a fully orbed and explicit approach to soteriology.[92] For the most part it has been reduced to forms of liberation, which have been important, but it has ignored the multifaceted nature of salvation in this context. Soteriology has been undermined by religious pluralism (all roads lead to God) and universalism (everyone is going to get there regardless), but also by consumerist secular culture that prioritizes the self at the expense of others and the created order. A practical theology that appreciates the nature of the work of the Holy Spirit in the church, as it is informed by *pneumatological mediation* in Luke-Acts, expects the work of the Spirit to be soteriological in focus. It cannot be otherwise.

## 4.6 Conclusion

This chapter has built upon the previous discussion of Pentecostal experience and mediation of the Holy Spirit in chapter 3 by focusing in some detail on key biblical texts in the book of Acts. A fresh analysis has revealed some interesting and useful insights about how these narratives can foster a better understanding of pneumatology and ecclesiology. It is clear from these narratives that the Holy Spirit can be seen as an intermediary between divine and human/creational realities. The Spirit is not merely a conduit for the presence of the other two members of the Trinity, but provides a distinctive

89. See Twelftree, *People of the Spirit*, pp. 47-51, who suggests: "For Luke, *salvation is the realization of the powerful presence of God in present as well as future experience*" (p. 51).

90. See Turner, *Power from on High*, pp. 346-47, 421.

91. David J. Bosch, *Transforming Mission: Paradigm Shifts in Theology of Mission* (Maryknoll, N.Y.: Orbis, 1991), p. 107.

92. Most authors do not have an entry for "salvation" or "soteriology" in the index or contents page.

"presence" orientated toward an eschatological and soteriological telos. The relationship between the created order and the church is important, and the Holy Spirit is present to and active in both domains such that both are independent at one level and intertwined at another level. This analysis is suggestive of an account of soteriology in a pneumatological key.

The next section in the book will address the implications of these findings for practical theology by suggesting two kinds of "intervention." First, following on from this chapter, and because practical theology is concerned with concrete practices, the import of these findings will be worked out in relation to an analysis of an existing congregational study, in which the concept of redemption is used to capture the significance of lived religion (chap. 5). Second, the discourse of practical theology in the academy is impoverished because of its limited articulation of soteriology. Therefore, the intention of chapter 6 is to begin to address this gap and to provide an appropriate intervention in order to develop a practical-theological conversation around soteriology. Other aspects could have been addressed, but given the limitations of space, these topics present themselves as both interesting and urgent.

# 5 Ecclesial Practices in Practical Theology

## 5.1 Introduction

Practical theology as a discipline has developed different ways of engaging with the church and the world. One of the most important contributions has been the empirical study of congregational life. This kind of inquiry has taken many forms, as different approaches and methodologies have been used in creative ways. To move from the P/C hermeneutical horizon back to the practical-theological horizon where I began, I have chosen as a key dialogue text a monograph based on a study of a single congregation. It is selected for a number of reasons. In the previous chapters I consulted and engaged a variety of texts because I wished to situate the study within two distinct, broad fields of inquiry, even as I wished to concentrate on key issues: the use of Scripture, pneumatological mediation, religious experience, and in particular, the day of Pentecost narrative. It is important to test whether this contribution to practical theology can be developed through a critical and close reading of a particular empirical study. In this way, the theoretical work so far developed can be grounded in relation to an example of contemporary practical theology. The pneumatological strategy can also be tested and refined in relation to a key text outside of the P/C frame of reference, thus potentially expanding the horizon of significance. The text chosen is fairly representative of feminist practical theology within the USA, and it provides a contrasting perspective with which to interact. It also focuses on the theology of practices within an ecclesial setting, which picks up one of the key themes emerging from chapter 4. Therefore, the author serves as an interesting dialogue partner with whom to engage creatively for the sake of illustrating how P/C theology might intervene in the academic discourse of practical theology.

This chapter describes the nature of the congregational study undertaken, including the theoretical perspective of postmodern place theory. In particular, it gives attention to the discussion of the relationship between ecclesial practices, the use of biblical texts, and pneumatology. Following these descriptions, I offer some critical observations before suggesting a couple of "interventions" from the perspective of pneumatological mediation and biblical hermeneutics, which have significance for ecclesial practice.

## 5.2 A Congregational Study

The monograph chosen for this part of the study is written by Mary McClintock Fulkerson, who is professor of theology at Duke University, USA.[1] It is the study of a multiracial congregation in the United Methodist Conference located in Durham, North Carolina, that existed for ten years before merging with another church. The membership of Good Samaritan United Methodist Church is comprised of different races, classes, and abilities. The theological inquiry proffered by McClintock Fulkerson seeks to be "adequate to the full-bodied reality that is Good Samaritan, one capable of displaying its ambiguity, its implication in the banal and opaque realities of ordinary existence, even as it allows for testimony to God's redemptive reality" (p. 7). It is a reading of the contemporary situation that takes seriously the lived faith of the congregation and the social interaction from out of which theological praxis develops.

For McClintock Fulkerson, this emergent theology originates at the "scene of a wound" (p. 13). This is because wounds generate new thoughts, offer a disjunction with past thinking, and create new possibilities for fresh ideas. The wounds here are those whose bodies are identified as different because they are people of color or people with disabilities — specifically, the wounds of racism and ableism, which are accompanied by social obliviousness (the not-seeing of difference) by those in dominance (here the educated and white) (p. 150). The congregation's "woundedness" in its social composi-

---

1. Mary McClintock Fulkerson, *Places of Redemption: Theology for a Worldly Church* (Oxford: Oxford University Press, 2007). Page numbers to this work have been placed in the following text.

tion is a symbol of its worldliness in the sense of reflecting the broader social realities of American life today. She states: "By reading it [the community's worldliness] as a wound — a situation characterized by interpersonal forms of obliviousness and aversiveness marked and sustained by larger social-political processes — I understand Good Samaritan as *a situation characterized by harm that demands redress*" (p. 17). The answer or redress is the provision of a shared space where difference can be seen, recognized, and acknowledged by others as essential to social and political life.

### 5.2.1 Theoretical Framework

Postmodern place theory is used as a lens through which to consider "place as a structure of lived, corporate, and *bodied* experience" (p. 25). It is regarded as fundamental in generating knowledge because the body provides an orientation in relation to the world and the world influences the body. Attending to the place of Good Samaritan means more than just knowing its geographical location, however. It means attending to its corporate and embodied experience, which generates meaning. It is this particularity that cannot be escaped and that shapes all knowledge because it emerges out of the lived situation. But the volume and complexity of the situation need to be expressed and understood, so McClintock Fulkerson identifies characteristics of place that connect the various elements contained there. These are (1) *resonances* via affective associations, which suggest a mode of connection that is indirect and yet obvious, mediated via bodies that are gendered, raced, and classed; (2) *narratives* (as resonances are consciously interpreted), which give a shape to the experiences of the situation, even if they do not include every detail available; and (3) *unity*, because a place has a territory marked out by buildings, land, and the forms of meanings produced by its members. "The place called Good Samaritan occurs as a gathering — a coalescing of language, rituals, stories, and tacit understandings as well as bodies, habits, buildings, and memories" (p. 30).

The place of a congregation is also associated with ongoing ecclesial practices. These practices constitute the particularities of place and are best understood as *habitus*. Following Bourdieu,[2] McClintock Fulkerson argues that practices are forms of social enculturation enacted by agents influenced

---

2. Pierre Bourdieu, *Outline of a Theory of Practice*, trans. Richard Nice (Cambridge: Cambridge University Press, 1977).

by dispositions and memories in specific actions; they can include disso-
nance as well as resonance. These actions are also influenced by wider social
and political forces. This means that places are fluid. They are shaped by both
centripetal and centrifugal forces, which also constitute the particularity of
specific places. Therefore, places are dynamic and are constantly being constructed and reconstructed over time. To begin to evaluate these practices
in light of Christian tradition, she employs MacIntyre's idea that individual
actions make sense only in the context of the larger story of a person's life,
which is also embedded in larger communal stories.[3] The chronological
pieces are therefore connected via narrative, and the notion of the good is
used to evaluate given behavior ethically. The good is defined by the wisdom
of the community's tradition. Practices are those actions that "instantiate and
extend the goods of a tradition." Only activity that is intelligible in terms of
the communal narrative counts as a practice, and it involves "participatory
development of a good."[4] This means that practices "tradition" a community, and participation in the communal practices enhances the traditioning
processes.

In addition, and following Connerton,[5] McClintock Fulkerson develops
the idea that corporate memory is displayed in communal practices, so that
there is a connection between Christian stories and the communal story.
These practices involve bodies that have been socially informed, displaying
corporeal knowledge as *habitus* in bodily skills and abilities. To illustrate
the point, she considers the way in which black bodies under slavery were
postured in relation to the white owner class (bowed heads, shuffling gaits,
and attempts at invisibility) in order to survive. A long-established *habitus*
may also be regarded as "tradition" because its meaning is conveyed in the
bodily performance. In this way, the "body is an assemblage of embodied
aptitudes, not a medium of symbolic meanings."[6] These bodily performances
are accompanied by practices of inscription whereby stories and verbal expressions of the ends and means of the vision are critical to the communal
identity. This position makes a significant move for the notion of normativ-

---

3. Alasdair MacIntyre, *After Virtue: A Study of Moral Theory*, 2nd ed. (Notre Dame:
University of Notre Dame Press, 1984).

4. McClintock Fulkerson, *Places of Redemption*, p. 39.

5. Paul Connerton, *How Societies Remember* (Cambridge: Cambridge University Press,
1989).

6. McClintock Fulkerson, *Places of Redemption*, p. 46; Talal Asad, *Genealogies of Religion:
Discipline and Reasons of Power in Christianity and Islam* (Baltimore: Johns Hopkins University
Press, 1993), p. 75.

ity. "The point here, however, is that the wisdom suggested by the *habitus* requires a shift away from a rule- or content-driven model of normative thinking about traditioning."[7] It is regarded as *improvised* knowledge, which combines identity with flexibility, that is, "regulated improvisation." The position is stated succinctly:

> In sum, the "understanding" of *habitus* is, first, a *competence,* one that is productive and creative. Importantly, the social and bodily character of this competence gives it a particular character, distinguishing it from certain kinds of abstract productivities. It is as Essed says, an "everyday" knowledge. It will draw from inscribed traditions, for ends and visions available, but it may outrun them and reconfigure them. Second, its wisdom is a capacity to respond improvisationally to a *situation;* it is competence to do or say something well *for a circumstance.* Third, while shaped by inscribing practices of a culture, *habitus* as incorporative practice is a distinctively presentist and performed bodily way of communicating meanings as well.[8]

For McClintock Fulkerson, this understanding has implications for how one makes normative judgments about the practices located in the congregation of Good Samaritan. What makes it a *faithful* place? Certainly, faithfulness cannot be limited to cognitive components; it is not simply about a set of beliefs. The wisdom contained in the *habitus* cannot be reduced to second-order reflection "and precludes prescribed, fixed forms of normative discourse."[9] The body is a condition and component of competence, which means that gospel communication cannot be reduced or limited to verbalization but must include bodily practices as well. Christian traditioning converges with existing practices such that there is an ongoing interplay between bodies and discourse that produces a "text." Such practices, incorporated and inscribed, can enhance capacities as they advance the goals of the community, as traditions are internalized and extended. "The ongoing faithfulness of those practices has to do not only with the complex criteria attending bodily and inscribed social memory, but with the enhancement of relevant capacities as well" (p. 51).

7. McClintock Fulkerson, *Places of Redemption,* p. 47.

8. McClintock Fulkerson, *Places of Redemption,* pp. 47-48; Philomena Essed, *Understanding Everyday Racism: An Interdisciplinary Theory* (London: Sage, 1991), pp. 48-49.

9. McClintock Fulkerson, *Places of Redemption,* p. 48. Page numbers to this work have been placed in the following text.

## 5.2.2 Ecclesial Practices, Biblical Texts, and Pneumatology

Given the perspective from which the study is positioned, McClintock Fulkerson elucidates four key practices that assist in the analysis of the theology of the church community in its context. These four practices are formation, worship, homemaking, and interpretation of the Bible. In the light of my concerns noted above, and to do justice to the details of each, I shall focus on just two key areas that are informed by or illustrate an approach to pneumatology and the use of Scripture in order to explore these features not just at the level of ordinary discourse but also at academic levels. So, pneumatological texts will function as entry points into the discussion.

First, McClintock Fulkerson traces the origins of the congregation and its emergent identity, considering the founding events as practices of formation. Social integration is regarded as one of the defining practices of the church. The initial vision for this practice emerged from a Bible study of Acts 8 and the encounter of Philip with the Ethiopian eunuch. From this example of evangelism emerged a conviction that God was calling them as a congregation to go and find people who — like the Ethiopian eunuch was to Philip — were not like them in race, nationality, and physical ability. In other words, this narrative gave the congregation a formational identity that inspired particular interpretive practices through which the community was sustained, at least for a period of its history. McClintock Fulkerson designates this significant interpretive event "a practice of inscription," which functions as a rationale for acting in a particular way and gives a basis for other kinds of practices (p. 84). This makes sense when one realizes that the Good Samaritan congregation emerged out of a failed all-white congregation called Wellspring United Methodist Church in Durham, amid the social complexity of North Carolina and the dynamics of race, politics, and economics. With the change in racial composition in the area, the church declined as an all-white church until it became unviable as a congregation, with only 10 members meeting for worship in 1987 (from 130 in its heyday). The denomination decided to sell the building and to plant a new congregation from the remnant of church members in a different area of the city.

The new emerging church, led by their pastor, Dan, decided that their identity would not be defined by homogeneity but rather by difference, based on a Bible study of Acts 8:26-39. Arising from a group Bible study, the remnant of the dying church met to read this passage. The passage caught their imagination, and in particular the role Philip played as he was led by the Holy Spirit to approach this unknown traveler. As a result of the encounter, the eunuch believed the gospel message and was baptized, before going on his way. To those ten people, the eunuch was a symbol of people who were different, or who were looked over or passed by. Originally, a eunuch was a castrated man responsible for an Oriental harem or employed as a state official. But in this context the meaning of the term took on a new twist. "Eunuch" was redefined to provide an image of the "other" that was relevant to their own context and to which they could relate analogously. As McClintock Fulkerson states, "[w]e might call Dan's an interpretive 'catachresis' — a resignification that indicates how a biblical story gains new meaning through a performance excess of meaning" (p. 64). The name The Good Samaritan was chosen to give expression to this founding identity of seeking the lost in the crowd in the surrounding racial context. Dan's style was informal and relaxed, but the style of the minister who replaced him, Gerald, originally from the Bahamas, was more formal and liturgical. The denomination decided to replace Dan with Gerald because of his race: he was judged to be black. Given the history of slavery and racism in North Carolina, and the continuing issues of racial integration in congregational life, it was understood as a positive move. However, the path toward greater racial diversity began under the ministry of Dan and his wife Linda. During their ministry, the congregation gradually became less "white." Subsequently they connected to people with disabilities living in local residential care homes. Members from two different residential homes began to attend regularly.

The cost of these moves, especially the move to make the church more multiracial, was discovered when the congregation wished to purchase land to erect a new church building. Initial contact with the local community suggested support, but opposition grew as the plans became firm, including the Ku Klux Klan targeting individual congregational members with acts of intimidation! Eventually, supporters significantly outnumbered detractors and the plans went ahead. At its numerical height, the congregation attracted 130 members, roughly one-third Anglo, one-third African American, and one-third African, with small numbers of Koreans and other Asians. Over time the *habitus* of "welcoming eunuchs" was challenged by those who found the church "too black"; that is, the color balance had been tipped too far in the nonwhite direction (p. 81). In reality, the numbers at the time did not support this understanding; what the challenge reflected was a broader cultural attitude, even among those who would reject racism (suggesting that attitudinal racism is a continuous measure rather than a discrete one). This forced the pastor at the time, Dan, to make a difficult decision, namely, to let some people leave over the matter. This was a challenge to the propriety into which most Americans have been socialized, namely, that they inhabit for the most part racially homogenous communities and that multiracial spaces can be controlled in favor of the dominant racial group. This is regarded as a practice rather than a cultural phenomenon by McClintock Fulkerson, and it is linked to notions of dominance and subordination. The multicultural congregation challenged the ownership of social space by white people, so-called white space (p. 86). Thus it exposed the underlying discomfort, fear, and loss of control.

Second, McClintock Fulkerson identifies different styles or kinds of worship associated with the two pastors — with Dan, who was informal and interactive, and with Gerald, who was more formal and "intellectual." All worship, however, is communal, and there is a dynamic interaction between the leader and the congregation, which includes bodily performances and affective experiences. These practices unite diverse members into a collective. They are categorized in terms of inscribed or incorporative practices.

During Dan and Linda's tenure as pastor and pastor's wife, the style of the church was exuberant and informal. The praise songs used in worship were of the black gospel style, and they were sung with great enjoyment. Arms were raised in the air and bodies swayed to the rhythm of the music. On Martin Luther King Day the congregation sang "We Shall Overcome" while holding hands. Dan's preaching style was interactive; he moved around and asked the congregation questions while preaching the sermon, and the worshipers responded with comments. There was a noticeable movement from a liturgical voice to a preaching voice, with the latter being more relaxed and conversational. These ritual practices produced a pleasurable effect as the congregation engaged with them, such that worship time had some fluidity, spilling out beyond set boundaries. The themes that emerge from this period of leadership are the following: reliance on God because nothing is our doing; celebration of the community's diversity; and affirmation of the ordinary, especially the ordinary believer. Dan's performance of informality created space for personal intimacy with God, but within this genre his style stayed ordinary, which was "somehow its redemption" (p. 101). By this, McClintock Fulkerson means that he connected the sacred and the secular in the very ordinariness of his persona.

Gerald appeared to be more formal, using colored liturgical coverings, a president's chair, vestments, and altar candles, to suggest transition from secular to sacred space. Nevertheless, his greetings were informal and he welcomed members by name. The sermon style was different, but his Pentecost Sunday sermon suggests some resonance with the style of the previous pastor. In the sermon he revisited the narrative of Pentecost, which he described as the church's birthday, an inclusive party. The disciples were bold, empowered by the Holy Spirit. They were gifted for ministry and mission, able to "witness to the mighty acts of God's salvation" rather than seeking "personal glorification" (p. 104). Gerald suggested that Christians often respond to the church's birthday with timidity and denial, when the opposite should be the case. McClintock Fulkerson describes Gerald's central theology of the Spirit:

> The Spirit's movement is always outward, he says, and its goal is always renewal. Repeating the prophet Joel's promise that God's Spirit would be poured out on all flesh, Gerald begins a litany of God's renewing acts. God's renewal is toward unity, he says, unity in Christ's body, and it will unite us with others "across all existing barriers and divisions." The divisions are cultural, he continues, they are religious and social and economic. And even racial, or class- or gender-based, these divisions will be overcome by the Spirit. (p. 104)

The implications of this position for race were given support by reference to the person of Christ, who was born a Jew but had Gentile blood; for gender because both sons and daughters will prophesy; and for age because the old will dream dreams and young will see visions. Class and occupation both submit to the lordship of Christ, as does nationality, because the earth is the Lord's and everything in it. The diverse audience of Parthians, Medes, Egyptians, Libyans, Jews, and Arabs heard the outpouring but refused to acknowledge it as the outpouring of the Spirit. Gerald associated these groups with contemporary American ethnic groups and others, to challenge attitudes toward Hispanic migrant workers, unemployed African Americans, Native Americans, single white mothers on welfare, wheelchair users, and "special needs" children. To all these examples the congregation responded with "Amen's." Everyone was invited to the birthday party of the church, which meant if you were white, then the "block of ice" in your gut was being melted; if you were black, the cynical trickles of ice water in your veins were no longer tasted. This is because whoever calls on the name of the Lord will be saved. The music that followed this sermon was vibrant and "full-bodied"; its rhythm connected with the movement of the people.

McClintock Fulkerson sees Gerald as someone who fits into a "liberationist" position theologically. He often portrayed God as liberator and the marginalized community as agent. He often used illustrations and examples from nonwhite authors and sources. Although Gerald is black, his white stepmother helped him become aware of race issues. For Gerald, Pentecost addresses the disunity of "othering" caused by socioeconomics and cultural politics. The congregation's culpability in colluding with these evils of marginalization is a denial of our calling to live up to life in the Spirit. All are invited to the church's party, and the praise and worship illustrate congregational unity in the Spirit through corporate bodily movement as an incorporative bodily practice (pp. 107-8).

### 5.2.3 Critical Observations

There are very many positive aspects to McClintock Fulkerson's study, and it is an important contribution to scholarship, full of careful reflection and insight. I have chosen it as a case study because I regard it as exemplary in many ways, well deserving of detailed engagement and yet not without weaknesses. The following, more critical comments should be understood alongside a very positive assessment of its value. They enable a case to be made for building on her achievements and moving beyond them in a constructive fashion. In this critical mode I make a number of points.

First, McClintock Fulkerson begins her study by entering at what she calls the scene of a wound; she enters via the lenses of race and ability. Clearly, these are significant issues in their own right and deserve to be studied as subjects in American society more generally. The metaphor of a wound is, however, undeveloped. For example, she does not discuss the causes of such wounds, like the concept of sin. Fractures in human relationships, such that people are not treated equally before God as bearers of the *imago Dei,* suggest attitudes that could be described as sinful. Of course, segregation, whether enforced legally or policed socially, contributes to a system of exclusion based on either ethnicity or ability. Related to this idea of exclusion based on these features is the remedy for the wound. How might the wound be healed? There is no discussion of soteriology in terms of healing. What might a therapeutic redemptive practice look like within the context of a congregation, a denomination, or a network of churches? How might such a soteriology challenge American culture at its deepest level? I am unclear whether McClintock Fulkerson has a network of theological themes able to do justice to the concept of sin and is able to articulate a Christian theology of redemption in a wider sense.

Second, McClintock Fulkerson suggests that normativity is always situational and combines identity with flexibility. It is embodied in faithful practices in the context of a faithful place. What is important about her argument at this point is the recognition that theology is not just about a set of beliefs articulated in propositional form. With this statement I am in wholehearted agreement. It is about a *habitus*, which includes a bodily performance. However, where I might be critical of her position is in the apparent loss of all forms of universality. If a form of Christianity is allowed to find relevance and authenticity only in its particularity, then there is always the danger that it becomes disconnected from the wider historical and contemporary tradition of Christianity. The problems surrounding such a move are myriad. However, I would argue that both consistency and innovation are required for authenticity. It is unclear how the "regulated improvisation" is indeed regulated, and by whom? This leads to the notion of faithfulness. Faithfulness suggests a holding on to both poles of identity and relevance,[10] but it is not clear how McClintock Fulkerson understands this notion; there may be confusion about theological universality. Postmodern theory tends to emphasize the particular and the partial over the universal and grand account, but in reality it often substitutes one form of universality for another form. The other form becomes an operational form of normativity that functions below the surface but is never fully named or owned; it is simply assumed by those of like mind.

Third, McClintock Fulkerson would fall into the sixth category of practical theologians identified in chapter 2 (an advocate of the excluded approach). She does not engage with Scripture in a meaningful manner in order to construct a theological account. Where biblical texts are cited, they form part of the first-order discourse of the leaders and congregation. In her analysis of the theological themes contained in these texts, she does not go behind the discourse produced in order to reflect on the range of meanings one might elucidate in relation to key biblical texts. They are simply described in a flat manner and form part of the larger analysis of the theological performance of the congregation. That is, they are subsumed under some larger theme. This methodological move does not take seriously the role of Scripture in the formation of the identity narrative associated with the congregation and mediated via their pastors as key interpreters. In other words, it plays down the mediatorial roles that both pastors play and the ways in which biblical texts are received and used by the congregation. Furthermore, there is no critical appraisal of the strategies employed or indeed the outcome of such strategies for congregational identity formation. This

10. E.g., Jürgen Moltmann, *The Crucified God* (London: SCM, 1974), pp. 7-25.

means that an exclusion occurs at both first-order and second-order levels, which compounds the original problem identified in chapter 2. Not only do exemplars of the excluded approach ignore biblical texts within theological construction, they also ignore the significance of the use of Scripture within first-order discourse.

Fourth, the problem identified for the use of Scripture can also be applied to pneumatology. The description of the congregation's life identifies two key passages that contain pneumatological themes: Acts 2 and Acts 8. These texts are used in reverse order in the description of the church, and provide a pneumatological basis for the overarching identity narrative of the congregation. However, McClintock Fulkerson fails to engage with pneumatology as a legitimate theological category that assists in the explication of the ordinary theology and might contribute toward a theological account of the congregation in relation to redemption. The question is, why is this excluded? When an important theological theme permeates the narrative, why would anyone ignore it? I can only suggest that she was either insensitive to its presence or deliberately chose not to engage with it. Either way, there is a problem, because a congregational study intentionally seeks to identify key themes and harnesses them for the sake of the theological account.

Fifth, there is an overarching framework that gives shape to the content of the theology, and indeed the framework and the content mutually inform each other, and necessarily so. It is here that one senses the lack of a Trinitarian framework of any sort. McClintock Fulkerson appears to function with a general theistic framework that is vague enough to allow for a variety of moves, depending on how the argument is developed. The person of Christ is mentioned, but, again, there is no real sense of a developed or informed Christology integrated within the theological discourse or informing it in any significant manner. Of course, this could raise an even more pertinent query, namely, whether in fact this is really an anthropological discourse under the guise of theology. If God-talk is fundamentally marginalized from the discussion such that redemption is framed within a social and cultural context to the exclusion of the transcendent, then is it not just a thinly veiled form of anthropology and not really theology at all? This, of course, begs the question as to whether such an account can be called *redemption* in a theological sense, since a theological conceptualization, however construed, will of necessity include a transcendent referent of some kind.

In my responses that follow, I shall endeavor to address all these points. In many respects the issues identified in this analysis can be mirrored in the wider literature, which means that this approach is both pertinent and useful as a way of approaching the issues I identified at the beginning of the study.

## 5.3 Intervention

Obviously, there are limitations to my intervention. I cannot reresearch the original congregation, even if I wanted to. So how might a P/C perspective suggest a contribution at a theoretical level? A number of possible interventions emerge from pneumatology in the biblical texts.

### 5.3.1 The Ethiopian Eunuch

One contribution is to discuss how a reading of Acts 8, via the lens of pneumatological mediation, might assist in engagement with the theology espoused in this congregation and used in its identity construction. Chapter 8 of Acts follows on from the stoning to death of Stephen (7:54-60), with the beginning of the chapter stating the approval of his death by Saul (soon to become Paul). Shortly after this event, Luke records that the church is scattered throughout Judea and Samaria because a great persecution has come upon it, led by Saul. Philip, based on his fullness of the Spirit and wisdom (6:3), is one of the seven chosen to assist in the distribution of food to widows (6:5). He travels to the city of Samaria to preach the message of Christ, and this is supported by signs and wonders, such as exorcisms and healings, which brought much joy to the city (8:4-8). As a result of Philip's ministry, many people believed the message and were baptized, including Simon the magician. The apostles Peter and John, having heard the news, visit Samaria, pray, and lay hands on the Samaritans, and they receive the Holy Spirit (8:14-17). Simon seeks to buy this power to mediate the Holy Spirit and is rebuked by Peter, so that he acknowledges his wrong attitude before Peter. At this point we come to the story of Philip and the Ethiopian eunuch.

The narrative states that an angelic intermediary instructs Philip to go south on the desert road that links Jerusalem to Gaza, and he obeys the command. En route he meets an Ethiopian eunuch, who is described as an important official in the queen of Ethiopia's household, being responsible for the treasury.[11] He was a God-fearer or proselyte and had been on pilgrimage

---

11. It was not unusual for a castrated male to hold a position of importance in an Oriental

to Jerusalem. In his chariot as he traveled he was reading the book of the prophet Isaiah. At this point the text says (8:29 NRSV): "Then the Spirit said to Philip, 'Go over to this chariot and join it'" *(eipen de to pneuma to[i] Philippo[i]: proselthe kai kollēthēti to[i] harmati touto[i]).*[12] So Philip runs up to the chariot and hears the man reading from Isaiah and asks whether he understands what he is reading. The eunuch replies that he cannot understand unless someone explains the meaning of the text to him. So the man invites Philip to sit with him in the chariot and explain the meaning of the passage from Isaiah, which comes from 53:7-8 (Acts 8:32-33 NRSV):

> "Like a sheep he was led to the slaughter,
> and like a lamb silent before its shearer,
> so he does not open his mouth.
> In his humiliation, justice was denied him.
> Who can describe his generation?
> For his life is taken away from the earth."

The eunuch asks Philip whether the prophet was talking about himself or someone else (8:34), at which point Philip expounds the meaning of the text in relation to the good news about Jesus Christ. Subsequently, as they pass some water the eunuch asks Philip whether there is anything that would stop him from being baptized. So they stop the chariot and Philip baptizes the eunuch there and then. As they come out of the water, we are told that the Spirit of the Lord suddenly took Philip away (8:39, literally "seized" him, *pneuma kuriou hērpasen ton Philippon).*[13] The eunuch did not see Philip again but went on his way rejoicing. Philip, however, traveled around the area preaching in the various towns until he reached the city of Caesarea.

In terms of mediation, this passage raises some interesting points that invite further comment.

First, there is something about Philip that makes him sensitive to the workings of the Holy Spirit. He has already been described as someone "filled with

---

court of the period; see Luke Timothy Johnson, *The Acts of the Apostles* (Collegeville, Minn.: Liturgical Press, 1992), p. 155.

12. Ling Chen, *The Characterisation of God in Acts: The Indirect Portrayal of an Invisible Character* (Milton Keynes: Paternoster, 2011), p. 24, suggests that it amounts to "divine intervention." We also note the move from angelic messenger in verse 26 to the role of the Holy Spirit in verse 29, which in effect eclipses the role of angels in this episode.

13. Intriguingly, some manuscript variants suggest that the Holy Spirit came upon the eunuch, but this evidence is not well attested; see Johnson, *Acts,* p. 159.

the Spirit and wisdom" (*plēreis pneumatos kai sophias,* 6:3) and has been set apart for service. But now this ministry extends beyond the original remit, as he has traveled in order to preach the gospel message. This preaching is accompanied by signs and wonders and a positive response, as people believe and are baptized. Here is a man who is a preaching, healing evangelist, who is prompted by the Holy Spirit to travel to Samaria, a place previously outside the realm of Jewish acceptance, to a people ostracized by the Jews of the period. He is being used to mediate the presence of the Holy Spirit through his speaking, his prayers for healing, and his involvement in the conversion-initiation process.

Second, instructions are given to Philip to do something. An angel is introduced into the narrative. The use of angelic messengers is reasonably common by Luke in both the Gospel and Acts.[14] So it is unsurprising that the first instruction comes from a heavenly messenger. The text does not give us very many details about this encounter. There is no description of what the angel looked like, or how the angel sounded. The reader is simply told in a straightforward manner that an angel gave an instruction to move in the direction of a particular location. Then Luke says the Spirit spoke directly to Philip, telling him to approach the chariot and remain alongside it. Again, we ask how this happened. What was the mechanism through which this occurred? It might seem as though this was a direct and unmediated experience, but some aspect of his humanity, not least his imagination, must have been used in the process. He obeys the Spirit's prompting, and so engages in a conversation with the eunuch.

Third, the eunuch is reading Scripture from the book of the prophet Isaiah. He is struggling to make sense of the text, and Philip gives it a christological meaning, thus allowing it to be interpreted in the light of Jesus. The outcome of this explanation is that the eunuch wishes to convert to Christianity and is baptized. Implied in the narrative, although not explicitly stated by Luke, is the idea that the Holy Spirit has prompted the man to read this text, allowing Philip to mediate a gospel interpretation, in order that he might convert. Implied also is the idea that the eunuch has believed and received the gift of the Holy Spirit — implied in the statement of joy but not explicitly stated. The narrative is circumscribed by the sovereign work of the Spirit, who then suddenly seizes Philip away from the eunuch, without so much as a bon voyage![15] In other words, it is implied that through the text

---

14. Luke 1:11, 13, 26, 28; 2:9-10, 13; 22:43; Acts 5:19; 10:3, 7, 22; 12:7-15; 27:23.

15. Luke's language suggests that Philip is "snatched away"; see J. D. G. Dunn, *The Acts of the Apostles* (Peterborough: Epworth, 1996), p. 115.

of Scripture and the person of Philip the presence of the Holy Spirit has been mediated to the eunuch.

In practical-theological reading terms, two features are worthy of note.

First, the narrative raises some questions about the hermeneutically re-flexive stance of McClintock Fulkerson.[16] There are, of course, different levels of reflexivity. She offers some commentary on the hermeneutical strategy of the Bible study group, for whom the eunuch represented "the other," the one lost in the crowd in the surrounding racial context. She regards this exten-sion as a resignification of meaning, whereby the original story gains new meaning. Just as Philip sought out the lost eunuch, so the church saw itself as receiving, if not seeking, those who might be considered lost. Of course, the name The Good Samaritan is taken from a completely different biblical text, with a whole different set of resonances (Luke 10:25-37). But in the ordinary hermeneutic exhibited by the congregation, their quite different meanings are conflated. The question to be raised is less about the ordinary herme-neutical posture and more about whether McClintock Fulkerson might have questioned her own hermeneutic in the light of her engagement with the original texts. There is some discussion of the original category of eunuch, but not a critique of whether it is responsible simply to equate this category in the contemporary discussion with race or ability. In the discussion by the church, the role of Philip is equated with congregational aspiration to offer a loving welcome to all. It misses an important set of features, namely, the role of the angel and the Spirit in directing Philip, the mediation of the text by Philip, and the evangelization of the eunuch, followed by the absolute aban-donment of the person by both Philip and the Spirit at the side of the road. There is no conversion aftercare here! In other words, the representation and reinterpretation of this text are highly selective at both hermeneutical levels. This resignification raises some important questions in relation to what is lost. Clearly the congregation was energized and empowered by the reading, but perhaps a fuller appreciation of the original sociocultural context might have led to a more nuanced understanding of who might represent the eu-nuch in contemporary American society.

Second, is it possible that in the attempt to explore race as a fundamental category of thought, a priori lenses of both congregation and researcher have so shaped the reception of the text that significant features have been sup-pressed or even distorted? It is here that the contemporary issue of racism in American society has been reflected in the texts to the extent that the range

---

16. This point aligns with my reading strategy point 1 (see 2.2.4 above).

of possible and legitimate interpretations has been constrained not by the text in its context but by the wider contextual issues in American society, of which the congregation studied by McClintock Fulkerson is a part.[17] This is acknowledged when she frames the discussion in terms of "a situation characterized by harm that demands redress."[18] While I have absolutely no doubt about the veracity of this statement, it nevertheless poses problems in terms of how it is handled. The feature is extended to ability/disability, but the congregation does not explore fully what the significance of the eunuch's conversion might have had on the reception of people with impairment or their process of conversion. Indeed, conversion, which is at the heart of this narrative, is simply not discussed in any real detail. This is because the issue of diversity becomes the dominant category to the exclusion of all else. Redemption is subsequently defined in terms of sociocultural acceptance rather than the conversion-initiation complex associated with Luke's horizon of thought. A different agenda of evangelism and church growth in a contemporary American context would, without doubt, have interpreted this narrative in a very different way, both at the ordinary and at the academic levels. Given the limitations of a study of a particular congregation, it is understandable that this wider agenda is not explored when the congregation under investigation does not exhibit such beliefs and practices. However, in a country where evangelistic activities are commonplace, and I would say as commonplace as existing racist attitudes, then it suggests that a fairly restrictive set of contemporary questions have been brought to the text from the contemporary context. This observation raises a fundamental question as to where our questions come from and how they are defined and used. I regard this as a crucial point for practical theology as a whole, because asking questions is a practice imbued with beliefs and values.

### 5.3.2 Pentecost

As described above, there is an interesting and illuminating interpretation of the church and its mission by the second pastor, Gerald, in relation to Pentecost. In the light of his theological discourse, and given our interests, it useful to revisit his narrative and how it is used by McClintock Fulkerson.

Gerald's statement that the day of Pentecost is the church's birthday is

17. This point aligns with my reading strategy point 5 (see 2.2.4 above).
18. McClintock Fulkerson, *Places of Redemption*, p. 17.

relatively uncontroversial, and the idea of an inclusive birthday party is a natural extension of the metaphor. However, it could be said that all groups have boundaries, and while the day of Pentecost offers a sociocultural critique both then and now, it also provides a redefinition of the included *and* the excluded. The birthday of the church is based not just on an anthropological dynamic of changing the boundaries, but also on a theological and ecclesiological ontology, whereby the Spirit of God constitutes the new temple of God, the *ecclesia*. The Spirit is poured out on all flesh in the sense that the boundary line shifts from an exclusively Jewish identity to one that includes Gentiles. The messiah of the Jews has become the savior of the Gentiles, and it is Christ who mediates the Spirit to the church and all who would be incorporated into it (Acts 2:33). There is a clear boundary marker evidenced by repentance, faith, baptism, and reception of the Spirit. The invitation is to all, irrespective of background, but a boundary line still exists and has not been eradicated. Inclusivist positions can also appear to be vacuous, and the Pentecost narrative, when attended to, challenges this kind of assumption. The social critique challenges the boundary marker based on anthropological privileges (race, nationality, gender, age, class, and occupation) by replacing it with a pneumatological one; reception of the Spirit cuts across the anthropological divisions. It is fundamentally based on an internal heart-based response by individuals and groups, hence the question after the hearers are "cut to the heart" (Acts 2:37): What should we do? McClintock Fulkerson in her analysis ignores or simply does not "see" this pneumatological dimension, or perhaps subsumes it under the anthropological category.

The disciples certainly were emboldened by the reception of the Spirit, as Gerald acknowledges in his sermon. They witnessed to the "mighty acts of God" rather than seeking personal glorification. This much is true. But the declaration of the mighty acts of God on the day of Pentecost is linked to doxological speech, specifically glossolalia. While McClintock Fulkerson notes praise and worship in her description, she does not really analyze the role of worship and, specifically, doxology in terms of witness and identity formation. The practices of worship shape communities; doxology in the Pentecost narrative mediated the presence of the Holy Spirit such that the community was united to the life of the Trinity. This union with the divine is an expression of ecclesial ontology. There is no theological framing of doxology either in Gerald's discourse or in the secondary discourse of McClintock Fulkerson. These omissions raise questions about what kind of ecclesiology is operative at *both* levels of interpretation. Practical theology is concerned with ecclesiology, and this narrative highlights the relationship between pneumatology and ecclesiology. While the Holy Spirit is not restricted to the church, and importantly the church does not "own" or "dispense" the Holy Spirit, there is a constitutive role of the Spirit in the church ontologically. It is not just a religious club or a national institution. It is the "body of Christ" united to its head by means of the Spirit. Once again, a limited ecclesiology appears to be normative in this kind of congregational study. But it is also reflected in practical theology at large, and therefore requires further sustained attention.

Gerald's central theology is a very useful way of capturing the heart of his pneumatology and of assessing McClintock Fulkerson's own pneumatology as reflected upon in her study. He suggests that the movement is always outward. I would agree in terms of the ultimate movement of the Spirit, but would add that it is first internal to the life of the Trinity (before creation) and the church. The language of Pentecost, using spatial metaphors, suggests "coming down," "coming upon," "coming inside," before the "sending out." In a sense the difference may be more logical than temporal, but on the day of Pentecost it was both temporal and logical. The goal of the Spirit's work espoused by Gerald is one of renewal upon "all flesh" that leads toward a breaking down of divisions and unity across barriers. This is certainly a legitimate aspect to the reading of the narrative, but it is a rather "thin" reading, and more can be said. The renewal is first about Israel. The nation of Israel is being reconstituted and represented via the new exodus liberation. This salvation has an eschatological horizon, and it comes not just from "above" but also from the "future" being rooted in apocalyptic imagery.[19] It signals not only the renewal of a nation, a people, a set of individuals, but also the *created order,* which is in the process of being sanctified for the residence of the glory of God. As Gunton observes, "the Spirit's work is best considered to be eschatological: as perfecting that which was created in the beginning, in the many and various particular ways in which that can take place, both ordinary and extraordinary."[20]

Finally, in this section I raise the central question of soteriology. What does it mean to be "saved" in this reading of Pentecost? McClintock Fulkerson characterizes Gerald as a liberation theologian, and there is good reason to use this designation for him. He understands God as the liberator,

---

19. See Max Turner, *Power from on High: The Spirit in Israel's Restoration and Witness in Luke-Acts* (Sheffield: Sheffield Academic Press, 1996), pp. 267-315.

20. Colin Gunton, *The Christian Faith: An Introduction to Christian Doctrine* (Oxford: Blackwell, 2002), p. 185.

identifies certain categories among the oppressed, and articulates the marginalized community as an agent of social inclusion. This is so far, so good. But from what are these excluded groups saved? Is the problem restricted to only a social one? Is it really about material resources and access to social and cultural goods? There are certainly social and communal dimensions to salvation as a category, but it would be highly reductionist to conceive soteriology exclusively in these terms. McClintock Fulkerson prefers to use the term "redemption," which has connotations of paying a ransom price to release a captive. But the language is not treated in any great detail, so we have to read between the lines to get a sense of its theological currency. If this congregation exhibits redemption and inhabits a place of redemption, what might be said of the nature, significance, and limitations of such a place? Furthermore, what would develop, enhance, and even transform such a place? The history of the congregation indicates that this "place" did not continue but was rather transferred to a different place. Does this mean that their experience of "redemption" was somehow lost or temporary? What did they leave behind when they moved, and what did they take with them? In other words, how far can a place-centered redemptive theology travel? What degree of universality can be said to exist? Is this a theology that is made in the world of contemporary southern American society with very little translation into other contexts? Or is it possible to detect some features, at the very least, of a transcontextual theology of redemption? Historically, Christianity is a religion of translation, which is why the text of Scripture has been translated into many different languages from around the world.[21] Theology is also part of the translation phenomenon; whether it is first-order or second-order discourse, the same question applies. Where can transcontextuality, or universality *through* particularity, be found?

## 5.4 Conclusion

This chapter has analyzed a concrete study of a Christian congregation and engaged with it critically in order to elucidate how a practical-theological study has the capacity to read previous studies in a new way. In particular, it analyzed the explicit and implicit pneumatology present in the study and observed how the author seriously underplayed this particular dimension

21. See the discussion of Christianity and translation in Lamin Sanneh, *Translating the Message: The Missionary Impact of Culture* (Maryknoll, N.Y.: Orbis, 1990).

of the congregational theology. Key pneumatological sections were given attention in the light of the concept of pneumatological mediation, and their contribution was rediscovered for the practical-theological account. Thus, the chapter illustrates how the central set of lenses established by this study can be used creatively to engage with existing studies to challenge and also affirm the value of congregational studies. Could the weaknesses in McClintock Fulkerson's study have been noticed by other perspectives? Quite possibly, but in reality they have not been identified and discussed. Therefore, as it stands, only a P/C perspective has been used to open up a new horizon in this regard. Other pneumatological perspectives may follow in due course, and I hope they do, but for now it is the insights and intuitions of P/C theology that have provided a critical intervention. It remains for new congregational studies to take up the challenge of integrating pneumatology within the set of theological questions to be explored at the outset rather than being read via a secondary examination as this chapter has done.

# 6 Soteriological Discourse in Practical Theology

## 6.1 Introduction

In this final chapter I propose that practical theology engage more consciously and rigorously with systematic theological loci. I realize that some practical theologians have rejected this strategy for a number of reasons. They do not wish to be dictated to by systematicians and their particular dogmatic agendas. They do not think that abstract philosophical and theological debates from history should influence the analysis of contemporary religious life. They regard the human sciences and their theories as important dialogue partners and do not wish them to be displaced by tight or exclusive theological discourse. There may be, of course, a host of other reasons for rejecting systematic theology, depending on the type of systematic theology one is discussing, because it is extremely diverse as a discipline. I have some degree of sympathy with all these objections. Indeed, it could be asked: Why should practical theologians "do" systematic theology for the systematicians? Surely, they should "do" it for themselves! I am not advocating a kind of re-colonization of the systematic theology lifeworld by a practical-theological approach. Rather, I am suggesting that just as practical theologians have marginalized Scripture, they have also become detached from key theological loci normally found in systematic theology. Some may see this as a positive development, but I suggest it has been detrimental because it has weakened the *theological* nature of practical theology. One way to expand and deepen that discourse is to reengage with the traditional theological loci, but from a distinctly practical-theological approach that pays attention to concrete value-laden practices, not just abstract ideas and systems of thought. Nevertheless, it would use these theological loci to reinvigorate and develop its discourse.

Therefore, in this chapter I shall cast the net wider, reflecting the oscillation inherent in practical theology between the concrete/particular and the theoretical/universal.[1] The detailed engagement with McClintock Fulkerson in the previous chapter highlighted an important theme, which was identified earlier in the discussion of the Pentecost narrative, namely, soteriology. A number of questions can be put to the wider practical-theological academy: (1) What does it mean to be "saved" in practical-theological discourse? (2) Who or what is saved, and from whom or what are they saved? (3) Who are the saviors, and how do they relate to each other? (4) What are the horizons (temporal, spatial, theological) of salvation? The majority of texts that I surveyed in chapters 1 and 2 did not use the category of soteriology as an explicit one; other themes were more usually in view, such as pastoral care, ministry concerns, and public issues. One could guess at the soteriological assumptions lying behind such discourse and the various dimensions of the concept that were implied in some way. But the implicit soteriology in many cases was *so embedded* that it would have taken considerable time, and not a little patience, to analyze and draw out the ideas assumed or hinted at. Therefore, I have selected only those sources that I regarded as implying soteriological categories sufficiently near the surface to be used relatively easily. This comment in itself is quite revealing, and says something about the nature of practical-theological discourse. Why does soteriology appear to be a largely missing or an implied category of thought? Where soteriological categories are explicit, they are limited to a number of themes and approaches.

This chapter outlines implicit and explicit discussions of soteriology among scholars before turning to ordinary theology and the ways in which soteriological discourse has been expressed at that level. Key positions are identified before a critical analysis of the material is offered. To bring insight from the perspective of P/C theology, the soteriology of Amos Yong is described before modifications to it are suggested. Finally, an intervention from a P/C perspective in relation to practical theology is suggested that draws upon pneumatological mediation derived in particular from Acts 2.

---

1. See Mark J. Cartledge, *Practical Theology: Empirical and Charismatic Perspectives* (Carlisle: Paternoster, 2003), pp. 24-30.

## 6.2 Soteriological Discourse

The designation "implicit theology" normally refers to theology that is embedded in everyday life as expressed in speech, cultural artifacts, literature, and media.[2] Here I am interested in the academic discourse of practical theology, so, similar to my review of practical theology in chapter 2, I restrict my sources to academic-level texts.

There are texts that suggest the benefit of interaction with a divine agent or a theological process of reflection or analysis, such that individuals and communities are themselves transformed in some measure; these texts, in other words, suggest an *implicit* soteriology. This kind of perspective could be said to be expressed by Don Browning with his use of transformation and restoration language,[3] as well as by Johannes A. van der Ven with his similar use of fullness, freedom, liberation, and integration language; he links the perspective to the person of Christ as the expression of God's love for humanity.[4] Similarly, R. John Elford suggests soteriological thought when he mentions grace and sin, but it seems as though the horizon of salvation is conceived in terms of social and political realities.[5] David Lyall roots the narrative of the church in God's self-revelation in Christ and understands the task of the church as reinterpreting it afresh for each generation. The salvific import of such reinterpretation is largely expressed in terms of liberation of the poor from oppression and the transformation of power relations. People are saved from either poverty or inequality through the work of those who make themselves vulnerable, modeling themselves on God, who in Christ has made himself vulnerable through the incarnation and the cross. This gives

2. Implicit religion has been described rather vaguely in my view as containing such ideas as commitments, integrating foci, intensive concerns with extensive effects and human depths; see Edward Bailey, *Implicit Religion: An Introduction* (London: Middlesex University Press, 1998). More promisingly, it has been described as an examination of "basic-but-nascent theological habits" or a "guessing at the hidden meanings in structures and practices" in the lives of congregations and denominations; see Martyn Percy, *Shaping the Church: The Promise of Implicit Theology* (Farnham: Ashgate, 2010), p. 2.

3. Don Browning, *A Fundamental Practical Theology: Descriptive and Strategic Proposals* (Minneapolis: Fortress, 1996; orig. 1991), pp. 280, 284.

4. Johannes A. van der Ven, *Practical Theology: An Empirical Approach* (Kampen: Kok Pharos, 1993), pp. 69, 70, 72, 73-75.

5. R. John Elford, *The Pastoral Nature of Theology: An Upholding Presence* (London: Cassell, 1999), pp. 92, 95, 97, 127.

hope for the transformation of the present situation.[6] This is very similar to the perspective of Terry Veling.[7] Finally, Ray S. Anderson's discussion of forgiveness, reconciliation, and healing assumes the kingdom of God as a therapeutic context and implies that reconciliation among people is ultimately based on the reconciliation established between humanity and God through Christ.[8]

There are a few practical theology texts that *explicitly* engage with the category of soteriology in detail. A number of these are worth noting and engaging in turn.[9]

Andrew Purves, working from within the Reformed tradition, seeks to offer a *christological foundation* to pastoral theology and inevitably touches upon matters of soteriological interest.[10] Salvation is conceptualized as "union with Christ," which indeed frames the whole of the Christian faith. This means that reconciliation becomes the dominant feature of soteriology, and everything else is viewed through this prism. "Union with Christ applies both to the objective work of salvation, our being forgiven, and to our personal transformation from sinners into saints, our regeneration and sanctification, the expression of which is Christian life and vocation."[11] For the benefits of Christ to become ours, humanity must be united to him via a mystical union. This union with Christ is through the Holy Spirit, who is the means by which salvation is mediated to humanity. The union through the Holy Spirit also takes on a Trinitarian dimension because the Holy Spirit is the bond of union between the Father and the Son. The gift of union is bestowed via the church's ministry of Word and sacrament, whereby people are brought to faith and nurtured in their union with Christ. Christ is the only mediator between God and humanity, the apostle and high priest (Heb. 3:1), who enables humanity to share in his righteousness before God, his knowledge of the Father, and his love of the Father. The ministry of the

---

6. David Lyall, *Integrity of Pastoral Care* (London: SPCK, 2001), pp. 21, 39, 41-42, 96-98, 104, 154, 158.

7. Terry A. Veling, *Practical Theology: "On Earth as It Is in Heaven"* (Maryknoll, N.Y.: Orbis, 2005), pp. 118, 162, 175.

8. Ray S. Anderson, *The Shape of Practical Theology: Empowering Ministry with Theological Praxis* (Downers Grove, Ill.: InterVarsity, 2001), pp. 291-310.

9. Sadly, the very relevant book by Wayne Morris, *Salvation as Praxis: A Practical Theology of Salvation for a Multi-faith World* (London: Bloomsbury T. & T. Clark, 2014), appeared too late to be included in this study.

10. Andrew Purves, *Reconstructing Pastoral Theology: A Christological Foundation* (Louisville: Westminster John Knox, 2004), pp. 78-104.

11. Purves, *Reconstructing Pastoral Theology*, p. 81.

church flows from this union with Christ and shares in Christ's mission from the Father.

Similarly, Gerrit Immink, in a study of the concept and praxis of faith from a practical-theological perspective, addresses the subject of salvation directly.[12] Also based in the Reformed tradition, he discusses salvation in terms of *justification* as the imputation of external righteousness upon believers and the internal working of that righteousness within believers as they make salvation their own.[13] A reciprocal relationship between God and humanity is established on the basis of Christ, whereby God knows humans and humans know God; as the image of God is being restored, intimacy with God increases. This is the work of the Spirit, who dwells within the believer, enabling a full reciprocity to exist. The inner work of the Spirit in the person is often called sanctification and enables greater conformity to Christ. Individuals cooperate with God's work in them, so that a new *habitus* is formed in them. It is a renewal that is linked to the broader historical and eschatological revelation of salvation in Christ.[14] Thus the social particularities of human lives are inescapably linked to salvation history, and people connect daily existence to the revelation of Christ and are, in turn, shaped by communion with Christ. A version of the *ordo salutis* within the Reformed tradition is used to frame a practical-theological approach to soteriology; this includes election, enlightenment by the Spirit, conversion, and sanctification.[15]

From a different perspective, James Poling's discussion of practical theology as a form of process theology brings doctrinal categories into conversation with pastoral issues, such as violence and abuse.[16] He explicitly considers the themes of Christology and soteriology as part of his discussion. He asks: "what cooperative work of God and humans will rescue the world from self-destruction and the loss of meaning, value and beauty?"[17] For Poling, salvation is fundamentally about *communion with God,* who has overcome evil and death and who rescues humans from sin and its effects. In this respect his work resonates with the Reformed tradition noted above.

---

12. F. Gerrit Immink, *Faith: A Practical Theological Reconstruction* (Grand Rapids: Eerdmans, 2003).

13. Immink, *Faith*, p. 84.

14. Immink, *Faith*, p. 105.

15. Immink, *Faith*, p. 108.

16. James Newton Poling, *Rethinking Faith: A Constructive Practical Theology* (Minneapolis: Fortress, 2011), pp. 43-46, 54.

17. Poling, *Rethinking Faith*, p. 43.

However, he is especially interested in listening to the voices of those who have survived domestic violence and is concerned for those who find the cross and its violence too problematic a symbol and leave Christianity altogether. He focuses on the person of Christ as Savior, although he considers feminist critiques of violence and womanist reinterpretations of the cross as a symbol of liberation. Finally, using the work of Kathryn Tanner, he places the cross within the doctrine of the Trinity in a way that suggests transcendence, generosity, and noncompetitiveness.[18] "As a fully human being, Jesus' crucifixion was an act of solidarity with humans. Because of his commitments to the disciples, the poor, and transformation of the religious and political systems, Jesus became a victim of human sin and evil. . . . As fully human and divine, Jesus can go to the cross and survive because Jesus is unified with the transcendent generosity of God. Human salvation is possible because we can be unified with Christ, and this unity can be lived out in generous and noncompetitive relationships with others."[19]

Although not known as a practical theologian, Alister E. McGrath was invited to address the British and Irish Association of Practical Theology annual conference in 2011. In a discussion on the relationship between theology and practice, he specifically explored the connection between salvation and *healing*.[20] The New Testament material suggests that the notion is complex and involves reconciliation, forgiveness of sins, authentic human fulfillment, restoration of humanity to its proper condition, and transformation toward its ultimate destiny. The word *sōtēria,* which is normally translated "salvation," "bears a rich range of meanings, including 'healing,' 'restoration' and 'rescue.'"[21] He observed how in the history of Christianity medical images have often been used to explain and illustrate the nature of salvation; one such image is spiritual sight being restored. Augustine of Hippo (354-430) conceived of the church as a hospital, which provides healing and care for the wounded and broken. Although the act of healing was God's, human beings were involved in the process as coagents with God. Similarly, in the depiction of the crucifixion by Matthias Grünewald (c. 1475-1528), which was painted for a monastery that specialized in the treatment of leprosy, Christ on the cross is portrayed as "pock-marked" and discolored. He is the one who is

18. Kathryn Tanner, *Jesus, Humanity, and the Trinity: A Brief Systematic Theology* (Minneapolis: Fortress, 2001).

19. Poling, *Rethinking Faith,* p. 55.

20. Alister E. McGrath, "Frailty and Flourishing: Good News for Humanity," *Practical Theology* 4, no. 3 (2011): 315-31.

21. McGrath, "Frailty and Flourishing," p. 323.

"carrying our infirmities" (Isa. 53:3-4), which implies that the one who bears human affliction is the one who provides for its renewal.[22]

The category of ordinary theology is also used to refer to those who have had very little formal academic training.[23] Some practical theologians have used this category as a lens through which to explore the beliefs and practices of ordinary Christians and thereby contribute to academic discourse in their work. Two studies have considered the category of salvation explicitly.

Ann Christie's work on ordinary Christology among rural Anglicans in North Yorkshire, UK, includes soteriology and thus provides an interesting example of how the category has been used as a focus of research.[24] By inquiring into ordinary soteriology, she explores two related concerns: (1) the meanings, if any, attached to the death of Jesus, and (2) the claim that Jesus is Savior. Ordinary theology espoused by the interviewees is supported by a discussion of various proponents of the positions discussed in Christian thought. Three types of soteriology are identified. First, an *exemplarist* soteriology describes Christ's death as a martyr's death; since he was a radical, he died a political death. It does not atone for sin; rather it shows humanity how to live in self-sacrificial terms. Thus, Jesus shows humanity how to live via heroic and costly action. His death also demonstrates God's love for humanity, such that humanity is compelled to respond in gratitude. Christie regarded this as the most dominant soteriological type and the "default position" accepted by over half of the sample.[25] Second, a *traditionalist* soteriology is held by people who accept and believe in the whole package of conventional Christian theology but cannot articulate why they believe what they do. It is simply taken for granted. They learn it through hymnody and liturgy, but when asked to explain it or articulate their views about it, interviewees were unable to do so. Jesus is their Savior, but they cannot easily say how this is the case. Therefore, Christie suggests that this kind of adherence

22. McGrath, "Frailty and Flourishing," p. 323.

23. Jeff Astley, *Ordinary Theology: Looking, Listening, and Learning in Theology* (Farnham: Ashgate, 2002), p. 139.

24. Ann Christie, *Ordinary Christology: Who Do You Say I Am? Answers from the Pews* (Farnham: Ashgate, 2012). Also see Ann Christie and Jeff Astley, "Ordinary Soteriology: A Qualitative Study," in *Empirical Theology in Text and Tables: Qualitative, Quantitative, and Comparative Perspectives*, ed. Leslie J. Francis, Mandy Robbins, and Jeff Astley (Leiden: Brill, 2009), pp. 177-96, and Ann Christie, "Jesus as Exemplar," in *Exploring Ordinary Theology: Everyday Christian Believing and the Church*, ed. Jeff Astley and Leslie J. Francis (Farnham: Ashgate, 2013), pp. 77-85.

25. Christie, *Ordinary Christology*, pp. 93-100, 144-47.

works primarily at the level of affect, that is, the hymns and liturgy elicit emotional rather than cognitive currency. It provides support for an understanding of salvation primarily conceived in otherworldly terms.[26] Third, an *evangelical* soteriology advocates a substitutionary theology of atonement, whereby the price for sin is paid by Christ on the cross in the place of the sinner, so that the guilty is pardoned. Rather than acquiring this theology via hymns and liturgy, evangelicals have been taught this specifically as a cornerstone of Christian discipleship. Christie notes that alongside this doctrine is the belief that salvation is based on a personal experience of being with Jesus. Becoming a Christian is often defined as acknowledging what Jesus has done on the cross and inviting him into one's life, thus experiencing personal conversion.[27]

My own work in the field of ordinary theology identified healing as an aspect of soteriology within a Pentecostal congregational study in Birmingham, UK.[28] Testimonies of healing were explained by reference to the atonement and Isaiah 53:4-6, Matthew 8:17, and 1 Peter 2:24, by which members of the congregation linked healing to the salvific work of Christ on the cross. This ordinary theology is connected to the discussion in Pentecostalism around the idea that "healing is in the atonement," namely, that Christ's saving effects extend beyond the realm of the forgiveness of sins to include wholeness and health. From my analysis, I concluded that healing or therapy was in fact the dominant soteriological motif within which other metaphors were subsumed. The therapeutic model of atonement is advocated by Bruce Reichenback, who argues that seeing healing as atonement means that the relationship with God is restored through the action of the Suffering Servant (the Messiah) on the cross, who personally takes on sin and punishment and by so doing grants "forgiveness, reconciliation, restoration and *shalom*."[29] The atonement on this account is multidimensional and holistic, including physical healing as an aspect of it. It extends to freedom from any burden in life that brings "dis-ease" with oneself, one's neighbor, and God. It is rooted in the incarnation as well as the cross, because, following Gregory of Nazianzus, we may say: "what is not assumed

---

26. Christie, *Ordinary Christology,* pp. 101-12.

27. Christie, *Ordinary Christology,* pp. 112-20.

28. Mark J. Cartledge, *Testimony in the Spirit: Rescripting Ordinary Pentecostal Theology* (Farnham: Ashgate, 2010), pp. 105-29.

29. Cartledge, *Testimony in the Spirit,* p. 123; Bruce R. Reichenback, "Healing View," in *The Nature of Atonement: Four Views,* ed. James K. Beilby and Paul R. Eddy (Downers Grove, Ill.: InterVarsity, 2006), pp. 117-42.

is not healed." Christ, through the incarnation, made possible the union of humanity with God and the healing of human nature in its entirety as part of the overarching gift of *shalom*.[30]

## 6.3 Critical Analysis

At least four theological frameworks can be discerned in the literature cited above, within which these theological themes are discussed.

1. A sociopolitical framework shapes salvific discourse largely in terms of transformation and liberation, not merely of the individual but also of the structures and systems in society. Communion with God and others may be considered an aspect of this framework (e.g., Poling), but it is largely interested in the this-worldly reality of social change. To be saved, we can infer (since this language is largely absent), means being liberated from forms of oppression through the actions of communities and individuals, acting on behalf of God or Christ, who challenge and change that which oppresses. The horizon is largely if not exclusively contemporary and particular. This framework appears to be the dominant one in contemporary practical theology. Alongside this framework is a worldview that downplays divine agency in favor of human agency. This may be supported by implicit deistic assumptions or emphasis on cooperation with God. Either way, what emerges is an emphasis on humanity or anthropology within the process of salvation. Solidarity with others and Jesus' solidarity with humanity are what come to the foreground in this sociopolitical framework. Interestingly, this theme is not as well represented as one might expect within ordinary soteriology. Chalcedonian Christology, with its emphasis on the Logos, or indeed Spirit Christology with its emphasis on pneumatology, is largely absent from these discussions. Ecclesiology also appears to play a very minor role. The church as the herald of the soteriological message in word and witness is often marginalized in favor of campaign groups of some kind or another, which may or may not have some link to a church denomination. This is not to say that campaign groups are unimportant, or that churches should not be involved in such groups as part of larger society, but to suggest that the soteriology articulated or implied is often too reliant on the latest sociopolitical agenda. Put simply: distinctive Christian soteriology is lost, which is ironic to say the least, when it has often been associated with the "saved."

---

30. Cartledge, *Testimony in the Spirit*, p. 127.

2. The Reformed framework understands that salvation is about individual union with Christ, and that this is part of an *ordo salutis* that includes justification and sanctification as historically understood in this tradition. By means of both justification and sanctification a person can be said to be reconciled with God and, by implication, also reconciled with others in the community of the church. The ordinary Anglicans observed by Christie could be included in this paradigm, as penal substitution lies behind the forensic understanding of atonement and the idea of imputed righteousness. To be saved means to be declared righteous upon repentance and union with Christ mystically by means of the indwelling Holy Spirit. The person is saved from sin and death by this union with Christ, and this union transcends all barriers of time and space, continuing into eternity. This framework owes more to traditional Reformed systematic theology than it does to contemporary practical theology. It provides an important perspective but lacks the breadth of theological metaphors found among the biblical writers and therefore needs some augmentation. For example, in what sense does the kingdom of God as a theological concept inform this soteriology? It is difficult to identify its impact in any meaningful way.

3. An evangelical/Pentecostal framework for understanding salvation emerges from the literature that focuses on healing as the central soteriological metaphor. This was noted by McGrath, among the other metaphors of restoration and rescue, and by me in a study of ordinary Pentecostal theology. In this framework, to be saved is to be healed, or more precisely to be located on a journey toward healing, a therapeutic *via salutis*. Healing is from sin, sickness, and death and applies to individuals and communities. Christ is the doctor in the house who heals by his Holy Spirit through the ministry of the church. The horizons of salvation are both present and future, because healing is interpreted in terms of the in-breaking kingdom of God, which is inaugurated but not yet consummated. In a sense this concept of the in-breaking of the kingdom of God brings a corrective to the Reformed position noted above, where mystical union with Christ appears to dominate but the impact of his reign on earth as in heaven often lacks elaboration. While this framework of healing and the kingdom of God might not be uppermost in the practical-theological academy more broadly, it deserves greater attention as a way of reconceptualizing the different metaphors associated with soteriology. It has the potential of incorporating other emphases and subsuming them as aspects of the overall *via salutis*. That is, other metaphors such as reconciliation, fellowship, victory over the forces of evil, and divine acquittal can be understood as aspects of this *via salutis*. It also has

the potential of connecting with the broader literature on health, medicine, and pastoral care.

4. The ordinary theology of Christie identified three soteriologies, the third being dealt with above under the Reformed category. The remaining two could be considered Anglican, although they may in fact reflect more general mainline or state church frameworks. To suggest greater generalization, I shall take them as reflecting mainline/state-type frameworks. Also, instead of marking two discrete categories of thought as suggested by Christie, they may really be two poles of a single spectrum of thought running from liberal to traditional. On the liberal pole Jesus is a good man who gave us a good example to live by, while at the other end all the traditional language found in the Anglican liturgy is affirmed in an unreflective manner. For the exemplarist, to be saved means to follow the example of Jesus in love and gratitude. One is saved from self-centeredness through a realization that there are good examples to follow, especially the example of Jesus. The horizon of salvation has to be the contemporary one because the action of modeling oneself on another person is limited to this present age even if the example is a historical figure. However, the traditionalist, on this account, is saved by participating in liturgical worship and affirming its theological content in a general sense. One could say that it is salvation via *lex orandi lex credendi*. The person is saved from sin and death by Christ, but the horizon of salvation is primarily life after death somewhere in the future. The liberal tradition in practical theology is fairly dominant, and where it is unaligned to liberation theology (as noted above), it could be the case that an exemplarist model predominates.

These different frameworks raise interesting questions about the relationship between agendas, issues, approaches, and perspectives in practical theology. This analysis has shown how one's positioning theologically can impact what is done and how it is done in significant ways. Therefore, given the argument of the previous chapters, in what ways might the insights derived from this argument inform soteriology within practical theology?

## 6.4 Reflections from Pentecostal Soteriology

To begin to answer this question, I shall argue for an intervention in practical-theological discourse, from the perspective of P/C theology. I shall use the sketch of pneumatological soteriology proposed by Amos Yong as a way into the discussion, before modifying it in the light of my own argument.[31] Yong is relevant to my argument because he uses Luke-Acts as the basis of his theological program, and his contribution dovetails with my own thinking (as well as diverging at certain points).

Yong proposes that "Christian salvation includes both the transformation of human beings into the image of Jesus by the power of the Holy Spirit and the transformation of all creation into the new heavens and new earth by the triune God."[32] It is initiated by God and received by people; it is a gift of the Spirit requiring a human response. He argues that salvation is a process of transformation that includes at least seven dimensions. (1) Salvation is personal insofar as individuals encounter the Spirit, are reconciled to God, and are transformed into the image of Christ. This includes the deliverance from oppression, from spiritual captivity of various kinds, including the "principalities and powers" of this age. At a basic level it is marked out by repentance, baptism, forgiveness of sins, and reception of the Holy Spirit. Individuals are always part of a community, yet they retain their own responsibility before God. (2) Salvation entails the family because the promise is for "you and your children." Individuals are members of families, and the experience of salvation is connected to other family members. This is seen in the household baptisms in Acts (11:14; 16:14-15, 31-33; 18:8). The salvific role that families play continues today. (3) Salvation is ecclesial insofar as there is a communal dimension to "being saved." The administration of the sacrament of baptism by the community is a significant marker of the ecclesial dimension. It signifies not only union with Christ, in his death and resurrection (Rom. 6:3-4), but also union with his body, the church. (4) Salvation is material because human beings are embodied, and it includes the healing of the whole person: mind, soul, and body; or the mental, the emotional, and the physical aspects. Yong suggests that material salvation is primarily directed toward the poor or the oppressed, since the good news is for the poor (Luke 1:52-53). (5) Salvation is social, as an extension of the ecclesial. It includes the reconciliation of relationships among people (especially in terms of race, class, and gender), as well as the redemption of socioeconomic and political structures. (6) Salvation is cosmic (Acts 2:19-20), which relates to the connection of humanity with its environment, as well as the redemption of the whole created order (Rom. 8:19-23). This means that ecological

---

31. See Amos Yong, *The Spirit Poured Out on All Flesh: Pentecostalism and the Possibility of Global Theology* (Grand Rapids: Baker, 2005), pp. 91-98.

32. Yong, *The Spirit Poured Out*, p. 91.

concerns should not be excluded or marginalized. (7) Salvation is eschato-logical. The arrival of the Spirit signals that the eschaton has already arrived in part, even as it has not been fully consummated. Soteriology looks back to the historical events of divine intervention and looks forward to the future transformation of creation.

This leads Yong to discuss the manner in which salvation is experienced by the believer, and in particular the relationship with the Holy Spirit. He does this in four steps. He considers Christian initiation and concludes that baptism of the Holy Spirit signifies salvation, "as nothing less than the gift of Jesus Christ himself to us in the totality of his Spirit-anointed life, death, and resurrection."[33] This means that the reception of the Holy Spirit is anticipated by Jesus' own offer to humanity (John 16:7-8); it is the culmination of the conversion-initiation process (Acts 2:38) and concludes the justification of the sinner because of its connection to the resurrection of Christ (Rom. 4:25). It is therefore connected to sanctification, as God declares sinners righteous on the basis of the righteousness of Christ and makes sinners righteous through the cleansing and restoring power of the Spirit.[34] Yong uses baptism in the Holy Spirit as a metaphor for salvation that includes both a process of experiencing the grace of God over time and crisis moments of radical encounter with God's presence. The past, "I was saved," reflects the initial experience of Spirit reception in repentance, conversion, regeneration, and justification. The present, "I am being saved," refers to ongoing experiences of the Spirit and includes sanctification as a process, as well as moments of empowerment. The future, "I will be saved," reflects the anticipation of future glory when the baptism of the Spirit is in its fullness and union with the triune God is fully realized.[35]

Yong does not appear to rank the seven dimensions, which can be re-categorized as referring to *recipients* (individual, family, and ecclesial) and *nature* (material, social, cosmic, and eschatological). Both of these categories can be interpreted in pneumatological terms, leading to a pneumatological soteriology, which is what Yong has attempted to do. That is, soteriology is read via the lens of pneumatology. However, it is possible to reverse this direction and read pneumatology via the lens of soteriology, which I shall do by reading the mediation of the Spirit in Acts 2 soteriologically. When this is done, I shall make a number of points.

33. Yong, *The Spirit Poured Out*, p. 101.
34. Yong, *The Spirit Poured Out*, p. 102.
35. Yong, *The Spirit Poured Out*, pp. 105-6.

First, the *recipients* upon whom the Spirit is poured out are all together in one place; this group obviously comprises individuals but more importantly suggests a community or *ecclesia*. Salvation as a process of knowing the presence of the Holy Spirit is received in community. Individual recipients experience this "coming upon them" in relation to others around them, and these others become part of the mediation and therefore the process. The Spirit was mediated by both the created order and the social context. This is followed by an explanation given by Peter, suggesting that the understanding of what was occurring was mediated by the sermon. Without experiences of the Spirit, there would not have been a sermon, and yet without the sermon, there would not have been a public explanation of the event. This process of receiving the saving presence of the Spirit comes first upon the *ecclesia*, suggesting the importance of the *ecclesia* above the family and indeed the individual, although both are included within the *ecclesia*. It also means that the *ecclesia* is the medium of salvation, although it would be extremely foolish to restrict salvation to the church because the kingdom of God is and has always been a wider category than the *ecclesia*. This point does not disagree with Yong, but rather reorders the categories such that the *ecclesia* emerges as the most significant one.

Second, at least in this discussion (if not elsewhere) Yong appears to ignore the category of the *context*. This event occurred at a particular time and in a particular place, which were both influenced by the contingencies of history, culture, and language. For sure, universality was present in the experience of the Spirit, but it was filtered through the matrix of particularity. In soteriological terms, this means that salvation and its expression will look different in various historical and cultural contexts. This does not mean that there are no transcontextual theological markers, for example, the rite of baptism, but it means that how that rite is practiced varies considerably around the world. This observation qualifies the role of the *ecclesia* and demonstrates that the *ecclesia* never really is an abstract reality but is always a concrete one. With this insight comes a corollary, namely, that the mediation of salvation through the life of the *ecclesia* is always influenced by contextual factors. It cannot be any other way. Sometimes these contextual factors facilitate and enhance mediation, and sometimes they inhibit and restrict it (perhaps giving some meaning to the idea of "quenching the Spirit," *to pneuma mē sbennute*, 1 Thess. 5:19). This mediation directly influences the soteriological reality experienced and is intertwined with the work of the *ecclesia*.

Third, with Yong, I agree that salvation is *holistic;* it includes the material, the social, and the spiritual. The doxology on the day of Pentecost was indeed an example of a holistic event involving action that was communal, individual, physical, emotional, and suprarational, if not altogether rational, as well as public. It was an event that was caught up in praise of the author of salvation. It provides a symbol of holistic soteriology that involves the physical dimension of vocal expression, the social dimension of corporate and synchronized action, the interaction with the presence and power of the Holy Spirit, as well as the transformative impact psychologically and spiritually upon individuals and groups. As this doxological speech is observed and witnessed by both insiders and outsiders to Christianity, it can promote a genuine sense of transcendence made immanent, which functions to radically critique materialist worldviews. Thus it offers a symbolic countertestimony rooted in soteriological reality and invites participation by all to join in this doxology. In this sense it could be called "doxological mission": a sending out of praise in order to gather others into this ongoing symbolic activity of salvation.

Fourth, an aspect of salvation that needs specific attention is its *eschatological* nature. A fundamentally new order of creation that stands in continuity as well as discontinuity with the present order is being established. It comes from the future and already impacts the present: it is the reign of God among people, so that the way things are appreciated is radically changed. This is seen in the egalitarianism of the Holy Spirit, where salvation is accessible to all, irrespective of social stratification. The boundary of the people of God is extended beyond the nation of Israel, and previous privilege is not only relativized by this new principle but also redefined by it. All previous forms of oppression or bondage are broken by this in-breaking new age of the Spirit: it represents a new exodus not just for Israel but also for the world. A new freedom to live authentically has been established, which is inextricably linked to the person of Jesus Christ, the Messiah, the King and Savior of the world. Therefore, soteriological discourse within the Christian tradition must contain at its heart discussion of the saving work of Jesus Christ.

Fifth, the *process* of receiving salvation follows a fairly similar pattern throughout the Acts of the Apostles. The Holy Spirit is active in preparing people to receive the gift of salvation. In the case of the day of Pentecost, people are brought to Jerusalem, allowing them to witness the church's doxology, followed by some form of reasoned explanation or exhortation. This in turn elicits some kind of response, including repentance, baptism, and reception of the Spirit. Throughout this process, individuals and households are incorporated into the *ecclesia* and participate in its life, which is itself a continuation of the process of conversion. Thus they receive instruction, enjoy fellowship, receive the eucharistic elements, and participate in prayer. Resources are shared for the common good, and a participation in communal life is established. A new family is constituted by the Spirit, and new members are added to its number through spiritual new birth, if not physical new birth. This understanding resonates with the work of Lewis R. Rambo, who advocates that conversion be described in seven stages: context, crisis, quest, encounter, interaction, commitment, and consequences. The latter two stages refer to the increasing integration of the individual into the religious community, in this case the church.[36]

## 6.5 Intervention

This reflection can offer a number of contributions to soteriological discourse within practical theology. It can be enhanced by using pneumatological mediation to modify existing categories. This form of theological intervention has not been suggested before, so it is appropriate at this point to ask the "so what?" question. In what ways might the insights from this study contribute to the enhancement of existing practical-theological discourse? I contend that the implications of this study suggest a soteriological agenda for practical theology, one that builds on its existing strengths but also moves beyond those strengths into new and important areas, or gives a distinctly "new take" on existing statements. In developing the earlier discussion, I address three main areas in this final section in order to make the points as generally applicable as possible, namely: recipients, nature, and process.

### 6.5.1 Recipients

The context is always important to practical theology, which in many respects is a form of contextual theology. The argument of this study is that the Holy Spirit is mediated through people situated in particular contexts, and that the particularities of the contextual dimension will always have an influence. These contexts will include sociocultural and social-psychological features. This does not mean that the soteriological work of the Holy Spirit

36. Lewis R. Rambo, *Understanding Religious Conversion* (New Haven: Yale University Press, 1993).

is necessarily compromised by such factors; but it is facilitated by them. In order to ask how the Holy Spirit is working in different contexts, it is always important to understand these different contexts in all their richness and beauty, as well as their ordinariness, even sometimes including their ugliness. People are always "people-in-context" as well as "people-with-history"; personal history and contextual history are always important aspects of research. Therefore, practical theology will always wish to research this context, but now it needs to be alert to how salvation is being mediated in this context. What are the narratives, actions, and symbols of such a soteriology, and how might we say the Holy Spirit is mediated? These questions are hardly ever asked in practical theology. The analysis of biblical texts earlier in this study suggests that a number of points might be usefully made.

Acts 2 describes the salvific and empowering work of the Holy Spirit as mediated through the gathered group. The gathered group is an important aspect of practical theology, especially when there is an expectation that God is about "to do" something. It is stated that the group was indeed waiting for the gift of the Holy Spirit, so this expectation and reason for gathering is perhaps a unique one. Not all gathered groups are waiting for the Holy Spirit to arrive in dramatic fashion. But ecclesial groups of different kinds gather in order to receive something from God. They may not talk about the Holy Spirit, nevertheless they engage in religious practice of some kind. There is a very definite interface between the gathered group and the practice of spirituality. The importance of "groups" in religious life and "units of mediation" deserves analysis in practical theology, not just in terms of group dynamics or how groups are led, which is indeed important, but supremely in terms of how the salvific work of the Holy Spirit is operational among the group.

Acts 2 also shows a relationship between groups, communities, and even wider society. There is an overflow of mediation from the smaller group to the larger group, which is significant in terms of the mission of the church. The examination of the text suggests that there is some debate regarding the nature of the interface between the space of the upper room, however constituted, and the space of the wider context. The doxological language was overheard and understood. Worship moved beyond the space of "church" and into the space of wider society. It had the character of spontaneity and freedom, and yet there was purpose in it. It was a form of what might be termed "doxological mission." Worship spilled out into the public square so that "others" overheard the Christian doxology, which in turn prompted questions of meaning, which are addressed and explained in terms that were understood within the history and theology of Israel at the time. Practical theology should be interested in exploring how Christianity is received by wider society and how the Holy Spirit might be orchestrating an engagement with wider society. In particular, it should be interested in understanding how worship is received by those who hear it perhaps by surprise: they simply eavesdrop on doxology. The phenomenon, the public reaction, and the ecclesial response are significant areas for study.

The languages spoken under the inspiration of the Holy Spirit are diverse: they are "the many tongues of Pentecost." A number of things occur in Acts 2 that are relevant to practical theology. Even though the people who overhear the speech understand the words, which they regarded as remarkable since the speakers would not have been expected to use those languages, an explanation is still required. Peter provides this explanation within his speech and draws on the Jewish tradition and Scripture, as well as the phenomenon witnessed by the wider group. This feature raises the important question of language and how language itself is a medium of reality, including the reality of the Holy Spirit. Practical theology will be interested in religious phenomena, as well as their reception, but it will also be interested in analyzing the reflective narratives provided by adherents to religious and, in particular, Christian groups. How these groups tell their story is a crucial feature of practical theology. How these narratives are composed, delivered, and defended against competing narratives is a significant area of research. The role of the Holy Spirit in these narratives will also be significant, whether explicit or implicit. Explanations are important; and practical theology will wish to use theology (espoused or enacted) as an *explanatory* factor, not merely as a dependent factor to be explained by other kinds of academic discourse, such as sociology or social psychology. This is a crucial move for practical theology and shifts the power balance away from the social sciences and toward theology. In other words: *(academic) theology interprets (ordinary and ecclesial) theology.*

Acts 2 also describes a movement of people for the purpose of pilgrimage to Jerusalem and then a return to their homelands. The site of Spirit reception is itself expanded and transcended via the movement of people. The recipients of mediation become themselves the mediators of the work of the Spirit, and this is exactly what the rest of the book of Acts narrates in terms of key figures in the story of early Christianity. But there is also the *untold* story of the many ordinary individuals who transmit their experiences and understandings to others because of their movement. Their movement includes a specific location (Jerusalem), followed by some kind of dislocation or liminality, and then a subsequent relocation. The mediation of the Holy

Spirit is caught up in this dynamic of being located and then being dislocated (liminality) before being relocated. It would appear that this oscillation is essential to the transcontextual dimension of Christianity and the mediation of the Holy Spirit. It is especially the case in contemporary transnational Pentecostalism, which is a religion made to travel. But it is not restricted to Pentecostal migration, because various forms of Christianity are on the move from the east to the west and from the south to the north. Once again, these people movements provide an agenda for practical theological research in the context of globalization.

Finally, we reflect once again on the tension between universality and particularity. In the narrative of Acts 2, both are present and, arguably, both are required. The mediation of the Holy Spirit is via particularity, and yet the Spirit is present universally across time and place. If the tension is resolved in terms of one or the other, then mediation is reduced to either a bland omnipresence of the "God is everywhere" variety or a fundamentalist solipsism of the "God is only here" variety. *People* are at the center of this tension, not ideas per se, but actual people in their concrete realities. Herein is the tension with the emphasis on context within practical theology. To emphasize particularity of specific contexts at the expense of universality and the possibility of transcontextuality is to weaken the significance of soteriology in the Christian tradition. To do this is to privilege a particular nonuniversalist theological narrative, which, ironically, contains its own implicit universalistic assumptions. Indeed, the transcendence and universality of the presence of the Holy Spirit may be lost if the accent is always on immanence in particularity. The challenge is to present soteriological discourse in ways that transcend the particular, and focusing on the mediation of the Holy Spirit across time and place is one way to achieve that.

### 6.5.2 Nature

One of the key features of soteriology is the fact that within the narrative of Acts, and among Pentecostals generally, its nature is regarded as holistic: the whole of humanity in all its complexity is in the process of being saved. The salvation of one's soul in terms of merely the spiritual component of an individual is a parody and must be named as such. Salvation as mediated by the Holy Spirit is multidimensional and includes all aspects of life: spiritual, psychological, physical, material, social, occupational, global, and cosmic. Indeed, no area of life is untouched by "saving grace." In many respects it is impossible to pull these different dimensions apart, and yet the challenge is how to study them in all their complexity at the same time. Indeed, that in itself is an impossibility. Therefore, practical theology must focus on particular aspects; this is inevitable. And what this looks like on the ground, wherever that "ground" is located, will be different.

Sin and sickness in all their forms have not been eradicated and will not be fully dealt with until the end, the eschaton. Practical theology does not discuss the concept of sin in any great detail, except perhaps in the context of social sin and human oppression. The nature of sin and the role of the Holy Spirit in convicting individuals and groups of their incapacity and culpability can be seen as challenging from an academic perspective. Understandably, academics are more than a little wary of pointing a moralistic finger. It may turn around and be pointed back at them with even greater force! But the issue of what is sin and whether it still has some usefulness in practical theology needs to be asked. On the whole, like a good number of theological themes, it is largely ignored. It is a kind of theological embarrassment for liberal-minded people. But in the context of a retrieval of the mediation of the Holy Spirit in Acts 2, we cannot ignore the statement that upon hearing the message proclaimed by Peter, some of the audience, at least, were "cut to the heart." They were convicted of sin and wanted to do something about it. Somewhere in the message there is a mediation of the Holy Spirit causing such a response. When people are convicted of something and wish to move toward the goodness of God revealed in Jesus Christ, surely we can discern the mediation of the Holy Spirit.

The new exodus liberation motif can be helpful in offering a way of expressing salvation. It recognizes the role that sin plays in limiting human freedom and flourishing, and in creating individuals and groups who are constrained and diminished. The mediation of the Holy Spirit enables humanity to fulfill its God-given potential, and in the new exodus motif it connects with some aspects of liberation. However, and crucially, it does not simplify power relations by constructing two fundamental social categories: the oppressed and the oppressors. That is far too simplistic in this global world of networked relationships. Rather, it sees the role of the Holy Spirit as mediating between a set of power relations, some of which may well be oppressive and others less so. Liberation theology has been a dominant perspective within practical theology, but very often its advocates appear to replace one oppressed group by another in a kind of circularity according to dominant ideologies. What the narrative of Acts does is to relativize this human analysis in the light of the Spirit's liberating presence, the corollary of which is a redefinition of social categories. This is especially seen in age and gender relations, where the Holy Spirit mediates an egalitarianism that challenges subordinationism based on age, biology, or culture.

This leads to a comment on the mediation of salvation eschatologically framed, which means that it always stands in relation to a wider set of references. These wider references of thought provide a framework that affirms the present as a realization of the presence and purpose of the reign of God as well as its lack of consummation. The presence of the Holy Spirit does indeed mediate salvific realities, but, given the "eschatological time," so to speak, these realities are inaugural and not complete. There is a "not yet" to the reign of God, and the mediating presence of the Spirit does not obliterate that "not yet." This eschatological tension characterizes the whole of the Christian life and indeed, from a Christian theological perspective, the whole of society as well. And yet it is largely ignored within practical theology. The implication of this feature for practical theology is that the world is indeed messy, despite the mediation of the Holy Spirit and the presence of salvific realities. The messiness of life is just as much a part of the situation to be researched. It also means that the very task of describing, analyzing, evaluating, and constructing theological discourse (and any discourse, for that matter) is inevitably shaped by a "between the times" condition reflected in "fallen" if sometimes "inspired" human reason. This should lead to modesty in soteriological discourse because it is always open to revision in the light of eschatological reality.

### 6.5.3 Process

What is the fundamental process through which this eschatological and soteriological reality is mediated by the Spirit of God? The answer is by means of the church, not exclusively but primarily. This is because the kingdom (= reign) of God is always greater than, and can never be restricted to, the church. In other words, there have always been people in the kingdom who have not technically and formally been members of some expression of church. But, having said this, I still wish to maintain that the church, the *ecclesia,* is in fact the normative way in which pneumatological mediation of salvation occurs, and I would argue that this is in fact the position found in the Acts of the Apostles. So how does this soteriological mediation occur? Once again we revisit Acts 2, but in terms of the process of mediation.

The *ecclesia* is called to be a people marked by doxology. Indeed, it could be argued that in terms of the "marks of the church," this is a "Pentecostal distinctive," which the tradition offers to the wider church for consideration. In doxology identity is shaped and the relationship with God sustained and strengthened. Therefore, it could be considered constitutive of the church: to belong to the church is to belong to a community worshiping the triune God, but not necessarily by means of glossolalia. I regard glossolalia as an important expression of doxology, as represented by Acts 2:11, but it does not exhaust the category. This is because doxology as a larger category is much more significant and inclusive of different expressions of authentic Christianity. From the analysis of Acts 2, we have seen that this action is itself a means of mediation of the Spirit to both the church and, via its doxology, to a wider public. It is also the means of participating in the Spirit, in a return movement, so to speak, back toward the triune God, but this time in union with the *ecclesia* and as part of the return journey of salvation, the *via salutis*.

From this central doxological practice flows communion with the triune God that extends to all in the community, so that at its heart there is indeed a deep connection beyond merely human association: it is a *koinōnia*. This participation in the fellowship of the Trinity is mediated by the Spirit and characterizes the fellowship of the community. In this sense worshiping practices function to pull individuals and groups into the *ecclesia*. At the center of the community's worship are central practices, namely, sacramental participation in the Eucharist, the reception of the teaching of the faith in the exposition of Scripture, reflections on it in light of the challenges of Christian discipleship, and finally prayer, which binds it all together. Here we see the integration of spirituality and spiritual practices within the context of the church and its mission in the world. The process of participation in salvation from the perspective of Acts 2 contains all these features. The rest of the book of Acts narrates how the *ecclesia* moved out in mission and took its practices into very different contexts in Asia Minor and Europe. We read of the message being communicated in a variety of settings, but each one being connected to the beginnings of a Christian community and salvation being associated with belonging to that community and experiencing the work of the Holy Spirit through the local *ecclesia*.

In practical-theological terms, the *ecclesia* is engaged in a range of practices that have theologically laden value. These practices provide concrete expressions not just of human actions and behavior but also of pneumatology: the Holy Spirit is mediated by all these means, which together provide a communal matrix for the reception of salvation. Therefore practical theology by virtue of being interested in the concrete practices of religious communities is also committed to researching the processes by which communities are sustained and renewed in these practices. How do new members gain entry? How are they integrated? How are they traditioned or socialized? And in all these various processes of access and maintenance, what are points of mediation whereby the salvific realities are understood to be experienced by believers and possibly benefit wider society, not just ecclesial communities?

Of course, the recipients, the nature, and the process of soteriolology are indeed interconnected categories, and necessarily so. Nevertheless, these categories transfer more readily and generally outside of Pentecostalism and indeed resonate with many different theological traditions. Therefore, they provide useful bridges to help us appreciate how a distinctively pneumatological reading of mediation offers new insight into how soteriology might be better appreciated, and in particular, how soteriological discourse might be constructed.

## 6.6 Conclusion

This chapter has focused on the important theme of soteriology as expressed in the discourse of practical theology. It identified some general trends in the discussion of soteriology and described contributions from different theological perspectives and traditions. This was followed by a critical analysis in which the strengths and weaknesses of four contributions were discussed. Following this analysis, I reflected critically on the contribution that is made from a P/C perspective and suggested how this approach might feed into the conversation. From this point, I was in a position to advance an intervention in the practical-theological discourse of soteriology based on *pneumatological mediation*. This intervention suggested that soteriology in practical theology should pay attention to the recipients of, the nature of, and the process of salvation. I would suggest that these features set an agenda for further inquiry and suggest a framework for understanding soteriology in practical theology. I would also suggest that this discussion offers a model showing how to integrate systematic theology within a discussion of practical theology. It is certainly not the only way to approach this kind of theological dialogue, but it is one way in which practical theology can become more attentive to theological loci and advance its own theological nature in the process. It is hoped that others will be able to build on this discussion critically and advance practical theology as a result.

# Conclusion

Research can be understood as a process of investigation that leads to findings or insights, which are in turn shared effectively with audiences of one kind or another. This book is the product of a theoretical research process, and it is written primarily for students and scholars of theology. As a book in the Pentecostal Manifestos series, it addresses a domain of Christian theology, specifically the discipline and field of practical theology, and is written by someone who straddles both P/C theology and practical theology. As a member of both the Society for Pentecostal Studies and the International Academy of Practical Theology, I consider this book an attempt to bring the former society into conversation with the latter academy, but also to prompt the former to challenge and potentially shape the discourse of the latter. Obviously, readers will have to decide how successful I have been in the attempt to address practical theology from a P/C perspective. Before suggesting what I regard as the significance of this study, I summarize the key points in the argument of the book.

P/C scholars who have engaged in work associated with practical theology have largely been located in seminary education, training professionals for church work, especially clergy. Therefore, there has been an emphasis on personal and professional formation within a fairly standard evangelical model of theological education augmented by P/C spirituality. In my view, this dominant approach has had very little engagement with the broader practical-theological academy. The influence of both liberation theology and empirical theology is present in only a limited manner, despite being significant strands in the wider practical theology academy. However, what can be discerned from this situation positively is that P/C theology brings together the use of Scripture with experience and pneumatology. This three-fold contribution was explored in relation to the wider practical-theological academy. It was discovered that a range of approaches to the use of the Bible is in fact present within practical theology, but that in general terms its usage is on the weak side. Experience is discussed as a general source and point of reflection for theology, but "religious experience" as a concept is underdeveloped, to say the least. Very rarely is pneumatology used either in relation to a discussion of experience or in relation to Scripture. Therefore, it could be said that the strength of P/C theology is the weakness of practical theology, and vice versa. In the light of these issues I asked: *How might a distinctively Pentecostal and pneumatological contribution be constructed that intervenes in the contemporary discourse of academic practical theology?* That is, in what way might pneumatology that pays attention to Scripture and experience speak to contemporary practical theology?

To address this question, I explored the relationship of Scripture, experience, and the Holy Spirit by means of the central concept of mediation. P/C theologians have recently begun to discuss mediation, and insights from these studies were used to define how the concept might be used to interpret Spirit baptism as a religious experience as well as worship rituals. It was argued that implicit in these discussions is a form of sacramentality whereby material reality can be understood to mediate the presence of the Holy Spirit, and this can be extended to the providential notion of *concursus,* whereby divine and human agency are understood to be coordinated. Of course, behind this creaturely mediation are both a Trinitarian and a christological mediation, because they provide the proper context to the reality of creation and ecclesiology. Setting this discussion in a broader historical and contemporary Protestant theological context reinforced ideas of divine-human relations in sacramentality and ecclesiology, as well as concerns about differentiation (between God and creation, Christ and the Spirit, and the Spirit and the church).

Following the P/C commitment to develop theological constructs by means of Scripture, experience, and the Holy Spirit, key texts in the tradition, namely, from Acts 2 and other places in Acts where the Spirit was received, were used to better understand the nature of *pneumatological mediation.* From the analysis of these key texts a number of propositions were articulated. These are as follows: Christ mediates the Holy Spirit to the church (M1); the Holy Spirit mediates Christ and the Father to the church (M2); creation mediates the Holy Spirit to the church (M3); the church mediates the Holy Spirit internally (to individuals, via worship and practices) (M4); and the church mediates the Holy Spirit externally (to individuals, via public worship and practices) (M5). This means that the mediation of the Holy Spirit is both subjective genitive (where the Spirit mediates the Trinity) and objective genitive (where the Spirit is mediated by Christ, creation, and the church). From this analysis it was suggested that Acts 2 might also provide an agenda for interventions in practical theology comprising attention to ecclesial practice and theological loci, in particular soteriology.

To test this construction as both legitimate and valuable for practical theology, I addressed two specific examples. The first was a case study of a congregation written from the perspective of practical theology. This case study verified the weaknesses of practical theology identified in the earlier discussion, namely, in the use of the Bible and in pneumatology. Thus, it provided a place to address these issues in a particular manner. A number of "interventions" were made to illustrate the ways in which sensitivity to pneumatological mediation might have contributed to the analysis of the congregation and its life. The second study considered the broader concept of soteriology in the practical-theological literature and, once again, using an understanding informed by pneumatological mediation, indicated how soteriological discourse in practical theology might be critically advanced by considering soteriology's context, nature, and process.

The significance of this study for Christian theology, and in particular practical theology, can be understood in terms of its insights arising from the process of investigation. (1) This study offers a unique analysis of practical theology found in the Pentecostal and charismatic literature. (2) It modifies the existing understanding of the use of the Bible in practical theology and proposes a new typology. (3) It offers a unique analysis of experience understood from the perspective of pneumatology within practical theology. (4) It provides a discussion of pneumatological mediation in relation to Pentecostal and charismatic studies, as well as broader Protestant theology. (5) It gives an original reading of Pentecost and the Spirit-reception texts in the Acts of the Apostles. (6) It interrogates an existing congregational study and provides an example of theological intervention. (7) It critiques and modifies the existing soteriological discourse in practical theology and provides an example of theological intervention. (8) It is the first study to propose a Pentecostal manifesto for practical theology as a distinct discipline (see below).

# A Pentecostal Manifesto for Practical Theology

This book has aimed to speak to a sector of the theological academy, namely, practical theology, from an orientation informed by Pentecostal and charismatic theology. To crystallize the proposal of this study and to aid the assessment of its contribution, I close with a "manifesto." It is hoped that the "public" of the practical theology academy will take note and engage with its content in order to develop its own self-understanding and engagement with religion and society.

1. *Practical theology should embrace the contributions that specific theological traditions make to its discourse, allowing distinctive tenets and practices to be critically evaluated and appropriated.* In other words, it should welcome, affirm, and celebrate a greater range of theological perspectives than it does currently. It is dominated by Western, liberal traditions and should be augmented, and even challenged, by non-Western, indigenous, Eastern, and independent forms of Christianity. Even if unintentionally, Pentecostal and charismatic forms of Christianity, in both their Western and non-Western forms, have been marginalized from the practical theology academy, and this should be addressed because of the phenomenal growth globally of this sector of Christianity.

2. *Practical theology should engage in a deeper and more serious manner with Scripture because of its significant role in theology historically and because of its central role in the life of the church.* In view of recent hermeneutical theory, it could develop a specific practical-theological strategy for reading Scripture. This approach would place contempo-

rary practical-theological questions at the heart of the exercise, while retaining a respect for and interaction with biblical studies, historical studies, and systematic-theological studies of biblical texts.

3. *Practical theology should pay more attention to the distinctive role that "religious experience" plays in the lives of contemporary individuals and communities.* It has given a fair amount of attention to the discussion of "experience" in more general terms and, of course, lived experience in its social and cultural contexts. However, it has failed, so far, to develop a distinctly practical-theological account of religious experience among the interaction of religious and nonreligious people. By developing this, it will move beyond the dominant abstract philosophical categories of religious experience, which tend to focus on mental activities rather than holistic embodied experiences.

4. *Practical theology should develop a deeper and more critical dialogue with systematic theology and an engagement with the full range of theological loci.* It is extremely rare for practical-theological studies to give attention to the classical theological themes of Trinity, Christology, and soteriology, not to mention ecclesiology and eschatology. The effect of this limited engagement is that the "theological" nature of the discourse can be considered rather "thin." "Thicker" theological descriptions and explanations need to be developed in the academy. Theology is not just a category to be described in other explanatory terms; it has genuine explanatory power in its own right. This explanatory power needs to be more fully developed.

5. *As a focused development of point 4, practical theology should pay specific attention to the theological theme of soteriology.* The concept of soteriology is crucial to theological discourse and historically has driven major debates in the church, but it is rarely mentioned in practical theology. In some ways, practical theologians seem rather embarrassed by the category. Chapter 6 of this book has attempted to begin a conversation in this area; nevertheless, I am aware that it is very much the beginning of a discussion that needs to be developed in a more rigorous and sustained fashion.

6. *Practical theology should become more interested in the study of spirituality in its contemporary forms and not just through the dominant lens of historical and mystical theology.* The fact that spirituality has been studied as a dimension of practical theology for a considerable period of time should be acknowledged, but it appears to be largely conceived in broadly Catholic and mystical traditions. In this regard, it follows the

mainstream academic study of spirituality. Without denigrating these traditions, and indeed their importance for theology, I maintain that the study of spirituality in its contemporary form is a much more religiously diverse field of study and needs to be recognized as such.

7. *Practical theology should pay even more attention to the research of concrete expressions of church (and other religious communities) by investing resources in congregational studies.* It should build on existing congregational research knowledge, and give attention to specific congregations around the world that provide crucial knowledge and information about how faith is being negotiated and practiced within specific social and cultural contexts. Religious congregations provide significant clues for understanding how issues of faith and society might be conceptualized afresh in dynamic contexts and amid globalizing forces.

8. *Practical theology should advance a much more sophisticated analysis of the relationship between divine and human agency.* This should be done with reference to pneumatology, without collapsing it into the category of the anthropological without remainder. Much practical theology is, in effect, deistic and anthropological, constrained by various forms of modern and postmodern rationalism. New ways of conceiving this relationship need to be advanced in a practical-theological manner consistent with the key commitments of the discipline.

9. *Practical theology should clarify the relationship between universality and particularity in its discourse.* On the one hand, there are major assumptions about what counts as universals, but these are never really discussed because the constituency tends to agree about their implied normativity. On the other hand, practical theology is concerned about the nature of religious life in all its particular expressions, even when the implied universals are at variance with the assumptions of religious others. The relationship between these universal, normative, and hermeneutical values and dissonant concrete particularities is rarely expressed in the discussions of the practical theology academic community.

10. *Practical theology should be prepared to analyze where the questions come from, how they are articulated, and by whom they are articulated.* Academy inquiry is fostered by intellectual curiosity, which is expressed in questions of various kinds. The kinds of questions that are asked can be extremely revealing about the nature of the community, and indeed of the individuals, asking the questions. The phrasing, tone, and timing of the questions are linked to power dynamics. Indeed, it could be argued that questions in and of themselves are never neutral but betray

commitments and prejudices. Of course, practical theology will tend to ask contemporary-orientated questions, but how they are constructed, and with what assumptions, is a significant issue for the reflexivity of academics and practitioners alike.

# Name Index

# Subject Index